ROYAL HISTORICAL SOCIETY
STUDIES IN HISTORY
New Series

QUEENSHIP AT THE RENAISSANCE COURTS OF BRITAIN

Studies in History New Series

Editorial Board

Professor Vanessa Harding (*Convenor*)
Dr D'Maris Coffman
Professor Peter Coss (*Past and Present Society*)
Professor B. Doyle (*Economic History Society*)
Dr Rachel Hammersley
Professor M. Hughes (*Honorary Treasurer*)
Professor Daniel Power
Professor Guy Rowlands
Professor Alec Ryrie
Professor Andrew Spicer (*Literary Director*)
Professor Richard Toye (*Literary Director*)

This series is supported by annual subventions from the
Economic History Society and from the Past and Present Society

QUEENSHIP AT THE RENAISSANCE COURTS OF BRITAIN

CATHERINE OF ARAGON AND MARGARET TUDOR 1503–1533

Michelle L. Beer

THE ROYAL HISTORICAL SOCIETY
THE BOYDELL PRESS

© Michelle L. Beer 2018

All Rights Reserved. Except as permitted under current legislation
no part of this work may be photocopied, stored in a retrieval system,
published, performed in public, adapted, broadcast,
transmitted, recorded or reproduced in any form or by any means,
without the prior permission of the copyright owner

The right of Michelle L. Beer to be identified as
the author of this work has been asserted in accordance with
sections 77 and 78 of the Copyright, Designs and Patents Act 1988

First published 2018
Paperback edition 2021

A Royal Historical Society publication
Published by The Boydell Press
an imprint of Boydell & Brewer Ltd
PO Box 9, Woodbridge, Suffolk IP12 3DF, UK
and of Boydell & Brewer Inc.
668 Mt Hope Avenue, Rochester, NY 14620–2731, USA
website: www.boydellandbrewer.com

ISBN 978-0-86193-348-8 hardback
ISBN 978-0-86193-355-6 paperback

ISSN 0269-2244

A CIP catalogue record for this book is available
from the British Library

The publisher has no responsibility for the continued existence or accuracy of
URLs for external or third-party internet websites referred to in this book, and
does not guarantee that any content on such websites is, or will remain, accurate
or appropriate

Typeset by Fakenham Prepress Solutions, Fakenham, Norfolk NR21 8NL

IN MEMORY OF MY FATHER

Contents

List of figures	viii
Acknowledgements	ix
Abbreviations	x
Introduction	1
1 Elizabeth of York	27
2 Material magnificence, royal identity and the queen's body	45
3 The social queen	70
4 Patronage in partnership	97
5 Queenship and pre-Reformation piety	122
Conclusion	149
Bibliography	158
Index	174

Figures

1. The family of Catherine of Aragon   xii
2. The House of York   xiii
3. The Woodvilles   xiv
4. The Tudors   xv

Acknowledgements

This book has been many years in the making, and I have acquired too many debts of thanks, both personal and professional, for me to adequately acknowledge here. Nevertheless, I shall endeavour to express my gratitude to some of the many people in my life who made this work possible. This project could not have been completed without the support and guidance of Caroline Hibbard, to whom I owe more than I can say. Her work on queenship inspired my own interest in the reigns of Catherine and Margaret and forged a path that many scholars of queens now follow. I would like to express my sincere thanks to Carol Symes, Clare Crowston and Derek Neal, and the many friends and scholars who read drafts of these chapters. Lastly, I would like to thank my editor Alec Ryrie for his thoughtful comments and Christine Linehan and the Royal Historical Society, who made publishing this work possible. The research for this work was made possible through the generous help of the Institute of Historical Research. I would also like to express my appreciation for the excellent staff of the National Archives at Kew, the British Library, the Scottish National Library and the Scottish National Archives, who were exceptionally helpful and efficient. Malcolm Underwood, archivist for St John's College, Cambridge, was very kind to me on my visits there and provided many welcome cups of tea and a great deal of help with the college archives.

Finally, I would like to acknowledge that a project as large as this was only possible to complete through the personal support of my family. My husband Michael survived many hours of dinner conversation about British queenship, and he probably knows more about British history than any other software engineer in the country. Without his encouragement and support this book would never have been published. Writing a book can be an isolating experience, and my siblings, Daniel and Sarah, have provided much-needed levity and perspective after long days in front of my books. My parents, Pamela and Colin, always gave me their love and support to see this project to the end. My father's shining example of stubborn perfectionism and determination gave me the confidence to see this work completed. His faith that all of his children could succeed at whatever we strove for made all of us the people we are today.

Michelle L. Beer
May 2018

Abbreviations

BL	British Library, London
CDS	*Calendar of documents relating to Scotland*, ed. Joseph Bain, Edinburgh 1881-8
CSP Spanish	*Calendar of letters, despatches, and state papers, relating to the negotiations between England and Spain, preserved in the archives at Simancas, Vienna, Brussels and elsewhere*, ed. G. A. Bergenroth and others, London 1862
CSP Venetian	*Calendar of state papers and manuscripts relating to English affairs: existing in the archives and collections of Venice, and in other libraries of Northern Italy*, ed. Rawdon Brown, London 1864
ERS	*The Exchequer rolls of Scotland*, ed. John Stuart and others, 1878-1908
JRL	John Rylands Library, University of Manchester
LHTA	*Accounts of the Lord High Treasurer of Scotland*, ed. Thomas Dickson and James Balfour Paul, Edinburgh 1877-1916
LP	*Letters and papers, foreign and domestic, of the reign of Henry VIII, 1509-1547*, ed. J. S. Brewer, and others, London 1862-1932
MS Add.	Additional manuscript
NRS	National Records of Scotland, Edinburgh
ODNB	*Oxford dictionary of national biography*, ed. H. C. G. Matthew and Brian Harrison, Oxford 2004, <http://www.oxforddnb.com>
Privy Purse expenses	*Privy Purse expenses of Elizabeth of York: Wardrobe accounts of Edward the Fourth*, ed. Sir Nicholas Harris Nicholas, New York 1972
RMS	*The register of the great seal of Scotland*, ed. John Balfour Paul, Edinburgh 1882-1914
RSS	*The register of the privy seal of Scotland*, ed. M. Livingstone, Edinburgh 1908
SJC	St John's College archives, Cambridge
State papers of Henry VIII	*State papers published under the authority of His Majesty's Commission: King Henry the Eighth* (Record Commission, 1830-52)
TNA	The National Archives, Kew
EHR	*English Historical Review*

ABBREVIATIONS

EM	*Early Music*
G&H	*Gender and History*
HJ	*Historical Journal*
HLQ	*Huntington Library Quarterly*
IR	*Innes Review*
JBS	*Journal of British Studies*
JEH	*Journal of Ecclesiastical History*
JMEMS	*Journal of Medieval and Early Modern Studies*
MET	*Medieval English Theatre*
Parergon	*Parergon: Journal of the Australian and New Zealand Association for Medieval and Early Modern Studies*
P&P	*Past & Present*
RS	*Renaissance Studies*
SCJ	*Sixteenth Century Journal*
TCH	*The Court Historian*

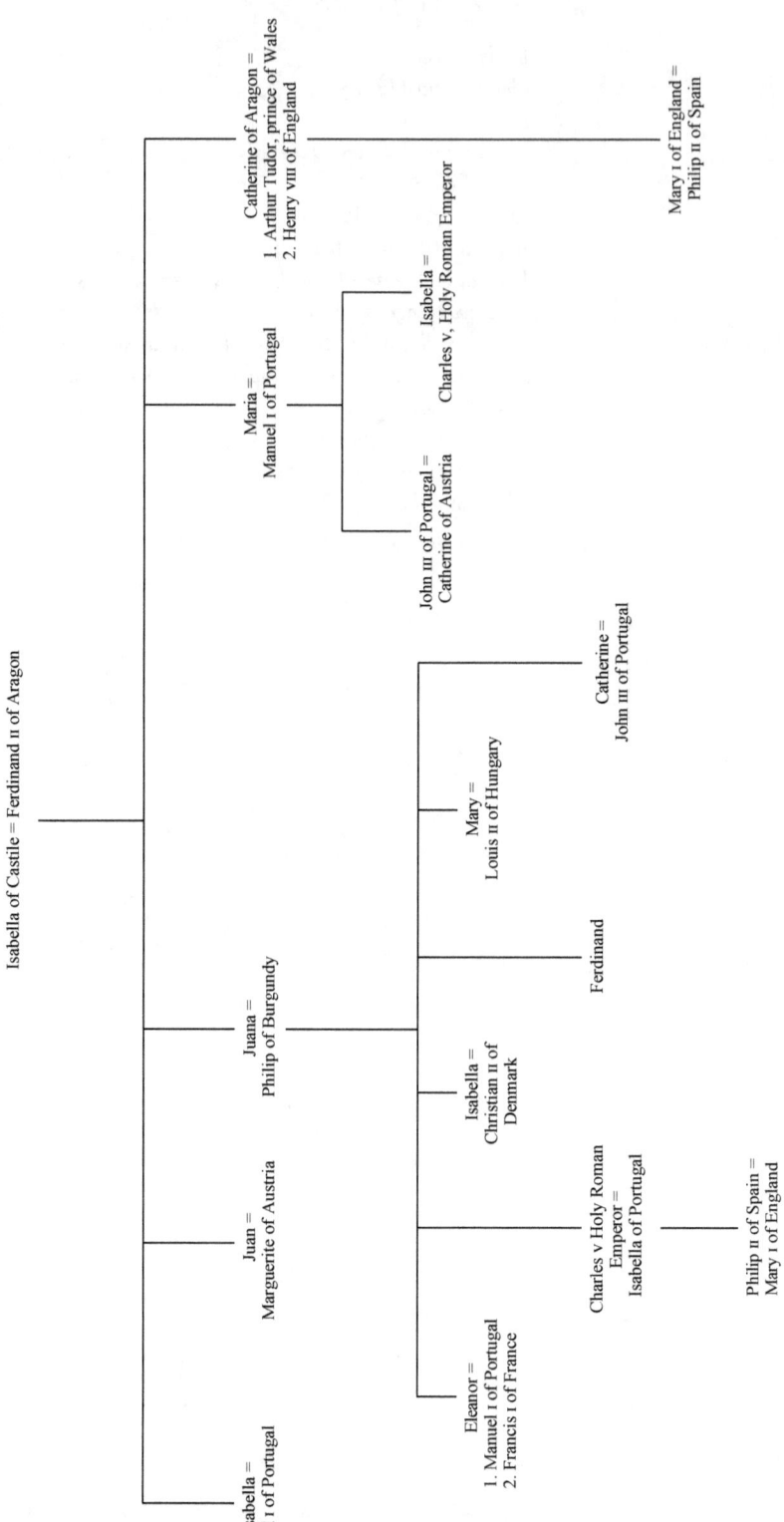

Figure 1. *The family of Catherine of Aragon*

Note: for the sake of clarity, not all spouses or offspring of each match are included.

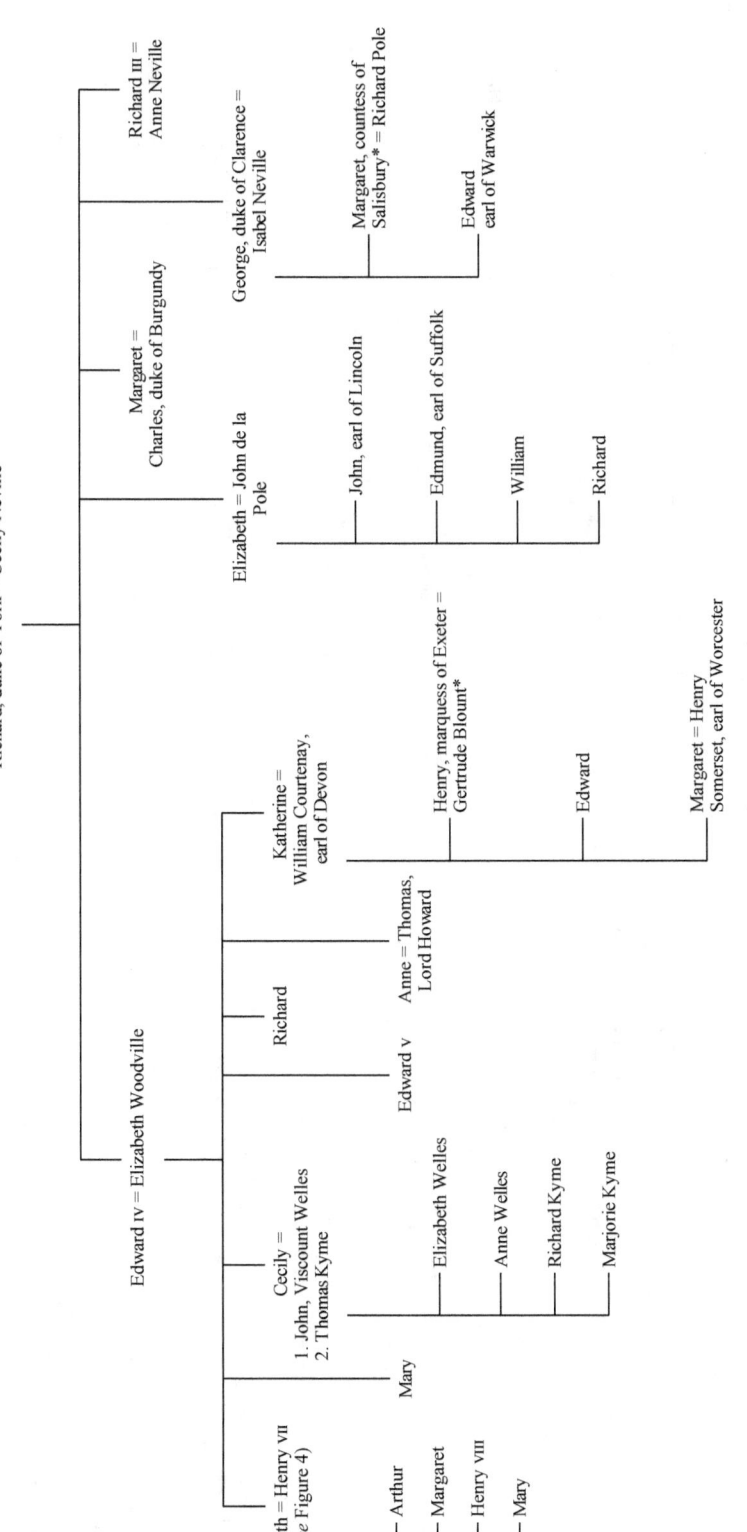

Figure 2. *The House of York*

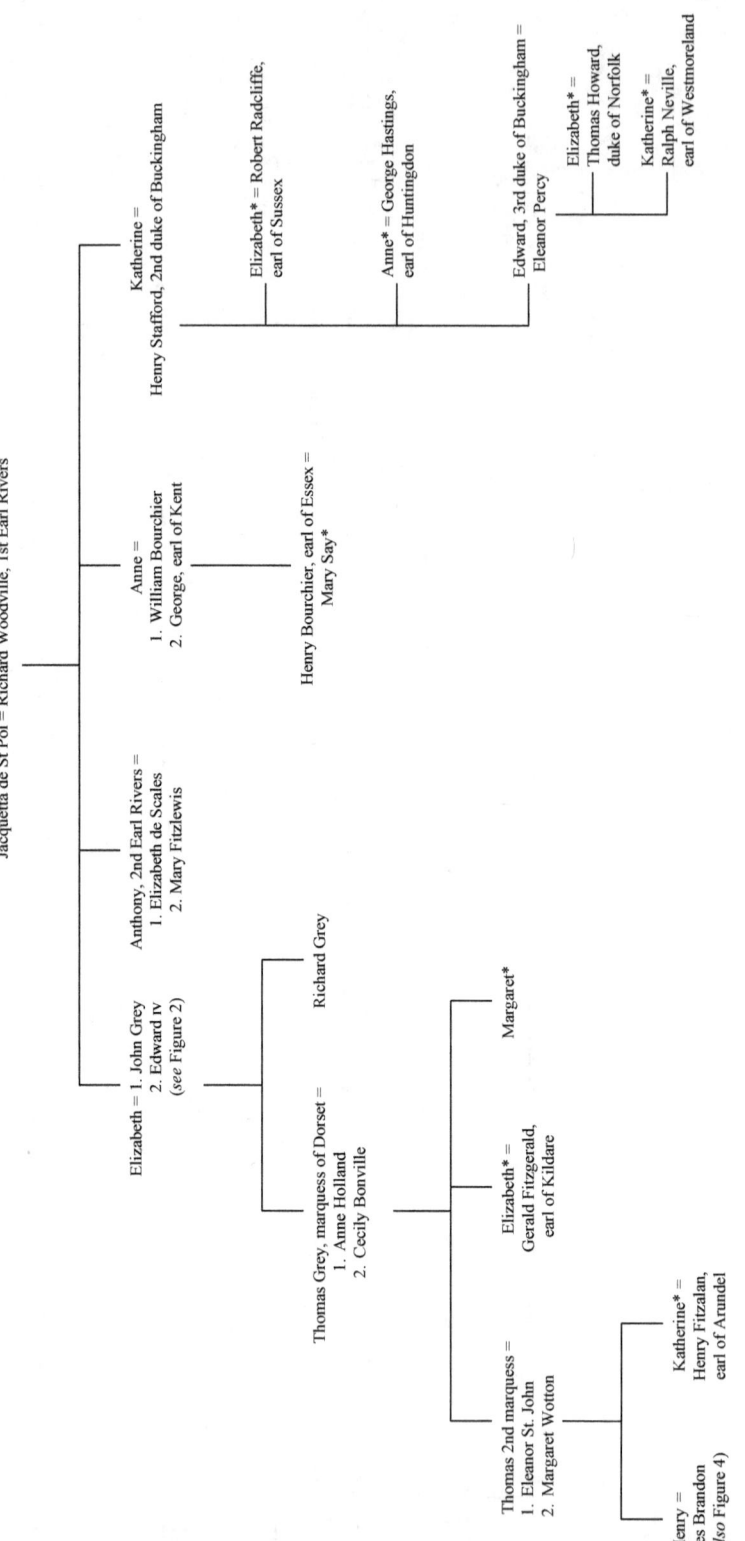

Figure 3. *The Woodvilles*

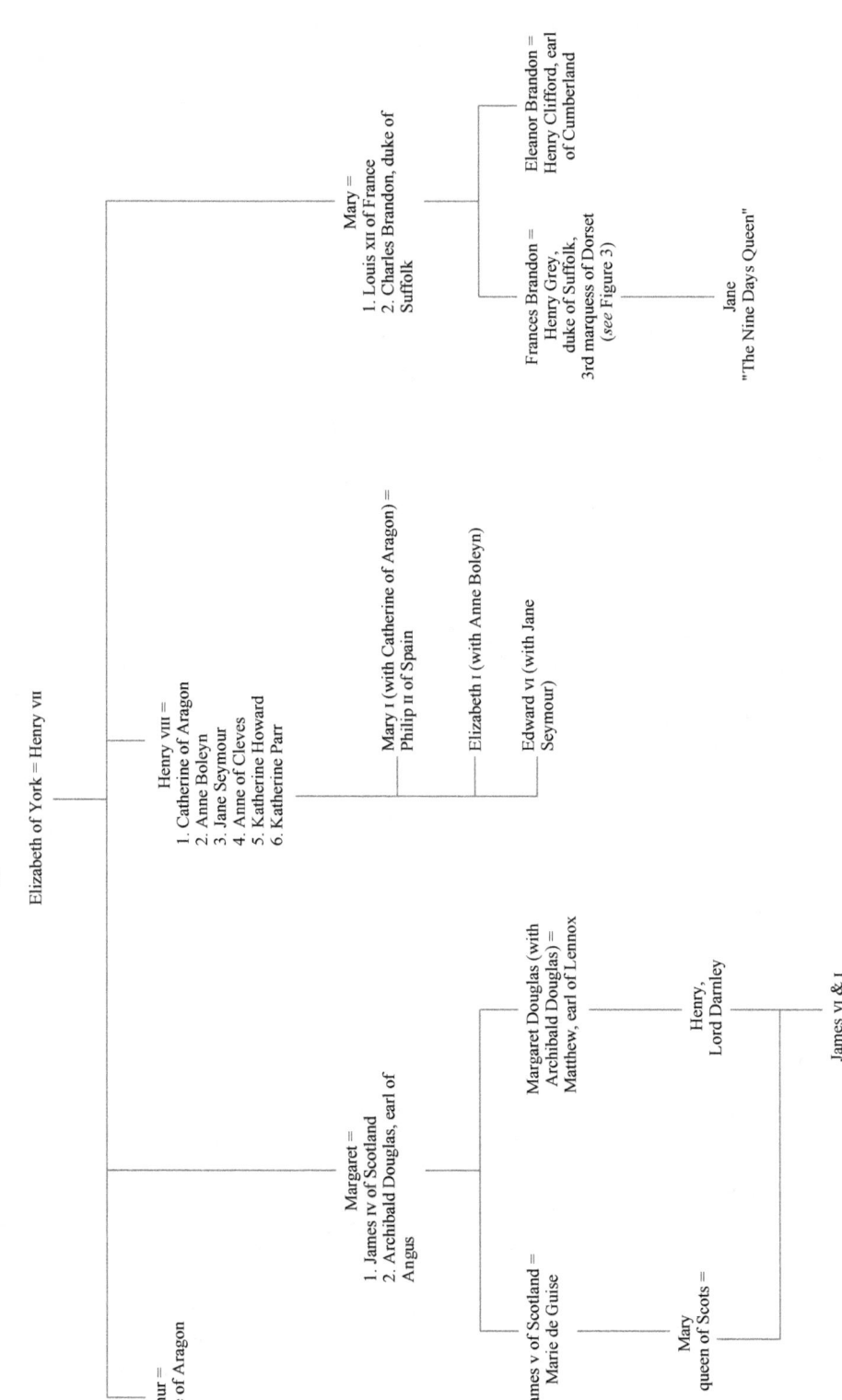

Figure 4. *The Tudors*

Introduction

On 5 October 1516 Catherine of Aragon, queen of England, and her sister-in-law, Margaret Tudor, dowager queen of Scots, sat together in Catherine's chamber at Westminster, surrounded by their waiting women. We do not know what these women spoke of, although if the two queens had conversed, it would have been in English. Catherine, the Spanish bride of Henry VIII, had lived in England for fifteen years and had become fluent in English, although she still spoke with an accent. We do know that they listened to music and watched their ladies dance.[1] They had first met when Catherine married Margaret's elder brother, Arthur, in 1501. Margaret had danced at Catherine's first wedding, and Margaret had probably become friendly with her sister-in-law before she left to marry James IV of Scotland in 1503. Thirteen years later, the two queens would have had a lot to discuss, as their reigns encompassed many of the same tragedies and triumphs. They had both experienced leaving family and friends for a strange, cold kingdom, the loss of a spouse and children, the joys of court life, the seriousness of pilgrimage and the honour and awe of coronation. As two queens in the British Isles, they had adapted to cosmopolitan court cultures with shared humanistic, chivalric and Christian values, not only between England and Scotland, but across Europe as well.

Whatever they discussed, Catherine and Margaret were soon interrupted by the king, Henry VIII, and the ambassador from Venice. Henry was a frequent visitor to his queen's chambers and, like his brother-in-law James IV, enjoyed informal pastimes with his wife and her ladies. Catherine, Margaret and their ladies would have known how to entertain the king and his guests through dancing, music and lively talk. Catherine would have been particularly interested in conversing with the Venetian ambassador, as Venice was an ally of France at the time and thus potentially an enemy of her nephew, the new king of Spain.[2] She probably already knew about the newly signed Treaty of Noyon, the peace between France, Venice, and Spain, and she may very well have discussed its implications with the ambassador on this occasion.[3] Catherine had always been a politically active queen consort, and her diplomatic experience and connections ranged across Europe to encompass the families of her sisters and their descendants.[4] Margaret was less experienced in politics

---

[1] Sebastiano Giustiniani, *Four years at the court of Henry VIII*, ed. Rawdon Brown, London 1854, i. 301.
[2] *CSP Venetian*, ii. 705, 773. Catherine's father, Ferdinand, had died in January 1516 and was succeeded by his grandson Charles of Burgundy.
[3] News of the treaty arrived in London *via* a French messenger in September: ibid. ii. 774.
[4] See Figure 1 above.

though, like Catherine, she had struggled to reconcile her loyalty to her dynasty with the duty that she owed to her husband and son.

Henry's appearance in his wife's chambers with an ambassador in tow illustrates the important roles of Catherine and Margaret at the Renaissance courts of their husbands, where their access to the centres of power and their personal and political relationships gave them influence, power and authority as queens consort. Throughout Europe the concentration of power and patronage in princely courts and households in the sixteenth century gave consorts like Catherine and Margaret visibility and influence at the cultural and political centre of the state. Scotland and England during this period saw an increasing importance of the royal court, as Henry VIII and James IV relied on a cult of monarchy and personal relations with their elites to enact their will.[5] This personal style of monarchy also manifested itself in an increased role for their queens consort, both of whom continued the medieval tradition of active and influential royal consorts while also participating in new styles of royal patronage, court life and public spectacle.[6] As queens Catherine and Margaret could wield significant power in the Renaissance monarchy through their positions as the public partner of the king, but their positions had to be asserted throughout their careers in order to maintain their status and authority. By considering their queenship in its own right and in the context of each other's queenship, this study will show how Catherine and Margaret adapted the court culture of England and Scotland to create and enhance their queenly identities.

While this study will primarily be focused on the activities of Catherine and Margaret, one of its key themes is how their queenship supported and was supported by their relationship and partnership with their husbands. Unless there are specific conflicts between the king and queen, it is easy to overlook how important the character of their relationship was to the queen's ability exercise power and authority.[7] This relationship was both public and private,

---

[5] Steven J. Gunn, *Early Tudor government, 1485-1558*, New York 1995, 43-4; Glenn Richardson, *Renaissance monarchy: the reigns of Henry VIII, Francis I and Charles V*, London 2002, 11-12; Roger A. Mason, 'Beyond the Declaration of Arbroath: kingship, counsel and consent in late medieval and early modern Scotland', in Steve Boardman and Julian Goodare (eds), *Kings, lords and men in Scotland and Britain, 1300-1625: essays in honour of Jenny Wormald*, Edinburgh 2014, 278-9; Katie Stevenson, *Chivalry and knighthood in Scotland, 1424-1513*, Woodbridge 2006, 82; A. A. MacDonald, 'Princely culture in Scotland under James III and James IV', in Martin Gosman, A. A. MacDonald and Arie Johan Vanderjagt (eds), *Princes and princely culture, 1450-1650*, Leiden 2003, i. 147-72.

[6] Barbara J. Harris, *English aristocratic women, 1450-1550: marriage and family, property and careers*, New York 2002, 210-12; James Daybell, 'Gender, politics and diplomacy: women, news and intelligence networks in Elizabethan England', in Robyn Adams and Rosanna Cox (eds), *Diplomacy and early modern culture*, Basingstoke 2011, 102.

[7] For a more wide-ranging discussion of the relationship between kingship and queenship see Theresa Earenfight, 'Without the *persona* of the prince: kings, queens and the idea of monarchy in late medieval Europe', *G&H* xix (2007), 1-21.

as the private relationship between the king and queen had public and political ramifications for the whole kingdom. That being said, it is nearly impossible for historians to determine the private nature of Catherine's and Margaret's marriages. The level of formality of life at court, combined with sparse primary source material, makes it unlikely that we will ever understand their emotional lives. What we can glean from sources is that both Catherine and Margaret got along well with their spouses and that they had relatively successful royal marriages. They seemed to have maintained good personal relationships, even when court life separated them at times. Catherine and Henry had a tradition of sending messages to each other every three days when they were apart, and Margaret and James exchanged letters and tokens when they were staying in different residences.[8] However, we must be careful not to assume that their relationships were modern, companionate marriages; both Henry and James had liaisons outside of their marriage vows, and both royal couples spent a significant portion of their lives in separate residences. When they were together, the king and queen had separate chambers and their own servants, all of which would have allowed them to live apart if they wished. Henry and James did enjoy socialising with their wives, which of course gave Catherine and Margaret the access that they needed to become successful queens. So, instead of a modern love-match, this study argues that Catherine and Henry, and Margaret and James, were royal partners, working together at times, but often at a distance, and they could be at odds with each other, too.

My assessment of Catherine and Henry's relationship as ultimately a positive and productive one may come as a surprise to those familiar with the bitter nature of Henry's campaign to divorce Catherine and marry Anne Boleyn in the 1530s, and his subsequent treatment of Catherine and their daughter Mary. One of the arguments of this study is that Catherine's relationship with Henry during the first two decades of their marriage should not be overshadowed by the marital crisis precipitated by Henry's later affair with Anne Boleyn. Henry's behaviour during that period was a highly anomalous and does not accurately reflect the more than two decades of relative marital peace that Henry and Catherine had experienced together. Likewise, there is very little evidence for any kind of serious disagreement between James IV and his young queen from their marriage in 1503 until the war with England in 1513, despite the fact that James kept mistresses before and during his marriage.

Queenship in Renaissance Europe

This complementary study of two queens embraces the transnational nature of queenship that had developed across Europe since the early Middle Ages,

---

[8] *CSP Spanish*, iv/2, 775; NRS, MSS E21/6, pp. 269, 287, 335; E21/7, fo.102r; E21/10, fo. 96r. See also *LHTA* ii. 401, 417, 464; iii. 145; iv. 310.

while also acknowledging the particularly close (though not often friendly) relationship between English and Scottish court culture in the early sixteenth century. Queenship was a truly international phenomenon as royal brides left their homelands, often with a large entourage from their natal kingdoms, to marry foreign rulers. Royal marriages benefitted both parties, and the royal dynasties of the Continent and the British Isles had long sought to use royal marriages to further their own diplomatic goals and to increase their own prestige.[9] Through dynastic marriages, queens and other elite consorts became 'vehicles for the transmission of dynastic wealth, power, and culture' across Europe.[10] This comparison of queenship across borders is particularly appropriate because we know that Renaissance monarchs were constantly (and jealously) comparing themselves and their courts with those of their fellow monarchs.[11] Moreover, English and Scottish monarchs specifically competed with each other and influenced each other's court culture, courtly literature and chivalric practices during this period. This study will show how the connections between Catherine and Margaret reflect that close relationship.[12]

Catherine's and Margaret's careers coincided with the emergence of a number of powerful and influential consorts in France and the Italian states, as well as female rulers and regents in Spain and the Low Countries. In France, Anne of Brittany (r. 1491-1514), heiress to the duchy of Brittany and consort to two French kings, worked to establish the French queen's household in parity with that of the king. She strove to protect her own considerable inheritance and resources as part of her agenda for maintaining control over an independent Brittany.[13] Ultimately, Anne failed to maintain Brittany's independence from the French kingdom, but her queenship significantly

[9] Janet L. Nelson, 'Medieval queenship', in Linda Elizabeth Mitchell (ed.), *Women in medieval western European culture*, New York 1999, 182, 185.

[10] Malcolm R. Smuts and Melissa Gough, 'Queens and the international transmission of political culture', *TCH* x (2005), 2.

[11] Richardson, *Renaissance monarchy*, 4.

[12] Katie Stevenson, 'Chivalry, British sovereignty and dynastic politics: undercurrents of antagonism in Tudor-Stewart relations, c. 1490-1513', *Historical Research* lxxxvi (2013), 1-18; Felicity Heal, 'Royal gifts and gift-exchange in sixteenth-century Anglo-Scottish politics', in Boardman and Goodare, *Kings, lords and men*, 283-300; Jenny Wormald, 'Thorns in the flesh: English kings and uncooperative Scottish rulers, 1460-1549', in G. W. Bernard and Steven J. Gunn (eds), *Authority and consent in Tudor England: essays presented to C. S. L. Davies*, Aldershot 2002, 61-78; Priscilla Bawcutt, 'Crossing the border: Scottish poetry and English readers in the sixteenth century', in Sally Mapstone and Juliette Wood (eds), *The rose and the thistle: essays on the culture of late medieval and Renaissance Scotland*, East Linton 1998, 59-76.

[13] Caroline zum Kolk, 'The household of the queen of France in the sixteenth century', *TCH* xiv (2009), 11-13. There has been a recent explosion of works on Anne of Brittany's political legacy and cultural patronage. Two works that consider her roles in the development of French queenship are Nicole Hochner, 'Revisiting Anne de Bretagne's queenship: on love and bridles', in Cynthia J. Brown (ed.), *The cultural and political legacy of Anne de Bretagne: negotiating convention in books and documents*, Cambridge 2010, 147-62, and Michel Nassiet, 'Anne de Bretagne, a woman of state', in Cynthia J. Brown (ed.), *The cultural and political*

raised the public and political profile of the office of the French queen consort. At roughly the same time, redoubtable Italian consorts such as Isabella d'Este (r. 1490-1519, d. 1539), wife of Francesco Gonzaga, were crucial participants in the administration of Italian city-states and acted as religious, literary and artistic patrons.[14] Meanwhile, Habsburg women such as Marguerite of Austria (d.1530), Mary of Hungary (d.1558) and Isabella of Portugal (d.1539) acted as powerful regents in the Netherlands and Spain for the often absentee emperor Charles V. Catherine and Margaret were related by blood and marriage to a number of these consorts. Two of Catherine's sisters, Isabella (r. 1497-8) and Maria (r. 1500-17), became queens of Portugal, while in her lifetime her nieces became queens of Portugal, France, Denmark, Hungary and Spain and Holy Roman Empress.[15] The Tudors were less prolific than their Trastámara in-laws, although Margaret's sister Mary did become queen of France in 1514. As queens at the dawn of the sixteenth-century, Catherine and Margaret were in powerful, influential company indeed.

Catherine, Margaret, and their queenly contemporaries were all expected to fulfil common duties and roles when they became queens consort, and although these expectations did vary slightly across northern Europe, the few surviving conduct texts for elite women tend to share similar ideals. The most important role model for all pre-modern European women was the Virgin Mary, the ultimate example of Christian chastity and motherhood. However, Mary represented a number of other important virtues for queens in particular. Queens had a special relationship with Mary, who, as Queen of Heaven, was the heavenly equivalent of earthly queens. Developed to complement Christ-centred kingship of the fifteenth-century, the queen's association with the Virgin Mary positioned her as an intercessor for her people, just as Mary interceded for mankind.[16] Queens, then, were expected to become mediators between kings and their people, just as Mary was in heaven.

More specific expectations for queens can be found in the writings of Christine de Pizan, whose familiarity with the fifteenth-century French royal court and in particular the controversial queen Isabeau of Bavaria makes her advice particularly practical.[17] The French courtly author of numerous texts,

---

legacy of Anne de Bretagne: negotiating convention in books and documents, Cambridge 2010, 163-76.

[14] Sharon L. Jansen, *The monstrous regiment of women: female rulers in early modern Europe*, New York 2002, 155-62. Jansen's work is a general overview of the lives and activities of female rulers and consorts in Europe. See also Roger J. Crum, 'Controlling women or women controlled? Suggestions for gender roles and visual culture in the Italian Renaissance', in Sheryl E. Reiss and David G. Wilkins (eds), *Beyond Isabella: secular women patrons of art in Renaissance Italy*, Kirksville, MO 2001, 37-50, and Natalie R. Tomas, *The Medici women: gender and power in Renaissance Florence*, Burlington, VT 2003.

[15] See Figure 1 above.

[16] Joanna L. Laynesmith, *The last medieval queens: English queenship, 1445-1503*, New York 2004, 30-4; Nelson, 'Medieval queenship', 180.

[17] Other prescriptive literature written during the adult lives of Catherine and Margaret

Pizan was one of the few authors to offer advice explicitly to royal consorts in *The treasure of the city of ladies* (1405). This text circulated in the libraries of royal women across northern Europe and the Iberian Peninsula, where it could be found in the library of Catherine's mother Isabella.[18] In England, Pizan's other works were well-known, although there is no surviving manuscript of her advice book from this period.[19] We have no way of knowing whether Pizan's work influenced Catherine and Margaret specifically, but it is likely that Pizan's advice reflected the values and expectations that were passed on from other elite women as they prepared and educated princesses to become queens.[20]

In her work Pizan provides a wealth of relatively practical advice, which shows the variety of roles that consorts were expected to perform. An ideal princess (Pizan does not use the term queen) was expected to provide hospitality and welcome to guests at her husband's court, even if the princess did not personally get along with them. Princesses were supposed to defer to their lords in public but were allowed (or even encouraged) to advise their husbands privately. Princesses should distribute largesse and charity to their subjects, and to do so in a public manner, because their behaviour would be emulated by others.[21] Pizan also touches upon other, more general, expectations for women, including the raising of children, modesty and sobriety in behaviour

---

directed their advice towards high-born women and occasionally echoed Pizan's guidance: Juan Luis Vives, *The education of a Christian woman: a sixteenth-century manual*, ed. Charles Fantazzi, Chicago 2000; *Anne of France: lessons for my daughter*, ed. Sharon L. Jansen, Woodbridge 2004.

[18] Iona McCleery, 'Isabel of Aragon (d. 1336): model queen or model saint?', *JEH* lvii (2006), 676; Elizabeth Howe, *Education and women in the early modern Hispanic world*, Aldershot 2008, 35.

[19] Her most famous work for modern audiences, *The book of the city of ladies*, was translated into English in 1521 by a member of Catherine's household specifically as part of a campaign on behalf of the right to rule of Catherine's daughter, Mary: Hope Johnston, 'How the *Livre de la cité des dames* first came to be printed in England', in Liliane Dulac, Anne Paupert, Christine Reno and Bernard Ribémont (eds), *Desireuse de plus avant enquerre*, Paris 2008, 385–96, and Cristina Malcolmson, 'Christine de Pizan's *City of ladies* in early modern England', in Cristina Malcolmson and Suzuki Mihoko (eds), *Debating gender in early modern England, 1500–1700*, New York 2002, 17–21.

[20] For a discussion of how women shared courtly traditions and educated younger women for their role see Sharon D. Michalove, 'The education of aristocratic women in fifteenth-century England', in Sharon D. Michalove and A. Compton Reeves (eds), *Estrangement, enterprise and education in fifteenth-century England*, Stroud 1998, 117–39, and 'Equal in opportunity? The education of aristocratic women, 1450–1550', in Barbara J. Whitehead (ed.), *Women's education in early modern Europe: a history, 1500–1800*, New York 1999, 46–74; Susan Broomhall, 'Gendering the culture of honour at the fifteenth-century Burgundian court', in Susan Broomhall and Stephanie Tarbin (eds), *Women, identities and communities in early modern Europe*, Aldershot 2008, 181–93; and Elizabeth L'Estrange, *Holy motherhood: gender, dynasty and visual culture in the later Middle Ages*, Manchester 2008, 82–3.

[21] Christine de Pizan, *The treasure of the city of ladies*, trans. Sarah Lawson, New York 2003, 24–7, 38, 40–1, 54–5.

and dress, and chastity.²² She also emphasises the importance a princess's of protecting reputation and cultivating the good opinions of others, including their subjects.²³ These ideals echo Catherine's and Margaret's activities as queens, and the thematic subjects of this study reflect the importance of these expectations to their queenship.

As queens in the British Isles, Catherine and Margaret may have also been aware of the influential legacy of St Margaret of Scotland, the eleventh-century English princess who became queen of Scots and was canonised in 1250. St Margaret's daughter Matilda married Henry I of England and the saint's *Vita* was probably intended as a guide for her daughter.²⁴ Her sainthood was closely tied to her queenship, and her connection to England meant that St Margaret was a potentially powerful model for both English and Scottish queens. In Scotland, there was a particular interest in her as both a model queen and nationalistic saint during the late fifteenth and early sixteenth centuries, undoubtedly encouraged by two successive queens Margaret during the reigns of James III and James IV.²⁵ St Margaret's ability to influence her husband and sons, and her role in their education, especially in spiritual matters, were considered a model for later queens.²⁶

As with Christine de Pizan's model for princesses, it is impossible to know if Catherine of Aragon or Margaret Tudor ever looked to St Margaret as a queenly example. It is tempting to assume that Margaret Tudor may have been named after the saint, although in reality she was named after her formidable grandmother and godmother, Margaret Beaufort.²⁷ Once she became queen of Scots, Margaret Tudor must have been aware of her saintly predecessor, especially since both she and James could claim descent from her. When she was pregnant in March 1512 with the future James V, she had a servant fetch St Margaret's shirt, a holy relic that was supposed to aid in childbirth, which had also been used by Mary of Guelders, James II's queen in 1451.²⁸ James IV and Margaret frequently stayed at the royal palace and monastery of Dunfermline,

---

[22] Ibid. 28-31, 41-3.

[23] Ibid. 46-50.

[24] Lois L. Huneycutt, *Matilda of Scotland: a study in medieval queenship*, Woodbridge 2003, 10.

[25] Fiona Downie, *She is but a woman: queenship in Scotland, 1424-1463*, Edinburgh 2006, 24-30; Audrey-Beth Fitch, 'Mothers and their sons: Mary and Jesus in Scotland, 1450-1560', in Steve Boardman and Eila Williamson (eds), *The cult of saints and the Virgin Mary in medieval Scotland*, Woodbridge 2010, 160-2; Louise Olga Fradenburg, *City, marriage, tournament: arts of rule in late medieval Scotland*, Madison 1991, 95; Leslie Macfarlane, *William Elphinstone and the kingdom of Scotland, 1431-1514: the struggle for order*, Aberdeen 1985, 231.

[26] Fitch, 'Mothers and their sons', 160-2.

[27] Michael K. Jones and Malcolm G. Underwood, *The king's mother: Lady Margaret Beaufort, countess of Richmond and Derby*, New York 1992, 148.

[28] NRS, MS E21/10, fo. 106v. See also *LHTA* iv. 334, and Downie, *She is but a woman*, 29.

the burial place of St Margaret and site of her principal shrine.[29] As both a royal saint and an English-born queen of Scots, St Margaret could have been regarded as a role model for Margaret Tudor in more ways than one.

Catherine's and Margaret's success as queens depended on taking these ideals and adapting them to fit their individual situations, not once, but many times over many years. As queenship studies have increased in depth and scope in recent decades, scholars have successfully argued that 'queens are not born, they "become"'.[30] Because their positions were so anomalous in early modern society – a foreign woman who outranked every man in the kingdom, save one, and who had close access to the centres of power and patronage – queens consort had repeatedly to assert their unique status while also conforming to the gendered expectations of pre-modern society, thus avoiding the negative stereotypes of ambitious, greedy or manipulative foreign queens consort.[31] The repetition of socially-agreed-upon norms allowed Catherine and Margaret to wield power and influence over men beyond the bounds of normal gender roles for women, without challenging the patriarchal *status quo* or harming their reputations.

Although proper fulfilment of the ideals of monarchy in general and queenship in particular was an ongoing process, certain moments of political crisis can illuminate what was at stake for pre-modern monarchs when performing their expected roles. For instance, Margaret of Anjou, queen consort to Henry VI of England, was slandered by her opponents when she was forced to go beyond the bounds of normal queenly roles because of the incapacity of her husband.[32] Later, the dismal failure of Henry VI and his supporters to rally the London crowds was due in large part to the king's poor performance when processing through London, to the extent that few would acknowledge his authority.[33] In contrast, Catherine's daughter Mary expertly used the material and symbolic trappings of majesty during her 1553 bid for the throne, which was 'determinative' in her success in defeating her opponents and becoming England's first queen regnant.[34] The proper performance of queenly (or kingly) roles and the maintenance of the honour and status needed to exert royal authority could have life or death consequences.

---

[29] NRS, MSS E21/11, fo. 16r; E21/12, fo. 39r. See also *LHTA* iv. 380, 418; NRS, MS E32/1, fo. 157r; and John G. Dunbar, *Scottish royal palaces: the architecture of the royal residences during the late medieval and early Renaissance periods*, East Linton 1999, 88.

[30] Earenfight, 'Without the *persona* of the prince', 14.

[31] In her study of French queens regent Katherine Crawford contends that 'early modern people deliberately measured gender behavior against cultural norms': *Perilous performances: gender and regency in early modern France*, Cambridge, MA 2004, 9.

[32] Katherine Lewis, *Kingship and masculinity in late medieval England*, New York 2013, 233.

[33] David Starkey, 'Henry VI's old blue gown: the English court under the Lancastrians and Yorkists', *TCH* iv (1999), 2–3.

[34] Jeri L. McIntosh, *From heads of household to heads of state: the preaccession households of Mary and Elizabeth Tudor, 1516–1558*, New York 2009, 164–9.

INTRODUCTION

Discussion of ideals, honour and reputation inevitably leads to questions of audience. Catherine and Margaret asserted their identity as queens before a variety of audiences, including their households, the royal court, foreign ambassadors and their subjects. There is no question that Catherine and Margaret understood that they were nearly continually before an audience of some sort. They were constantly attended by their ladies, even in their most private chambers. The arrangement of their chambers at court, which strictly limited and defined who could gain access to the queen, provided a natural transition from the semi-private space of the queen's inner chambers to the outer chambers and the wider court, thus defining who their audience would be at any given moment. For example, we know that dancing in the queen's outer chamber would have been limited to a select group of courtiers. Conversely, the different spaces of queenly duties – tournaments, for example – presuppose a wider audience for the queen's actions. Most important, because Catherine and Margaret were well aware of the protocols governing their chambers, they too would understand the differences in the audiences that they were trying to reach.

While it is clear that queens such as Catherine and Margaret would have understood that most of their actions were observed and commented upon by a variety of audiences, it is more difficult to understand the reactions of the audiences themselves. Public interaction and engagement with royal actions and issues could occur across a wide spectrum of society; however, evidence for public opinion exists in isolated and haphazard sources which do not allow for a comprehensive definition of 'the public' in the sixteenth century. Instead, historians have found isolated incidents of engagement in political and social issues by a broad range of social groups, from alderman and churchwardens to apprentices and travelling friars. Steven Gunn and Timothy Elston have convincingly argued that a wide range of the English populace was aware of royal events and had their own views on royal actions.[35] Our understanding of the sixteenth-century public, therefore, must necessarily be nebulous, but its existence or importance should not be dismissed. This perhaps best reflects how Catherine and Margaret understood their public audiences, as indistinct subjects who occasionally emerged into focus at specific moments, but who nevertheless were always part of their potential audience.

Some types of queenly interactions, such as royal entries into cities, pilgrimages across the countryside, or coronations and weddings, attracted large crowds. Margaret was greeted by large crowds during her journey to Scotland, for example, and Catherine drew a large audience of supporters

---

[35] Steven J. Gunn, 'War, dynasty and public opinion in early Tudor England', in Bernard and Gunn, *Authority and consent*, 131-49; Timothy G. Elston, 'Widow princess or neglected queen? Catherine of Aragon, Henry VIII and English public opinion, 1533-1536', in Carole Levin and Robert O. Bucholz (eds), *Queens & power in medieval and early modern England*, Lincoln 2009, 16-30.

during the 1529 Blackfriars trial of her divorce.[36] Recent work on late medieval civic plays suggests that pre-modern audiences who witnessed spectacles saw themselves as participants in the performance of various types of power, potentially including queenly power.[37] This 'spectatorial sensibility' suggests the possibility that queenly acts, such as the distribution of alms at the queen's gates, were witnessed by pre-modern individuals who understood these acts to be constitutive of the queen's power and authority.[38] Unfortunately, there are few first-hand accounts of audience reaction to queens, as most of the eyewitness accounts of their public actions come from foreign ambassadors, whose political and personal motivations were not shared by the audience at large. However, these ambassadors' accounts occasionally comment on the size or mood of the audiences in general, and they certainly indicate that a variety of audiences witnessed and responded to their queenship.

Catherine's and Margaret's assertion of their queenly identities and status had the potential to reach even wider audiences through the circulation of rumour, news and gossip. Foreign ambassadors spent a great deal of time and ink describing the festivities that they witnessed at court, and courtiers too kept those outside the court updated on the king and queen's movements and activities. For example, Anne Boleyn's gift of a gold chain to Lord Leonard Grey before he left for Ireland in 1535 was reported back to Lord Lisle, deputy of Calais, by John Grenville.[39] It is reasonable to assume that, given the importance of the court as a centre of influence, patronage and fashion, courtiers and their servants sent news about the court to their families and employers who were away from court during the period of this study.[40] In all likelihood, Catherine or Margaret would have been subjects of similar such reports, and their actions would have been widely reported and helped to form their queenly identity to a multiplicity of audiences.

Catherine and Margaret took their place as queens in a Europe that saw a number of influential consorts in the early sixteenth century. By responding to the ideals of queenship in order to assert their status, both Catherine and

---

[36] John Young, 'The fyancells of Margaret, eldest daughter of King Henry VIIth to James king of Scotland', in *Joannis Lelandi Antiquarii de Rebus Britannicis Collectanea*, ed. John Leland, London, 1770, iv. 282.

[37] Seth Lerer, '"Representyd now in yower syght": the culture of spectatorship in late-fifteenth century England', in Barbara A. Hanawalt and Gail McMurray Gibson (eds), *Bodies and disciplines: intersections of literature and history in fifteenth-century England*, Minneapolis 1996, 31–2.

[38] Ibid. 31.

[39] *The Lisle letters*, ed. Muriel St Clare Byrne, Chicago 1981, ii. 468. There is no collection of letters for this period in England or Scotland that even comes close to the depth and range of the Lisle (1533–40) or Paston (1422–1509) letters, which do not cover Catherine's or Margaret's reigns.

[40] For a discussion of the circulation of courtly and royal news during Elizabeth's reign see Natalie Mears, *Queenship and political discourse in the Elizabethan realms*, Cambridge 2005, 142–4, 166.

INTRODUCTION

Margaret continued queenly traditions developed through religious texts and secular chivalric and humanist ideals. Their adaptation of these values in numerous performative settings was effective because the audience for their queenship, at court and beyond, understood power and authority to be constituted through the fulfilment of these queenly ideals in word and deed. Catherine and Margaret were not born queens, they became queens, and their early education and experiences demonstrate how their families sought to prepare them for this role.

The lives and afterlives of Catherine of Aragon and Margaret Tudor

Catherine of Aragon, and to a lesser extent Margaret Tudor, have been the subjects of popular and scholarly interest for many years. The narratives of Catherine's and Margaret's lives have been continually told, reassessed and reimagined by scholarly and popular historians, not to mention filmmakers and novelists. This is both a blessing and a curse, as the wealth of detail is offset by the ossification of their stories at the expense of deeper scholarly understanding. Biographical narratives have a natural tendency to make value judgements about their subjects, through either an outright defence or condemnation of their behaviour. The complex lives of Catherine and Margaret thus become an inevitable march towards martyrdom (Catherine) or political failure (Margaret). This work's thematic structure will allow scholars to consider their role as queens through fruitful comparisons and detailed analysis of specific aspects of their careers, placing Catherine and Margaret within their sixteenth-century historical context and the recent historiography on queenship. To that end, at this point it may be helpful to briefly consider Catherine's and Margaret's lives and how their stories tend to be told.

Catherine was born in 1485, the youngest daughter of Isabella of Castile and Ferdinand of Aragon, the famous Catholic kings whose marriage united most of what is now called modern Spain under their rule. Isabella carefully educated Catherine and her three elder sisters to prepare them to become queens consort and to further Spanish ambitions. Isabella ensured that her daughters had excellent tutors, and Catherine and her sisters were known throughout Europe for their humanistic education, especially their knowledge of Latin. This education included lessons in music, dance, weaving and sewing as well as religious instruction, history and literature. Many scholars agree that Catherine's learning went beyond that of conventional princesses, and later in life she gained recognition from humanist luminaries such as Desiderius Erasmus and Sir Thomas More for her Latinity and wisdom.[41] It

---

[41] Maria Dowling, *Humanism in the age of Henry VIII*, London 1986, 16–7; Timothy G. Elston, 'Transformation or continuity? Sixteenth-century education and the legacy of Catherine of Aragon, Mary I and Juan Luis Vives', and Judith M. Richards, 'Mary Tudor:

is worth remembering that Isabella did not intend to educate her daughters to rule kingdoms in their own right; instead, she prepared them to become influential, accomplished and powerful representatives of Spanish interests abroad as queens consort. Significantly in light of their future careers, Isabella's educational programme gave her daughters the universal language of Europe, Latin, and the ability to seek out sources of learning on their own. In Catherine's case, her education seems to have fostered an interest in books and reading from a young age. For example, when Catherine was unhappy with homesickness in 1501, Henry VII took her to his library in Richmond to brighten her spirits.[42] Regardless of the obstacles that her daughters would face later in life, Isabella ensured that Catherine and her sisters had the skills to navigate the glittering and treacherous world of sixteenth-century European court politics and diplomacy.

Margaret Tudor was four years younger than Catherine, born in 1489. The eldest daughter of Henry Tudor and Elizabeth of York, Margaret's dynasty was less illustrious than Catherine's, but as the eldest daughter her marriage was an important component of her father's diplomacy. Very little is known about Margaret's own education in England. Hester Chapman, one of her biographers, asserts that 'Margaret Tudor was more carefully educated than most princesses of her day', although she was never celebrated for her learning in the way that Catherine of Aragon was.[43] She shared a household and tutors with her younger siblings, Henry and Mary, probably until she left for Scotland in 1503. The Tudors were widely known for their musical abilities, and Margaret was definitely musical, playing the clavichord and the lute for her future husband when they met in 1503.[44] The rest of her education may have been more haphazard. Giles Duwes, a French lutenist and librarian to Henry VII and Henry VIII, was her lute teacher and later claimed to have taught Margaret and her siblings French as well.[45] Margaret may have joined her brother in his lessons in Latin and history, as we know that Henry had an excellent education. Latin instruction had started early for her eldest brother Arthur, who at thirteen could write letters in Latin to Catherine of Aragon, his betrothed, so Margaret may have been fairly advanced in her studies, whatever

Renaissance queen of England', in Carole Levin, Jo Eldridge Carney and Debra Barrett-Graves (eds), 'High and mighty queens' of early modern England: realities and representations, New York 2003, 11–26, 30; Theresa Earenfight, 'Raising infanta Catalina de Aragón to be Catherine queen of England', Anuario de Estudios Medievales xlvi (2016), 417–43.

[42] *The receyt of the ladie Kateryne*, ed. Gordon Kipling, Oxford 1990, 77.
[43] Hester W. Chapman, *The sisters of Henry VIII*, London 1969, 26.
[44] Young, 'The fyancells of Margaret', 285.
[45] *Privy Purse expenses of Elizabeth of York: Wardrobe accounts of Edward the Fourth*, ed. Nicholas Harris Nicholas, New York 1972, 29; Giles Du Wés, *An introductorie for to lerne to rede, to pronounce, and to speake Frenche trewly compyled for the right high, excellent, and most vertuous lady, the lady Mary of Englande, daughter to our most gracious souerayn lorde kyng Henry the eight.*, London 1533, fo. A2r.

they were, by 1503.[46] Whatever book learning she did manage to pick up, her education was undoubtedly interrupted by her marriage and departure for Scotland at the age of thirteen. Unlike Catherine, who brought a tutor with her to England as one of her chaplains, none of Margaret's chaplains were known to have tutored the young queen before or after her marriage.[47]

Both Catherine and Margaret were celebrated for having skills and accomplishments, such as religious instruction, dancing, etiquette and public comportment, that today we do not immediately recognise as learning. In the sixteenth century, however, these subjects were important for young elite women to master. Margaret was well-trained in these crucial areas of public performance, as can be seen in her participation at the English court in tournaments and celebrations for her brother Arthur's marriage to Catherine and her own proxy wedding ceremony.[48] These skills would allow Margaret to fulfil her duties as hostess and social leader of her husband's court, an important part of her queenship.[49]

Margaret and Catherine, like the rest of their siblings, married into foreign royal dynasties as part of their parents' concerted efforts to further their dynastic goals. The Spanish monarchs sought to combat French expansion in Italy and the Pyrenees through the marriages of their offspring into nearby kingdoms. They hoped that Catherine's marriage would encourage Henry VII to oppose France, while Henry hoped that Catherine's family would help him neutralise threats to his dynasty on the Continent. In all likelihood, Catherine would never have known a period in her life when she was not destined to become queen of England, as her parents began negotiating for her marriage to Arthur, Prince of Wales, when she was just two years old (this possibly sheds some light on her subsequent determination, in the early 1500s and later in the 1530s, to fight for her place in England).[50] The 1489 Treaty of Medina del Campo officially sealed the match, and Catherine, at the age of three, became princess of Wales. From a long-term perspective, the Anglo-Spanish alliance renewed a much older relationship between the two regions, going back to dynastic intermarriages between Castile and England as early as the twelfth century.[51]

---

[46] Steven J. Gunn, 'Prince Arthur's preparation for kingship', in Linda Monckton and Steven J. Gunn (eds), *Arthur Tudor, prince of Wales: life, death and commemoration*, Woodbridge 2009, 7.

[47] Margaret's two known chaplains, Dr Henry Babington and James Carvenall, acted as treasurers and almoners for her household, but there is no indication that they tutored the queen.

[48] Michalove, 'Education of aristocratic women', 129-30.

[49] See chapter 3 below.

[50] For a more detailed discussion of the negotiations and the European context of Catherine's first marriage see Ian Arthurson, '"The king of Spain's daughter came to visit me": marriage, princes and politics', in Monckton and Gunn, *Arthur Tudor*, 21-2.

[51] Alexander Samson, 'A fine romance: Anglo-Spanish relations in the sixteenth century',

Henry VII also used his children's marriages to legitimise his dynasty. In the late fifteenth century, England had recently emerged from decades of the civil unrest known today as the Wars of the Roses. Henry VII claimed to have ended the conflict with his victory at the Battle of Bosworth in 1485, but his rule and dynasty were still new and potentially unstable.[52] Thus the marriage treaty with Spain was a significant confirmation of Henry's success and legitimacy as a monarch. Prince Arthur's marriage to Catherine was the first step in raising England's international profile, and Margaret's marriage to James IV, negotiated shortly after the Spanish match, continued to secure Henry's throne by neutralising Scotland as a safe haven for rebels.[53] The motivations for Catherine's and Margaret's marriages were so intertwined that Catherine's parents sent an envoy to Scotland in the 1490s to help negotiate a peace between the English and the Scots, a peace that would also benefit Spain.[54] Ferdinand and Isabella had even considered marrying Catherine's older sister, Maria, to James IV, in an effort to unite England and Scotland through the two sisters. When Maria's hand was needed to reinforce their Portuguese alliance, however, the Spanish kings quickly pivoted to supporting Margaret's marriage to James. Both Catherine's and Margaret's marriages complemented and reinforced the goals and policy of the other for both England and Spain.

Catherine's dynastic connections were significant and complex assets to her as queen, and therefore it is important to bear in mind the multiple alliances that her marriage cemented for England beyond the Spanish kingdoms. The most important of these connections came from the marriage of Catherine's elder sister Juana to Philip of Burgundy, the Habsburg heir to the Holy Roman Emperor, in 1496. After the deaths of Catherine's older siblings Juan and Isabella, in 1498 Juana and her children became Ferdinand and Isabella's heirs. Eventually, Juana's son Charles would become the Holy Roman Emperor, king of Spain and duke of Burgundy, in addition to holding numerous other lands and titles. Since he was her nephew and king of Spain, Catherine would regard Charles and his Habsburg family as England's natural allies against their mutual enemy, France. Catherine's other surviving sister Maria married into the royal house of Portugal, and Maria's son became John III of Portugal.[55]

JMEMS xxxix (2009), 78; Rose Walker, 'Leonor of England and Eleanor of Castile: Anglo-Iberian marriage and cultural exchange in the twelfth and thirteenth centuries', in Maria Bullon-Fernandez (ed.), *England and Iberia in the Middle Ages, 12th–15th century: cultural, literary and political exchanges*, New York 2007, 67–88.

[52] Henry VII's claim to the throne was weak, as it came through his mother's descent from a bastard line of the royal family, and he faced several challenges to his throne by pretenders claiming to be princes of the rival dynasty of York.

[53] David Dunlop, 'The "masked comedian": Perkin Warbeck's adventures in Scotland and England from 1495 to 1497', *Scottish Historical Review* lxx (1991), 127-8.

[54] Arthurson, 'Marriage, princes and politics', 21-2.

[55] See Figure 1 above.

After much negotiation and some delays, Catherine arrived in England to marry Arthur in 1501, accompanied by a splendid escort and Spanish servants carefully chosen by her mother. Arthur and Catherine's wedding was possibly the greatest celebration of Henry VII's reign, and its magnificent pageantry was recorded in a detailed narrative chronicle.[56] Given the years of strife and dynastic uncertainty that had preceded Henry VII's reign, Catherine and Arthur's marriage was a major accomplishment at its inception, regardless of the events that followed. The marriage of an heir to the throne during his father's lifetime had not occurred in England since Edward III's son the Black Prince married Joan of Kent in 1361, so the marriage of an adolescent heir to the throne to a foreign princess was an extraordinary statement of the stability and prosperity that the Tudor dynasty brought to the throne of England.[57] It indicated the health and vigour of the heir and signalled his coming-of-age and maturity. The marriage also indicated the confidence and power of Henry VII, who, unlike his recent predecessors, did not need to marry his children to noble English families in order to secure their support.

Tragically, young Arthur died a few months after the wedding, and Catherine was left a young widow in a strange land. Her parents immediately began negotiations for a second marriage for Catherine, to Arthur's younger brother Henry, the new heir. These negotiations appeared to be finalised in 1503, although Catherine would have to wait until Henry came of age for the marriage to take place officially. It was forbidden in canon law for a woman to marry her husband's brother, so in 1502 Catherine's parents obtained a papal bull that allowed Catherine to marry Prince Henry.[58] Although the dispensation and the status of Catherine's marriage to Arthur would become a crucial issue in the 1520s and 1530s, in 1503 it was quickly dealt with as a minor obstacle to the new marriage. Shifting European politics and English alliances, however, meant repeated delays to Catherine's second marriage. She remained in England in royal limbo, neither widow nor wife, for six years.

For Margaret's marriage alliance, it took years of careful diplomacy to bring England and Scotland, traditional enemies, together. Having put off marriage for years in the hope of obtaining a prestigious match with a French, Spanish

---

[56] *Receyt of the ladie Kateryne*. See also Sydney Anglo, 'The London pageants for the reception of Katharine of Aragon: November 1501', *Journal of the Warburg and Courtauld Institutes* xxvi (1963), 53-89.

[57] Henry VI's heir Edward was technically married during his father's lifetime, in 1470, to Anne Neville, the daughter of the earl of Warwick. However, this was during the Yorkist period of ascendancy and shortly before the final Lancastrian defeat and Edward's murder.

[58] Garrett Mattingly, *Catherine of Aragon*, New York 1960, 51-4, 59. This dispensation may have been unnecessary, as Catherine's household, led by her duenna Elvira Manuel, swore that the princess was a virgin. Thus her marriage to Arthur was unconsummated and could be considered invalid in the eyes of the Church. For a detailed discussion of the canon law of Catherine's divorce, including a consideration of the dispensation obtained in 1503, see J. J. Scarisbrick, *Henry VIII*, Berkeley 1968, 164-95, and David Starkey, *Six wives: the queens of Henry VIII*, New York 2003, 84-7.

or even Burgundian bride, James IV appears to have decided in 1499 seriously to pursue an English marital alliance.[59] The sixteen-year age difference between James and Margaret was one of the reasons the Anglo-Scottish alliance had many false starts; in 1499 James was twenty-six, while Margaret was only ten. Margaret's mother and grandmother refused to let her be sent to Scotland at such a young age, and so James was ultimately forced to wait for his bride to grow up.

In 1502 a formal peace treaty between in England and Scotland was signed, optimistically entitled the Treaty of Perpetual Peace. Margaret's marriage contract was signed at the same time. A year later, Margaret left the English court and began her journey to Scotland with a full train of supporters, including some of the highest nobility of the land and a lavish amount of wedding goods. This was the first major court event following the death of Margaret's mother, Elizabeth of York. The queen had died of a childbed fever in early February 1503, at the age of thirty-seven. Her death weighed heavily on the Tudor court and must have greatly affected the young Margaret as she prepared to leave her home. Margaret's journey to the northern borders of England was more than a wedding procession. In the waning years of Henry VII's reign, it was celebration of Tudor rule and an affirmation of the king's power and support in the north.

After the final round of wedding festivities in Edinburgh, most of Margaret's retinue returned to England, leaving her in Scotland with a handful of English attendants to make up her household. Margaret then began fully to assume her role as queen consort to James IV, travelling with the Scottish court, which led a peripatetic existence typical of the royal courts of the sixteenth century. Although relations between England and Scotland were never completely cordial, from the time of Margaret's marriage until the death of her father in 1509, Scotland and England were officially at peace. Scottish and English leaders began to administer justice in the borderlands between the two kingdoms, and James sent a steady stream of messengers south with news of Margaret and orders to buy goods from London.[60]

Henry VII's death in 1509 brought his son Henry VIII to the throne. The new king, who appears to have been of a romantic disposition, immediately married Catherine in a private ceremony, and she was crowned queen alongside Henry in Westminster Abbey. The quietness of Catherine's second wedding might suggest some 'lingering doubts about the propriety of the marriage',[61] but Catherine's history should not be rewritten with the benefit of hindsight. In truth, Catherine's second wedding was vastly eclipsed by a greater event, her joint coronation with Henry. It is far more likely that Henry's youth, and the

---

[59] David Dunlop, 'Aspects of Anglo-Scottish relations from 1471 to 1513', unpubl. PhD diss. Liverpool 1988, 210–13.
[60] NRS, MS E21/8, fos 81r, 90r. See also *LHTA* iii. 55, 351, 369.
[61] Starkey, *Six wives*, 109.

somewhat precarious nature of the Tudor succession given that he had no surviving brothers, necessitated a quick wedding that could then be publicly celebrated with his coronation.[62] Henry was, at eighteen, a youthful king, and the presence of a queen consort would provide further support to the new reign through her own magnificence and comparative maturity (Catherine was five years older than Henry). It would also further legitimise the Tudor dynasty, as Catherine was a member of one of the most celebrated royal houses in Europe. Henry VIII was the first English king to successfully claim the throne by a regular act of succession since 1422, and now he had as his allies his wife's illustrious family, renowned throughout Europe as the 'Most Catholic Kings' of Spain.[63]

Accounts of Catherine's life and career as queen have focused primarily on two themes, the English alliance with Spain and the need for an heir. These themes are prominent in a large part because they reflect the controversies over Henry VIII's later attempts to divorce Catherine, but it is certainly important to note that from the early years of her marriage, Catherine played a large part in the diplomacy between her father Ferdinand and her husband. David Loades, Garrett Mattingly and more recently Sharon Jansen have all emphasised Catherine's behind-the-scenes role as the true Spanish ambassador at the English court.[64] In fact, she was Europe's first female accredited ambassador, a post she was granted by her father in 1507.[65] After her father's death in 1516, Catherine's connections to Spain became more irregular but still remained an important part of her queenship.

As in the case of Catherine, much of the history written about Margaret's career as queen consort has focused on the diplomatic implications of the 1503 Anglo-Scottish alliance, and the ceremonial significance of her wedding celebrations. Although these are important studies, they are not primarily concerned with Margaret's career as a queen of Scots. Their interest in her is focused on her role as a symbol of peace and the alliance that her marriage represented. In a variety of articles written by historians and literary scholars, the negotiations, ceremonies and meaning of Margaret's marriage have been subjected to academic scrutiny.[66] Douglas Gray's article 'The royal entry in

---

[62] Nearly all of Henry's weddings occurred 'privately' with only a few witnesses, regardless of the propriety of the bride in question. None of them were lavish, public ceremonies on the scale of Catherine's wedding to Arthur in 1501, which took place in St Paul's Cathedral, although some of Henry's marriages were celebrated afterwards with processions and tournaments. See Maria Hayward, *Dress at the court of King Henry VIII: the wardrobe book of the Wardrobe of the Robes prepared by James Worsley in December 1516; edited from MS Harley 2284, and his inventory prepared on 17 January 1521, edited from Harley MS 4217, both in the British Library*, Leeds 2007, 53-5.

[63] Henry VIII was also the first adult monarch to succeed his father since Henry V succeeded Henry IV in 1413.

[64] Mattingly, *Catherine of Aragon*, 134-5; D. M. Loades, *Henry VIII and his queens*, Stroud 1996, 23; Jansen, *Monstrous regiment*, 117-19.

[65] CSP Spanish, i. 520

[66] Louise Olga Fradenburg, 'Sovereign love: the wedding of Margaret Tudor and James

sixteenth-century Scotland', argues that Scotland developed a vibrant tradition of royal entries in the sixteenth century, beginning with Margaret's wedding celebrations.[67] Sarah Carpenter has used the English account of Margaret's wedding to analyse the meaning of display and performance in early modern court culture.[68] Margaret's ceremonial entry into Edinburgh was one of the first recorded Scottish royal entries, and its position as a pioneer for Scottish entries contributes to its importance in Scottish historiography. Margaret's marriage has also attracted notice because of its long-term implications for the history of Britain. For many years Margaret's son James V and her granddaughter Mary queen of Scots were plausible claimants to the English throne, and eventually her great-grandson, James VI of Scotland, would succeed Elizabeth I as king of Great Britain.[69] With the benefit of historical hindsight, Margaret's marriage to James IV becomes a highly significant event in British history.

The other significant, and shared, theme in the lives of Catherine and Margaret was their struggles with childbearing. In 1506 Margaret became pregnant for the first time, probably an indication that James had waited to consummate their marriage.[70] Only one of Margaret's children with James IV, born in 1512, survived to adulthood and eventually became James V. Catherine's only surviving offspring was a daughter, who became Mary I of England. Both queens experienced the stillbirth or infant death of many of their children (at least five that we know of in the case of each woman). Catherine and Margaret each produced one surviving child in ten years of marriage, but while Catherine's pregnancies have been subject to detailed historical scrutiny because of Henry VIII's subsequent attempts to divorce her in order to sire more legitimate children, Margaret's childbearing, with its similar outcome of one surviving child with James IV, has not received the same attention.[71] This is yet another example of how the later events of Catherine's life have dictated which aspects of her life have become the focus of her history.

IV of Scotland', in Louise Olga Fradenburg (ed.), *Women and sovereignty*, Edinburgh 1992, 78-100, and *City, marriage, tournament*; Lorna G. Barrow, '"[T]he kynge sent to the qwene, by a gentylman, a grett tame hart": marriage, gift exchange, and politics: Margaret Tudor and James IV, 1502-13', *Parergon* xxi (2004), 65-84; David Dunlop, 'The politics of peacekeeping: Anglo-Scottish relations from 1503-1511', *RS* viii (1994), 138-61.

[67] Douglas Gray, 'The royal entry in sixteenth-century Scotland', in Mapstone and Wood, *The rose and the thistle*, 10.

[68] Sarah Carpenter, '"To thexaltacyon of noblesse": a herald's account of the marriage of Margaret Tudor and James IV', *MET* xxix (2007), 104-20.

[69] See Figure 4 above.

[70] John Carmi Parsons's study of aristocratic and royal women shows that, even when married at a very young age, most of these women did not have their first child until they were fifteen or older: 'Mothers, daughters, marriage, power: some Plantagenet evidence, 1150-1500', in John Carmi Parsons (ed.), *Medieval queenship*, Stroud 1998, 65-6.

[71] John Dewhurst, 'The alleged miscarriages of Catherine of Aragon and Anne Boleyn', *Medical History* xxviii (1984), 49-56; Catrina Banks Whitley and Kyra Kramer, 'A new explanation for the reproductive woes and midlife decline of Henry VIII', *HJ* liii (2010), 827-48.

INTRODUCTION

After her first pregnancy, Margaret began to assume a more independent role from her husband, indicating that her queenship had entered a more mature phase. Her household was briefly administered separately from the king's, and it began to include more Scottish personnel as the majority of her English attendants left Scotland between 1507 and 1508.[72] This change in staff meant that Margaret could forge new links with the Scottish court and the king's household, as many of Margaret's new officials had previously served the king.[73] Margaret was also increasingly in the public eye, as she and James went on joint pilgrimages and progresses to more remote areas of the kingdom. Margaret took on some public roles on her own, as in 1511 when she made a formal entry into the city of Aberdeen without the king.[74] While Margaret seems to have flourished in Scotland, after 1509 relations between Scotland and England became strained as her brother Henry VIII became more belligerent towards France, Scotland's traditional ally. Margaret attempted to keep the peace between her husband and her brother, but in 1513 James invaded the north of England in response to Henry's invasion of France. James was killed at the battle of Flodden Field by English troops under Catherine's command. At twenty-three Margaret became queen regent for her infant son, James V.

It is the later period of Margaret's life, from 1513 until her death in 1542, which has attracted the disapproving attention of historians since the sixteenth century. As Louise O. Fradenburg has pointed out, this history has been dominated by a type of modern nationalist historiography that vilifies the foreign 'interference' that Margaret represented.[75] Margaret's time as queen regent in 1513-14 has recently been reassessed by Amy Blakeway, who shows that Margaret was initially on her way to becoming an active, influential regent who had the support of some Scottish lords.[76] Margaret lost her position of regent when she married Archibald Douglas, earl of Angus, in 1514. While this study will not focus on Margaret's regency, understanding her previous experience as the public partner of her husband James IV will contribute to the ongoing reassessment of this complex historical figure.

Over the course of her lengthy marriage, Catherine's role at the English court also changed as her relationship with the king and her connections to England changed. In the early years of their marriage Henry looked to her for

---

[72] Athol L. Murray, 'The Exchequer and crown revenue of Scotland, 1437-1542', unpubl. PhD diss. Edinburgh 1961, 219-20. In February of 1508, which was the last time Margaret's English household members were paid separate fees, only nine of the original twenty-five Englishmen and women were still being paid by James IV: NRS, MS E21/9, fo. 60r. See also *LHTA* iv. 67.

[73] *LHTA* i. 146; ii. 109.

[74] *Extracts from the council register of the burgh of Aberdeen, 1398-1570*, ed. John Stuart, Aberdeen 1844, 81.

[75] Louise Olga Fradenburg, 'Troubled times: Margaret Tudor and the historians', in Mapstone and Wood, *The rose and the thistle*, 41.

[76] Amy Blakeway, *Regency in sixteenth-century Scotland*, Woodbridge 2015, 30, 71-2.

advice and counsel, to the extent that he named her regent and governess of England while on campaign in France in 1513. This moment was perhaps the apogee of Catherine's public power: under her command England won its greatest military victory of Henry's reign at Flodden. After 1520 Catherine seems to have withdrawn somewhat from the political and courtly stage, in part because of the ascendancy of Cardinal Thomas Wolsey as Henry VIII's chief minister. She devoted more of her energies to the education of her surviving daughter Mary, but she continued to perform her public duties in patronising scholars, corresponding with foreign monarchs, administering her lands and running her household. These activities continued up to and during the divorce crisis, whereupon the loss of her income and status, and her forced retirement in 1533 effectively ended her queenship. Catherine died three years later at Kimbolton.

Early histories of Catherine of Aragon, which began appearing soon after her death in 1536, were heavily influenced by the author's opinion of the Henrician Reformation and rarely considered her history in its own right. Catherine became either a virtuous Catholic martyr or a woman whose marriage to Henry VIII had never been valid and whose daughter was a bastard. However, by the late seventeenth century, Catherine's reputation had begun to solidify around the themes of dutiful wife, pious Catholic and wronged woman.[77] In the nineteenth century, Catherine's reputation as a politically able wife and mother began to take shape in a biography written by Agnes and Elizabeth Strickland.[78] The definitive modern account of Catherine's life is the masterful biography written by Garrett Mattingly in 1941.[79] Mattingly, who was familiar with foreign archives and had a keen understanding of the web of sixteenth-century European diplomacy, presents Catherine's life in the context of the domestic and foreign politics that shaped her world. It is still the best study of Catherine's life to date.

The recent interest in queenship studies has led to articles that address specific aspects or moments of Catherine's life, such as the education of her

---

[77] Judith M. Richards, 'Public identity and public memory: case studies of two Tudor women', in Broomhall and Tarbin, *Women, identities and communities*, 206-8; Richards makes an interesting point that Catherine's reputation may reveal the survival of oral traditions, which favoured the queen, in opposition to the print propaganda put forth by Henry VIII and his son. For Catherine's reputation after the death of Henry VIII see also Betty S. Travitsky, 'Reprinting Tudor history: the case of Catherine of Aragon', *Renaissance Quarterly* 1 (1997), 164-74, and Matthew C. Hansen, '"And a queen of England, too": the "Englishing" of Catherine of Aragon in sixteenth-century English literary and chronicle history', in Levin, Carney and Barrett-Graves, *'High and mighty queens'*, 79-100.

[78] Agnes Strickland and Elisabeth Strickland, *Lives of the queens of England: from the Norman Conquest*, Philadelphia 1847, iv. 63-121. For a modern appraisal of the Strickland sisters' work see Judith M. Richards, '"Unblushing falsehood": the Strickland sisters and the domestic history of Henry VIII', in Thomas Betteridge and Thomas S. Freeman (eds), *Henry VIII and history*, Burlington, VT 2012, 165-78.

[79] Mattingly, *Catherine of Aragon*.

daughter Mary, her cultural patronage and her own preparation to be queen, but there has been no full-length scholarly study of Catherine's queenship since Mattingly's work.[80] There are many modern partial and full-length biographies of Catherine, although these tend to be written for popular audiences.[81] More often than not, biographies of Catherine form a part of the 'six wives' story, a narrative history of Henry VIII's reign written through the lens of his six wives. Antonia Fraser, David Loades, Alison Weir and David Starkey, among many others, have written Catherine's life story within this context.[82] These narratives ensure that many features of Catherine's life – her marriages, diplomatic activities, physical decline and the fight over her divorce – are well-known. In these works, Catherine is most often cast as the 'virtuous queen' or wronged women in opposition to Anne Boleyn, and as in her earlier biographies more is revealed about Henry VIII's reign than about Catherine's queenship. While this type of history presents an entertaining narrative, it does not and cannot present Catherine within her proper context, as a queen consort with international standing and as a public partner in the first decades of Henry VIII's monarchy.

In a similar manner to the collective biographies of Henry's wives, Margaret Tudor has frequently been written about with her younger sister, Mary Tudor, who briefly became queen of France before marrying Charles Brandon and returning to England. The comparison between Margaret and Mary is less useful than Margaret and Catherine because Mary Tudor was only queen for a few months, unlike her sister and sister-in-law.[83] Patricia Buchanan's *Margaret*

---

[80] Elston, 'Transformation or continuity?'; Aysha Pollnitz, 'Christian women or sovereign queens? The schooling of Mary and Elizabeth', in Anna Whitelock and Alice Hunt (eds), *Tudor queenship: the reigns of Mary and Elizabeth*, Basingstoke 2010, 127–44; Valerie Schutte, '"To the illustrious queen": Katherine of Aragon and early modern book dedications', in Julie A. Chappell and Kaley A. Kramer (eds), *Women during the English Reformations: renegotiating gender and religious identity*, New York 2014, 15–28; Emma Cahill Marron, 'Una Lucrecia del siglo XVI: los libros de Catalina de Aragón', in Sandro De Maria and Manuel Parada López de Corselas (eds), *El imperio y las Hispanias de Trajano a Carlos V: clasicismo y poder en el arte español*, Bologna 2014, 419–28; Theresa Earenfight, 'Regarding Catherine of Aragon', in Carole Levin and Christine Stewart-Nuñez (eds), *Scholars and poets talk about queens*, New York 2015, 137–57, and 'Raising infanta Catalina'; Maria Hayward, 'Spanish princess or queen of England? The image, identity, and influence of Catherine of Aragon at the courts of Henry VII and Henry VIII', in José Luis Colomer and Amalia Descalzo (eds), *Spanish fashion at the courts of early modern Europe*, Madrid 2014, 11–36.

[81] Some of the most recent examples include Giles Tremlett, *Catherine of Aragon: the Spanish queen of Henry VIII*, New York 2010; Patrick Williams, *Catherine of Aragon*, Stroud 2012; Amy Licence and Philippa Gregory, *Catherine of Aragon: an intimate life of Henry VIII's true wife*, Stroud 2017.

[82] Antonia Fraser, *The six wives of Henry VIII*, London 1993; Loades, *Henry VIII*; Alison Weir, *The six wives of Henry VIII*, London 1997; Starkey, *Six wives*.

[83] Maria Perry, *Sisters to the king: the tumultuous lives of Henry VIII's sisters, Margaret of Scotland and Mary of France*, London 1998; Nancy Lenz Harvey, *The rose and the thorn: the lives of Mary and Margaret Tudor*, New York 1975; Chapman, *Sisters*. Nevertheless, Mary was an important figure at the court of her brother Henry VIII and a close friend of Queen

Tudor (1985), is the only modern work to discuss Margaret's life in full without comparing her to her younger sister; it is a curious biography that blends popular history with scholarly background.[84] In contrast to these biographical narratives, this work considers Catherine's and Margaret's queenship thematically, in hopes of not only avoiding a teleological analysis of their lives, but also revealing aspects of their reigns – such as the importance of patronage, court life and material culture – that are difficult to discern in a linear narrative.

Sources

Queens are difficult to trace within the royal archives because their records are often subsumed within the records of the king and his court. Eric Ives noted this problem in his study of Anne Boleyn: 'much of the necessary record material no longer exists or is almost inextricably mixed up with the king's archive. This partial submerging of a queen in the overall royal entourage is one explanation for there being less notice of Anne Boleyn's active participation in public affairs after 1533 [precisely when she became queen consort]'.[85] This is a common challenge facing historians of queens, as even figures as seemingly dominant as Anne Boleyn fade into the background of the archival record. Margaret especially suffers from this type of obfuscation because her household was not accounted for independently from the king's household (except for a few months in 1508) and her administration only partially appears in the records.

Despite the remarkable survival of state papers in England, records relating to queens have an uneven survival rate until the seventeenth century. Because Catherine, like several of Henry's wives, ended her reign in disgrace, there seems to have been little institutional or personal motivation for preserving documents relating to her reign, especially any which might have called into question the legitimacy of her successors' reigns.[86] Moreover, although some of Catherine's and Margaret's expenses appear in the Exchequer rolls of their kingdoms, there does not appear to have been a systematic accounting to the English or Scottish Exchequers of the queen's own officials in the sixteenth century.[87] Instead, only a handful of documents created by Catherine's officials

---

Catherine. For a nuanced approach to Mary's life and career see Erin A. Sadlack, *The French queen's letters: Mary Tudor Brandon and the politics of marriage in sixteenth-century Europe*, New York 2011.

[84] Patricia Hill Buchanan, *Margaret Tudor, queen of Scots*, Edinburgh 1985.

[85] Eric W. Ives, *The life and death of Anne Boleyn*, Oxford 2004, 205.

[86] Ibid. 215.

[87] This process was considerably more systematic in the Middle Ages, where the dominance of the Exchequer over royal finances ensured that the revenue and finances of Queen Isabella of France (1295–1358) as well as her some of her predecessors, are in fact more fully documented than those of Catherine of Aragon: Hilda Johnstone, 'The queen's

INTRODUCTION

have survived, and most of the sources related to her queenship are part of the familiar chronicles, state papers and diplomatic correspondence of the reign of Henry VIII.

There is an even smaller number of surviving sources for Margaret's time as queen consort of Scotland, possibly in part due to Margaret's chaotic later career as queen regent and queen mother. Her active political life after 1513 included numerous attempted coups and a temporary exile, any of which may have resulted in her official and personal papers being confiscated at some point. For instance, in September 1516, after she had fled to England, an indenture was made of the goods taken into custody by the new regent, John, duke of Albany. Listed amongst the valuable jewels and costly fabrics was a packet of letters regarding the surety of Margaret's lands in Kilmarnock, four books and an obligation for a debt of 2,000 marks, none of which have survived.[88] In addition to the uneven survival of the queen's records, Scottish royal records in general suffered from losses as a result of the unsettled nature of Scottish affairs in the sixteenth and seventeenth centuries.[89] Scottish secretaries also tended to treat their papers as personal documents, and thus they were not systematically kept once they left office.[90] The principal surviving sources concerning Margaret are accounts of expenditure of the royal household, kept by the Treasurer, which include expenses for Margaret's wardrobe and household amongst those of the king's household.[91] These accounts also provide evidence of life at court under James IV, replacing or in some instances supplementing, the descriptions usually provided by chroniclers and ambassadors. The poems of William Dunbar, a court poet patronised by James and Margaret, are also useful in constructing a picture of the Scottish court, although these must be approached with the caution due to any literary source.[92] Margaret's wedding journey was chronicled by the English Herald, John Young, who accompanied Margaret to Scotland and was a witness to the

---

exchequer under the three Edwards', in J. G. Edwards, V. H. Galbraith and E. F. Jacob (eds), *Historical essays in honour of James Tait*, Manchester 1933, 143-53.

[88] NRS, MS SP13/23.

[89] Unlike England, Scotland suffered numerous invasions in the sixteenth and seventeenth centuries. After Cromwell's 1650 invasion and occupation of Scotland, he had the records taken to England, and although they were returned in 1660, one of the ships carrying the records sank on the voyage home: Scottish Record Office, *Guide to the National Archives of Scotland*, Edinburgh 1996, pp. x-xi. Incomplete inventories makes it difficult to know what was lost in the wreckage.

[90] Ibid. 1. To a lesser extent, this was a problem in England as well, as can be seen by the wealth of documents that survive in the state papers simply because they were confiscated after the disgrace of their owners, such as Wolsey or Cromwell.

[91] NRS, MSS E21/6-12. See also *LHTA* i-iv.

[92] See also William Dunbar, *The poems of William Dunbar*, ed. James Kinsley, Oxford 1979, and William Hepburn, 'William Dunbar and the courtmen: poetry as a source for the court of James IV', *IR* lxv (2014), 95-112.

betrothal and marriage festivities.[93] Young's account, with its particular focus on courtly ceremony and etiquette, is invaluable.

It is important to acknowledge how the survival of specific sources alters our ability to understand Margaret Tudor's career and encourages us to accept that her history, and Catherine's, will always be contingent and piecemeal. Noting the absence or lack of sources for Margaret potentially reveals unconsidered problems or limitations on her queenship, problems that can be mitigated by studying these two women together. I have sought to craft a juxtaposition of Catherine's and Margaret's reigns in a way that illuminates not merely their commonalities and differences, but also their shared connections and experiences that when seen together present a clearer understanding of both their reigns. The manuscript sources on Catherine's queenship not only reveal details about Catherine, but also point to missing sources relevant to Margaret's queenship. For instance, Margaret's dependence upon her husband for administering her household and estates significantly affected her ability to become a patron and to assert her own control over finances once she was a widow. This argument is supported by an understanding not only of Margaret's patronage but also of Catherine's patronage and household finances. As is probably evident from their histories, the personal details of their queenships, including their age upon accession (Catherine was twenty-three and Margaret was thirteen) and duration of their reigns (Catherine reigned for over twenty years, Margaret only ten), would make a strict comparison unfair and unhelpful. Catherine and Margaret were queens in kingdoms that had developed different but related traditions of queenship, and this study acknowledges the contingency of their queenships on an individual level while also speaking to the nature of queenship in early modern Europe more generally.

Structure

This work begins with a discussion of the influence of Catherine's and Margaret's immediate predecessor in England, Elizabeth of York (r. 1486-1503) on early sixteenth-century British queenship. Elizabeth of York was Margaret's mother and Catherine's mother-in-law, and her reign provided an important precedent for Catherine and Margaret to follow when they established their own courts and households in England and Scotland. Elizabeth's queenship connected Catherine and Margaret beyond their shared family ties. For both women, Elizabeth was the only queen consort whom they had experience observing (Catherine's mother was a queen regnant), and her participation in English court culture influenced Catherine's and Margaret's activities at their own courts. When Margaret left for Scotland, she brought with her not only the memories and example of mother, but several members of her mother's

---

[93] Young, 'The fyancells of Margaret'.

household, who stayed in Scotland for many years and thus helped to establish the early patterns of her queenship. These servants then returned to the English court, where they served Catherine when she became queen. Elizabeth connected these two queens in many ways; this chapter also demonstrates the importance of studying Catherine and Margaret together.

The second chapter considers Catherine's and Margaret's clothing and material goods, and the relationship between magnificence, queenly identity and honour. The chapter focuses on moments of tension and political crisis during their queenships, when clothing and material goods became important means of asserting their queenly honour and virtue. Both queens used material culture during their first pregnancies to maintain their position at court during their confinement and after difficult births. After she returned to England in 1515, Margaret relied on material culture to assert her political importance after losing her position as queen regent for her son. In 1520 Catherine skilfully manipulated the magnificence of the royal court to argue for a Spanish alliance during the Anglo-French summit at the Field of Cloth of Gold. In order to understand how their authority and status at court were assessed and understood by their contemporaries, this chapter argues that we must look to the material culture of their surroundings, including their clothing, linens and furniture, to see how clothes could literally make a queen.

Chapters 3 and 4 turn to the relationship between the king and queen at the English and Scottish courts. The third chapter considers the close connections between the royal couple, demonstrated by the queen's participation in courtly hospitality and royal spectacle which gave queens the opportunity to work with the king to distribute patronage. By hosting entertainments, often in their chambers, and witnessing the tournaments and disguisings at court, Catherine and Margaret facilitated Henry and James's diplomacy and the display of their magnificence, which were morally and politically important duties for a sixteenth-century prince. One of the outcomes of their sociability is then discussed in chapter 4, which focuses on patronage. Catherine and Margaret were able to capitalise on their public association with the king to access their husbands' patronage in order to reward their own followers at court, and this in turn provided their husbands with new connections and opportunities for reward through their queens' households.

Chapter 5 is a discussion of the public practice of Catherine's and Margaret's pre-Reformation piety, in particular through their almsgivings and pilgrimages. These two pious activities were important aspects of their religious practice and closely tied to their sacred and moral status as queens. Almsgiving, especially the rite of the Royal Maundy, connected Catherine and Margaret with the life of Christ and divinely-sanctioned monarchy. Pilgrimage for both queens was deeply linked to their trials and triumphs in childbirth, and thus to their primary duties as queens. Their journeys were public royal progresses which brought their faith out to the wider world and echoed the journeys made by many of their subjects, thus connecting their faith with that of the people.

The conclusion discusses one of the most unusual periods of Catherine's and Margaret's lives, their regencies in 1513 and 1514. It may seem perverse to relegate one of the most potentially interesting periods of their queenship to the concluding chapter, but doing so allows the themes of the previous chapters, including the importance of material culture and magnificence, hospitality, patronage and piety, to come together in understanding Catherine's and Margaret's successes and failures as regents. As much as regency was a unique event in their careers, it was also a continuation of their identities as queens of England and Scotland. The power and authority that Catherine and Margaret wielded as regents was directly related to the development of their identities as queens consort across many years. For Catherine, her roles as public partner, honoured wife and sacred consort, developed through court ceremony, material culture, royal patronage and religious practice, gave her independent status and a close relationship with her husband, a prerequisite for a successful regency. As this study will show, Margaret's queenly roles were less developed than Catherine's in 1513, and this is reflected in the difficulties that she faced during her regency. The interaction between Catherine's and Margaret's queenly identity and partnership with their husbands produces a complex understanding of queenship at the Renaissance courts of Britain.

1

Elizabeth of York

'[F]irst and foremost we wish and desire from our heart that we may often and speedily hear of the health and safety of your serenity, and of the health and safety of the aforesaid most illustrious Lady Catherine, whom we think of and esteem as our own daughter.'[1]

In her letter to Isabella of Castile in 1497, Elizabeth of York took a maternal interest in the health of her future daughter-in-law, which foreshadows the close connections between these two successive queens of England. Daughter, sister, niece and wife of kings, Elizabeth of York's queenship is often dismissed as passive, and she is frequently overshadowed by her politically shrewd husband Henry VII and influential mother-in-law Margaret Beaufort.[2] Historians of English queenship have begun to show that Elizabeth was an important, if conventional, English queen consort, who survived a politically turbulent adolescence to make a dynastically significant royal marriage and become a well-loved queen.[3] For both Catherine and Margaret, Elizabeth of York was a profoundly important model of English queenship whose influence on the composition of the Tudor court continued after her death. Elizabeth's daughter Margaret and her successor Catherine of Aragon personally observed Elizabeth's performance of queenly duties at the Tudor court and continued to benefit from Elizabeth's familial and household connections; their relationship with Elizabeth would significantly inform their behaviour as queens.

Although Catherine, and to a lesser extent Margaret, were well-educated princesses in the academic sense, much of their understanding of how to behave and succeed as a queen consort came from observing their mothers, Isabella and Elizabeth. While Isabella of Castile undoubtedly had a profound influence on her daughter Catherine's education, for both Catherine and Margaret, Elizabeth of York offered a more direct example of what an English queen consort should be.[4] Most elite women, including princesses, learned a great deal about their roles by observing their elders and gaining experience in

---

[1] *Letters of royal and illustrious ladies of Great Britain, from the commencement of the twelfth century to the close of the reign of Queen Mary*, ed. M. A. E. Green, London 1846, i. 115.

[2] See, for example, Malcolm G. Underwood, 'The pope, the queen, and the king's mother; or, the rise and fall of Adriano Castellesi', in Benjamin Thompson (ed.), *The reign of Henry VII: proceedings of the 1993 Harlaxton symposium*, Stamford 1995, 73–4.

[3] See, for example, Arlene Okerlund, *Elizabeth of York*, New York 2009; Laynesmith, *Last medieval queens*; and Earenfight, 'Regarding', 144–5.

[4] Earenfight, 'Raising infanta Catalina'.

a variety of court contexts.[5] Young princesses might stand beside their mothers to greet dignitaries or ambassadors, in part to display them as prospective brides, but also to familiarise them with their future duties as queens. Both Catherine and Margaret had the opportunity watch and learn from Elizabeth of York's example before her untimely death, and their relationships with her show that the English queen cared for and watched over them both.

For Margaret Tudor, her mother was a constant presence in her early adolescence, and in the last year of Elizabeth's life the queen began to prepare her daughter to become queen of Scots, providing her with necessary goods and clothing and encouraging Margaret to preside over court ceremonies.[6] Elizabeth would have been a natural role model for the young princess, who would have understood from the age of six that she might become queen of Scots. Before her death, Elizabeth presided over the major ceremonies related to Margaret's betrothal, and the young princess would have followed her mother's lead in the numerous pageants, banquets and audiences at her father's court.[7] Margaret seems to have cherished the memory of her mother, and the Scottish court would consistently mark the anniversary of Elizabeth's death with a special mass and offering.[8]

Catherine's relationship with Elizabeth of York began before she arrived in England to marry Arthur Prince of Wales; Elizabeth exchanged letters with Catherine's mother Isabella and she wished to hear about the princess's health and happiness in Spain.[9] Elizabeth greatly prized letters from both Isabella and Catherine, and she even refused to relinquish them to her husband, sparking a (presumably good-natured) marital spat in front of the Spanish ambassador.[10] When she arrived in England, Catherine experienced Elizabeth's hospitality during her first eighteen months at court. After the death of Arthur in 1502, Elizabeth took a close interest in her daughter-in-law, providing the litter that took the newly widowed and still recovering princess back to London.[11] Elizabeth continued to send messengers and small gifts to the widowed princess and received messages in return.[12] Her death in early 1503 was a significant blow to Catherine and altered the princess's status at the Tudor court. Without Elizabeth's presence, Catherine's mother Isabella insisted that Catherine needed to return to Spain immediately, arguing that it was inappropriate for the young princess to reside at court without the queen,

---

[5] Downie, *She is but a woman*, 183-4; Michalove, 'Education of aristocratic women', and 'Equal in opportunity'.

[6] *Privy Purse expenses*, 19, 22-3, 29, 88-9, 93.

[7] *Receyt of the ladie Kateryne*, 31, 53; Laynesmith, *Last medieval queens*, 149.

[8] NRS, MSS E21/6, pp. 81, 230; E21/7, fo. 34r; E21/9, fo. 32r; E21/10, fo. 21r. See also *LHTA* ii. 249, 362; iii. 56, iv. 38, 183.

[9] *CSP Spanish*, i. 185.

[10] Ibid. i. 202.

[11] *Privy Purse expenses*, 103.

[12] Ibid. 43.

who had acted to her as a mother (and chaperone).[13] Isabella's fears seemed to have been assuaged, and Catherine remained at the Tudor court until she married Elizabeth's second son, Henry VIII in 1509.

For Catherine of Aragon and Margaret Tudor, Elizabeth of York was both a public model and a continuing influence on their own style of queenship in England and Scotland. This influence came both through their personal relationships and through the way in which Elizabeth shaped the composition of the early Tudor court and her role within it. Even after her death and the accession of her successor, Elizabeth's familial connections and her household servants permeated English court structures, and her family's legacy of Burgundian culture and pageantry remained at the core of the magnificence and spectacle of the Tudor dynasty. Margaret in turn carried these influences to Scotland, where she participated in Scottish tournaments and court pastimes and surrounded herself with servants and gentlewomen with close connections to her mother. Through both her style of queenship as the supportive spouse and proud dynast and the enduring legacy of her dynastic connections and patronage, Elizabeth of York's influence and legacy as queen of England continued to influence the style and substance of the reigns of her daughter and daughter-in-law.

Family and dynasty, 1485-1500

Elizabeth of York was born in 1466, the eldest daughter of Edward IV and Elizabeth Woodville, and for many years she was her father's heir presumptive. After the birth of her brothers, her role became that of a conventional English princess, destined for a foreign marriage to further her father's foreign policy. After the early death of her father and her uncle Richard's usurpation in 1483, Elizabeth's future looked uncertain; declared a bastard by her uncle, any chance of a prestigious foreign match was probably lost. Once the disappearance of her brothers became widely known, Elizabeth became an important focus for Yorkist opposition to her uncle and a key component in the attempts of Henry Tudor and his mother Margaret Beaufort to seize the throne from Richard III. Henry Tudor, then in exile in Brittany, swore that he would marry Elizabeth, thereby uniting the Lancastrian and Yorkist oppositions.[14] Because Elizabeth was Edward IV's surviving heir, she could have claimed the throne for herself. However, Henry Tudor's victory at the Battle of Bosworth in 1485 ensured that she would become his queen consort and transmit her dynastic claims to her children.

Henry VII had won the English throne in battle, but dynastically his royal legitimacy relied on two women: his wife and his mother, Margaret Beaufort.

---

[13] *CSP Spanish*, i. 360, p. 296.
[14] Polydore Vergil, *Three books of Polydore Vergil's English history, comprising the reigns of Henry VI, Edward IV, and Richard III*, ed. Henry Ellis, London 1844, 203.

Margaret Beaufort, descendant of Edward III through a legitimised bastard line, was an heiress in her own right and a political survivor who had devoted much of her life to supporting and protecting her only child. When Henry became king, he entrusted his mother first with the custody of his future wife, and then with numerous other lands and responsibilities.[15] Margaret Beaufort was a powerful force at the Tudor court, managing vast estates, which allowed her to live in a style that befitted the king's mother. She also was a pious and devoted woman, who spent much of her wealth supporting educational foundations and devotional works. Her strong presence at the Tudor court has often overshadowed the activities of her daughter-in-law, in part because many more records regarding her activities survive at her foundation, St John's College, Cambridge, whereas Elizabeth's papers are widely distributed across the royal archives, if they survive at all. Some observers at court assumed that Margaret Beaufort and Elizabeth did not get along, but their actual behaviour suggests that their relationship was warm, and they worked together on numerous occasions to influence the king's policies.[16] Both women were important figures in the creation of the early Tudor court, and both provided Catherine and Margaret with support and guidance.

Margaret Beaufort and Elizabeth worked with Henry VII to create a 'blended' court and household that would combine Lancastrian and Yorkist supporters and mould them into a new nobility loyal to his and Elizabeth's heirs.[17] Although Elizabeth was forced by political circumstances and gender politics to become a transmitter of her dynastic claims to her children, this did not mean that Elizabeth's dynastic identity as a Yorkist princess disappeared when she married Henry. Henry found it useful to emphasise his wife's dynastic connections once his heir, Arthur, was born, and thus inherited his mother's dynastic claims.[18] Elizabeth, meanwhile, worked to support other members of her dynasty, including her sisters, at the Tudor court, and their presence in her household and at key dynastic events continued into the reign of her son and of her queenly successor, Catherine of Aragon. Once he became king, Henry VIII found it useful to celebrate his mother's Yorkist ancestry as a legitimate royal lineage (unlike his Beaufort forebears), and in the early years of his reign he and his wife favoured his mother's kin.[19]

Elizabeth of York's mother and queenly predecessor, Elizabeth Woodville, had received a great deal of criticism for her efforts to promote her family's

---

[15] Jones and Underwood, *King's mother*, 67-70.

[16] For the comment that Margaret Beaufort dominated Elizabeth see the remarks that a Spanish informant sent to Ferdinand and Isabella in 1498: *CSP Spanish*, i. 205, p.164. For a more detailed discussion of their 'more than cordial relations' see Laynesmith, *Last medieval queens*, 211-12.

[17] Sean Cunningham, *Henry VII*, London 2007, 202.

[18] Sydney Anglo, *Spectacle, pageantry, and early Tudor policy*, Oxford 1997, 49-50; Laynesmith, *Last medieval queens*, 184.

[19] C. S. L. Davies, 'Tudor: what's in a name?', *History* xcvii (2012), 26-7.

interests at court, including securing advantageous marriages for her siblings and her sons by Sir John Grey, her first husband.[20] While these criticisms were fundamentally unfair, and primarily based on anti-Woodville propaganda put out by court rivals, it is significant that her daughter sought to promote her own siblings, nieces, nephews and cousins at court in much the same way. As an English queen consort, Elizabeth of York, like her mother, had a web of family connections that became the focus of her major patronage activities.[21] Her successful negotiation of marriages for her sisters and support for her cousins, half-brothers and nephews meant that her dynastic connections would continue to flourish at the English court.

As the eldest of seven sisters, Elizabeth of York sought to provide for her surviving siblings once she became queen because her father's plans for their foreign marriages had never come to fruition. Edward IV had planned to marry his daughters into the royal houses of Europe. His second daughter Mary was betrothed to the king of Denmark before her death in 1482, and he had betrothed his third daughter Cecily to the heir of James III of Scotland.[22] Princess Anne had originally been destined to marry Philip of Burgundy, heir to the Austrian Habsburgs.[23] As the eldest daughter, Elizabeth's marriage was the most significant; at the age of nine she was betrothed to the French dauphin, although this match fell through in 1482.[24] After the death of their father, these princesses' futures were increasingly uncertain, and all of their marriage plans were overturned with the usurpation of Richard III.

When Elizabeth became queen all the surviving Yorkist princesses were unmarried, with one exception, and she set out to arrange matches for her sisters as they came of age.[25] In 1495 she arranged for Anne to marry Thomas Lord Howard, heir of the earl of Surrey. She was intimately involved in the practical arrangements of the marriage, overseeing the transfer and administration of Anne's jointure and providing material support for her.[26] Some years later, Elizabeth made similar arrangements for her sister Katherine's marriage to William Courtenay.[27] Significantly, for both of these arrangements, Elizabeth entrusted the administration of their jointure lands to her half-brother the marquess of Dorset and her son Henry, relying on dynastic

---

[20] For a discussion of the marriages of the Woodville family see Laynesmith, *Last medieval queens*, 195-9.
[21] Ibid. 17-18.
[22] Charles Ross, *Edward IV*, Berkeley 1974, 212-13, 247.
[23] Ibid. 284.
[24] Okerlund, *Elizabeth of York*, 13-14.
[25] See Figure 2 above. Richard III had arranged for Cecily, Elizabeth's eldest surviving sister, to marry Ralph Scrope, one of his allies, but her marriage was quickly annulled after Bosworth: Laynesmith, *Last medieval queens*, 199.
[26] Thomas Madox, *Formulare anglicanum: or, A collection of ancient charters and instruments*, London 1702, 109-11.
[27] Laynesmith, *Last medieval queens*, 217.

connections from both her mother's family and her marital dynasty to protect her sisters' marriages. Elizabeth's sisters also became part of Henry VII's careful strategy of controlling members of the Yorkist dynasty by marrying them to his trusted lieutenants and extended family. Instead of marrying into Scotland, Cecily of York married John Lord Welles, Henry VII's half-uncle and loyal supporter.[28] These marriages may not have been the prestigious foreign matches that Edward IV had originally planned for his daughters, but they had the effect of keeping the sisters in England, where they and their children became members of the queen's household.

Because Elizabeth's sisters remained in England after their marriages, they supported the queen in Tudor dynastic ceremonies alongside her Yorkist and Woodville aunts, cousins and nieces. In addition to her sisters Anne, Katherine and Cecily, Elizabeth's cousins Margaret Pole and Elizabeth Stafford, and her aunt Countess Rivers, served as ladies-in-waiting to the queen during her reign.[29] Their presence around the queen meant that at significant royal occasions, such as the christening of Prince Arthur and Elizabeth's own coronation, there would be a strong Yorkist and even Woodville representation at the Tudor court.[30] This was important for Henry's attempts to weld Yorkist loyalties to his new dynasty, but it also meant that Elizabeth's lineage, her dynasty and kin, were a significant asset and source of support for the queen even after her marriage.

Elizabeth's mother-in-law Margaret Beaufort supported and even echoed her efforts to create a blended Tudor aristocracy. Margaret sheltered former Yorkists in her household, and members of her own extended family married into Elizabeth's family.[31] Princess Cecily's marriage to John Lord Welles, Margaret Beaufort's half-brother, was just one of several matches that brought together Elizabeth and Margaret's families. In 1487 Elizabeth's cousin Margaret, daughter of George duke of Clarence, married Richard Pole, son of Margaret Beaufort's half-sister Edith St John. Henry VII arranged the marriage to safeguard this dynastically dangerous woman, by linking royal Yorkist blood with a family whose non-royal, shared blood with Margaret Beaufort and her son made them both reliable and non-threatening.[32] Other marriages continued this trend, including the marriage of Thomas Grey, Elizabeth's cousin of the half-blood, to Eleanor St John, Margaret's niece of the half-blood.[33]

This web of familial marriages was a unique source of strength for English queen consorts such as Elizabeth of York, and it was one that consorts who came

---

[28] Ibid. 199.

[29] Harris, *English aristocratic women*, 218. See Figure 2 above.

[30] Laynesmith, *Last medieval queens*, 205-6; P. W. Hammond, 'The coronation of Elizabeth of York', *The Ricardian* vi (1983), 271.

[31] Jones and Underwood, *King's mother*, 85.

[32] Hazel Pierce, 'The king's cousin: the life, career and Welsh connection of Sir Richard Pole, 1458-1504', *Welsh History Review* xix (1998), 187-8, 206. See also Figure 2 above.

[33] Jones and Underwood, *King's mother*, 101.

from foreign dynasties, such as Catherine of Aragon or Margaret Tudor, could not re-create when they arrived in their new homelands. However, Catherine did inherit many of Elizabeth of York's familial connections at the English court. Several of the English ladies closest to Catherine had family connections to her predecessor, and many of these ladies remained loyal to Catherine throughout her life. Catherine's household included at least five high-ranking noblewomen with dynastic connections to her husband's maternal dynasty.[34] Gertrude Blount, lady-in-waiting and close friend of Catherine, married Henry Courtenay, Elizabeth of York's nephew.[35] Several of Catherine's other ladies had Woodville lineages, such as Elizabeth and Anne Stafford, descendants of Elizabeth's aunt Katherine Woodville, and Mary Say Bourchier, countess of Essex, whose husband was the son of Anne Woodville.[36] Finally, some of Elizabeth of York's female relatives continued their service to Catherine, such as Margaret Pole who became a close friend of Catherine and lady mistress to her daughter Mary.[37]

It was not only the women of the Yorkist and Woodville families that Elizabeth of York and her husband incorporated into the new Tudor court; in the mid-1490s Elizabeth's male relatives and in-laws came into their own as a potential new generation of Tudor courtiers. In 1494 four young knights with close ties to Elizabeth participated in the tournament marking young Prince Henry's creation as duke of York.[38] Thomas Grey Lord Harrington, son of Elizabeth's half-brother; William Lord Courtenay, her sister Katherine's husband; and Henry Bourchier earl of Essex, Elizabeth's first cousin, were all related to the queen on her mother's side, and thus did not share potentially threatening royal Yorkist blood. Only one of the young knights, Edmund de la Pole, the queen's cousin through her paternal aunt, carried the potential to claim the throne, and in the 1490s it appeared that he too was willing to support his cousin and her new family.[39] Together, these young lords 'formed a vibrant social group that caught the king's attention through jousting, dances, and other entertainments'.[40] Unfortunately, this amity was not to last, as three of these young men fell under suspicion by the end of the reign. Edmund de la Pole, probably resentful of his loss of status after his elder brother's attainder and jealous of the favour shown to other young nobles, fled England in 1501.[41] After the betrayals of the de la Pole family, Henry VII became more suspicious

---

[34] See Figures 2, 3 above.
[35] TNA, MS SP1/233, fo. 264r. See also LP, Add. i/1, 367, and J. P. D. Cooper, 'Courtenay, Gertrude, marchioness of Exeter (d. 1558)', ODNB. See Figure 2 above.
[36] LP i/1, 474; Harris, English aristocratic women, 218.
[37] TNA, MS LC9/50, fos 210v, 192r. See also LP iii/1, 491.
[38] Alison Hanham, 'Edmund de la Pole, defector', RS ii (1988), 240.
[39] See Figures 2, 3 above.
[40] Cunningham, Henry VII, 203.
[41] Hanham, 'Edmund de la Pole', 241.

of the queen's kin, and both Courtenay and Grey narrowly escaped execution at the end of the reign.

With the accession of Henry VIII, the new king's maternal kin were rehabilitated at court, including Courtenay and Grey (now marquess of Dorset), and their children would go on to serve both Henry and Catherine in a variety of capacities.[42] Early in the reign Henry also raised up his cousin Margaret Pole, making her countess of Salisbury in her own right and thus restoring some of her inheritance as a Yorkist princess.[43] Henry VIII's desire for war meant that he needed to re-establish good relations with leading members of the nobility, such as Grey and Courtenay, but he also seems to have favoured men and women in his mother's service.[44] Elizabeth's family thus became a legacy within the court of Henry VIII and the circle of his wife, whose closest English companions were part of Elizabeth's family and their networks.

Pageantry and diplomacy, 1501-3

Elizabeth's role at court as a participant in early Tudor diplomacy and pageantry offered Catherine and Margaret a model of how medieval ideals of chivalry and Renaissance concepts of spectacle and magnificence could be combined to promote the queen's family and dynasty. As with the influence and importance of her family at the courts of her husband and son, Elizabeth's cultural achievements and influences are easily overlooked.[45] While sources concerning Elizabeth's involvement in diplomacy and pageantry are scanty, those that do survive hint that her cultural influence and diplomatic activities at Henry VII's court were significant in shaping the tone of early Tudor entertainments and the diplomacy that those events so often celebrated.[46] And, because both Catherine and Margaret witnessed the apogee of these entertainments – the wedding celebrations for Catherine and Arthur – they would have understood the importance of the queen's role in courtly entertainment and diplomacy.

The court of the first Tudor monarch owed a great deal to the development of chivalric codes of honour and entertainments by the Burgundian court of Charles the Bold, and the assumption of these values by Elizabeth's Woodville relatives during the reign of her father Edward IV. Gordon Kipling has convincingly argued that Henry VII's cultural orientation towards Burgundy set the stage for the adoption of Burgundian pageantry, literary culture and

---

[42] Robert C. Braddock, 'Grey, Thomas, second marquess of Dorset (1477-1530)', *ODNB*; J. P. D. Cooper, 'Courtenay, Henry, marquess of Exeter (1498/9-1538)', *ODNB*.

[43] Hazel Pierce, *Margaret Pole, countess of Salisbury, 1473–1541: loyalty, lineage and leadership*, Cardiff 2003, 32.

[44] Laynesmith, *Last medieval queens*, 155.

[45] W. R. Streitberger, *Court revels, 1485–1559*, Toronto 1994, 41; Okerlund, *Elizabeth of York*, 178-9.

[46] Harris, *English aristocratic women*, 233.

painting in the reign of his son, and ultimately the reign of his granddaughter Elizabeth.[47] The flowering of Burgundian culture at the court of Henry VII was made possible through the return to court of the Woodville families and their Burgundian influences.[48] The Woodvilles were intimately connected to the Burgundian court through Queen Elizabeth Woodville's mother, Jacquetta de St Pol, who was descended from the Flemish counts of St Pol. Anthony Woodville in particular used his mother's illustrious heritage (which was significantly grander than her husband's, who was a mere member of the Lancastrian gentry) to claim honour and status in the chivalric competitions and diplomatic exchanges at the court of Edward IV.[49] In turn, the young men who became the elite participants in Henry VII's Burgundian-style tournaments of the 1490s were the heirs to this Woodville tradition. Moreover, the 1501 marriage of Catherine of Aragon to Arthur prince of Wales was a continuation of England's Burgundian connections. Catherine's sister Juana had married Philip of Burgundy in 1496, and the two sisters' marriages linked their natal and marital courts in a series of trade agreements, forming an Anglo-Burgundian-Spanish axis of cultural and economic links that continued well into the sixteenth-century.[50]

Elizabeth was significantly involved in the courtly ceremonies surrounding Henry VII's diplomacy, especially the betrothal and wedding ceremonies of her children. By far the largest and most complex of these ceremonies was the wedding reception for Catherine of Aragon in 1501. Elizabeth was responsible for ordering and providing the transport, including litters, chairs and palfreys for Catherine's ladies, and her master of the horse was in charge of outfitting the harnesses and saddles for the princess and her pages.[51] Elizabeth also chose the ladies who would greet the princess when she arrived in England, an important honour as they would be expected to keep her company and begin the process of introducing English customs to the Spanish princess and her entourage.[52] Elizabeth extended her personal welcome to Catherine after the princess had entered London. The night before her wedding, Catherine and her escort rode from their lodgings to Baynard's Castle, where Elizabeth was staying with the king. Catherine and her ladies arrived around three or four o'clock, and she was greeted by the queen, 'with pleasure and goodly commynycacion, dauncyng, and disportes thei passed the season full conveniently'. The

---

[47] Gordon Kipling, *The triumph of honour: Burgundian origins of the Elizabethan Renaissance*, The Hague 1977.
[48] Ibid. 15.
[49] Laynesmith, *Last medieval queens*, 187-90.
[50] Samson, 'A fine romance', 73-7, 79-80.
[51] BL, MS Cotton Vespasian C XIV, fos 83r, 85r-v; Kate Harris, 'Richard Pynson's "Remembraunce for the traduction of the princesse Kateryne": the printer's contribution to the reception of Catherine of Aragon', *Library* xii (1990), 104.
[52] *Receyt of the ladie Kateryne*, 5.

princess's visit lasted so long that she and her entourage returned to their lodgings at the bishop of London's palace by torchlight.[53]

Elizabeth's welcome for Catherine has unsurprisingly been overshadowed by the royal pageantry designed to emulate or even surpass Burgundian celebrations, but her less showy, behind-the-scenes contributions were nevertheless important. Henry VII clearly expected his wife to oversee the components of the reception that were within her expertise, such as the choice of ladies to serve the princess or the provision of female saddle gear and litters. While Elizabeth's role in this major celebration may seem retiring or marginal, in fact she was fulfilling many of the same ideals of queenship that her daughter-in-law would continue years later as the hostess and audience for her husband Henry VIII's celebrations at the Tudor court.

Elizabeth also modelled queenly hospitality for her daughter Margaret during the ceremonies that marked Margaret's proxy marriage to James IV in January 1502. Elizabeth's involvement in diplomatic ceremonial was often tied to the marriages of her children, and her chambers were especially associated with the celebrations involving her daughter Margaret's marriage.[54] The ceremony itself was held in the queen's chamber, where Margaret swore to marry James IV and formally sought the blessing of both her mother and father.[55] Elizabeth's chamber remained the centre of celebrations as the new Queen of Scots (as Margaret was now known) and her mother dined together at the same table. The festivities for the betrothal also included jousts featuring some of the young lords, such as the marquess of Dorset and the duke of Buckingham, who were connected to Elizabeth's dynasty. Margaret rewarded the winners of the jousts including her uncle (by marriage) Lord William Courtenay, in her mother's Great Chamber.[56] Under the watchful, and presumably encouraging, eye of her mother, Margaret began to take part in some of the same public duties that she would need to fulfil in Scotland.

Both Catherine and Margaret witnessed Elizabeth's personal involvement in early Tudor court revels, and they followed her example when they became queens in their own right. A close reading of existing sources show that Elizabeth was an important patron of courtly entertainments. Elizabeth's role has been easy to overlook in part because very few sources reveal her explicit involvement in planning or influencing court ceremony.[57] Elizabeth's Privy Purse accounts, which only survive for the last year of her life, indicate that she funded and created some of the entertainments at court. For example, she provided costumes for disguisings, including the fanciful spangles, stars

---

[53] Ibid. 38.
[54] Laynesmith, *Last medieval queens*, 148–9, 246.
[55] Young, 'The fyancells of Margaret', 261.
[56] Ibid. 263.
[57] Streitberger, *Court revels*, 41.

and points for decorating jackets used in a disguising in June 1502.[58] She was heavily involved in the Christmas entertainments of 1502, which were probably attended by both Margaret and Catherine. Elizabeth paid for a setting of a Christmas carol by William Cornish and provided funds for the king's disguising earlier in the month. She also paid 20s. to the Lord of Misrule, a traditional yuletide entertainment in large elite households.[59] Taken together, these examples show that Elizabeth was active in contributing to Tudor court culture and pageantry, and her contributions from previous years, although now lost, were probably on a similar scale. Both her daughter and daughter-in-law witnessed Elizabeth's personal involvement in early Tudor diplomatic ceremony and court revels, and they would have expected to follow her example when they became queens in their own right.[60] They probably would have seen the English queen as an active participant in court culture, and their queen-ships reflected the lessons that they had learned at the early Tudor court.

Elizabeth of York's participation and influence in early Tudor pageantry emerges most clearly in the diplomatic celebrations of the early years of the sixteenth century, but pageantry and ceremony were not the only way in which Elizabeth contributed to Henry VII's diplomacy. Like her daughter and daughter-in-law, Elizabeth was a diplomatically aware and active queen, especially concerning the negotiations for her children's marriages. Henry included her in lengthy meetings and discussions with ambassadors and other monarchs, which suggests that her involvement was important and not a mere formality. In 1498 the queen and Margaret Beaufort were present for a four-hour discussion with the Spanish ambassador and the king about letters that had arrived from Spain.[61] In 1500 she accompanied the king to Calais, where they met Philip of Burgundy, heir to the Holy Roman Emperor, and husband of Juana of Castile, Isabella and Ferdinand's eldest surviving daughter and heir.[62] At the meeting, Elizabeth joined in conversation with Philip and Henry. Although we cannot know how Elizabeth participated in these meetings, her presence for lengthy meetings, and not simply on ceremonial occasions, indicates that her involvement in diplomacy was not merely a courtesy.

Like her husband, Elizabeth also understood the important role that ambas-sadors played in the emerging world of European diplomacy. During Henry's reign, England had not only begun to send its own ambassadors abroad in semi-permanent residencies, but it had also hosted a resident Spanish ambassador,

---

[58] *Privy Purse expenses*, 21.

[59] TNA, MS E36/123, fo. 93r; Streitberger, *Court revels*, 249. Currency will be given in English sterling, unless otherwise noted in the text. There were 20 shillings to a pound and 12 pence to a shilling.

[60] Theresa Earenfight has also noted Elizabeth of York's influence on her successors: 'Raising infanta Catalina', 436.

[61] *CSP Spanish*, i. 202.

[62] Ibid. i. 268. See also Figure 1 above.

Dr Roderigo de Puebla, since 1495.[63] De Puebla had been sent to England by Ferdinand and Isabella at least three times during Henry's reign, and in 1495 he arrived as a residential ambassador. He was primarily responsible for concluding the marriage alliance and treaty between England and the Spanish monarchs. After its ratification in 1496, Elizabeth of York moved to reward the ambassador by arranging a marriage for him with one of her ladies. Not wishing to fall out of favour with his own sovereigns, de Puebla repeatedly refused the offer of marriage until he received permission from Spain (which was not forthcoming).[64] Nevertheless, Elizabeth's enthusiasm for the plan, mentioned in Spanish dispatches across two years, indicates that she was actively involved in the negotiations, understood de Puebla's importance and initiated the idea as a way of rewarding good service.

Elizabeth seems to have had a practical appreciation of the difficulties of international exchanges, especially for foreign brides. In July 1498 she requested that Catherine (then in Spain) begin to learn French so that she could communicate with the English queen and the king's mother, neither of whom knew Spanish or Latin. Three years later, Elizabeth's attention to detail bore fruit when she heard that Catherine had made great progress in learning French.[65] Elizabeth also suggested that Catherine learn to drink wine, which was the common drink in England for elite ladies, but not often drunk by ladies in Spain.[66] Catherine did learn to drink wine in the English fashion, and in later life she developed a taste for Spanish wine, which she had trouble obtaining after her divorce from Henry VIII in 1533.[67]

Elizabeth was also significantly involved in the negotiations and arrangements for her daughter Margaret's marriage to the king of Scots. As early as 1498, she joined with Margaret Beaufort to stop the princess from being sent to Scotland too early for marriage (Princess Margaret was only nine at the time).[68] In October 1501 Elizabeth sent one of her Chamber servants to accompany the king's herald to Scotland, as part of the final negotiations for the marriage treaty.[69] Although there is no way of knowing why Elizabeth sent her servant into Scotland, he travelled in the company of one of the king's

---

[63] John M. Currin, '"Pro expensis ambassatorum": diplomacy and financial administration in the reign of Henry VII', *EHR* cviii (1993), 590-91; Garrett Mattingly, 'The reputation of doctor de Puebla', *EHR* lv (1940), 29.

[64] *CSP Spanish*, i. 188, 268.

[65] Ibid. i. 294.

[66] Ibid. i. 203. The Spanish had a reputation for sobriety, while the English elite drank mostly wine (water was associated with the poor, prisoners and punishment): A. Lynn Martin, 'National reputations for drinking in traditional Europe', *Parergon* xvii (1999), 174, and 'The baptism of wine', *Gastronomica* iii (2003), 24-5.

[67] *CSP Spanish*, v/1, 26.

[68] Ibid. i. 210, p.176; Laynesmith, *Last medieval queens*, 211.

[69] *LHTA* ii. 122. The marriage contract and Treaty of Perpetual Peace were signed in January 1502; *CDS* iv. 1680, 1681.

frequent messengers, and it is likely that they were there to deliver messages regarding the ongoing marriage negotiations. His presence certainly suggests that Elizabeth was keeping a close eye on the Scottish negotiations, and she may have even sent messages or letters to the James *via* her servant.

Elizabeth's early death coincides with a general reduction in Tudor spectacle, which certainly suggests that she was a driving force behind early Tudor pageantry, but it is impossible to say if this is a mere coincidence.[70] If her Privy Purse accounts for 1502-3 are at all representative of her involvement in pageantry in previous years, then she was probably more active in sponsoring and directing entertainments at court than existing records can show. There is no doubt, however, that her presence was a powerful and useful symbol of the new political order, and that she presided over tournaments, banquets and disguisings at the Tudor court, just as her daughter and daughter-in-law would a few years later.

In the service of royal women, 1503-9

Like the presence of Elizabeth's family at the English court, the continuation of service between the households of Elizabeth of York, Margaret Beaufort, Margaret Tudor and Catherine of Aragon is perhaps one of Elizabeth's most enduring, yet invisible, legacies as queen. This may be surprising, as the queen's household appears to be an ephemeral institution that officially disappeared in the six-year interval between the reigns of Elizabeth of York and Catherine of Aragon, or in Scotland, the seventeen-year gap between Margaret of Denmark, wife of James III, and Margaret Tudor. Yet, when the households of queens in the early sixteenth century are examined more closely, it seems that there was a significant degree of continuity between the households of royal Tudor women. Elizabeth of York's influence on the queenships of both Margaret and Catherine survived after her death through the continuity and connections amongst their households.

Continuity between queenly households was not uncommon, but due to both political and personal circumstances, the continuity between Elizabeth of York, Margaret Tudor and Catherine of Aragon was more pronounced than that of their fifteenth-century predecessors.[71] Before Elizabeth's reign, years of civil war and factional fighting disrupted the continuity of the queen's household. When she became queen, Elizabeth of York returned to the tradition of continuity by including men and women from her mother's household in her new queenly household.[72] Queens in Scotland during the

---

[70] Okerlund, *Elizabeth of York*, 178-9.
[71] Derek Neal, 'The queen's grace: English queenship, 1464-1503', unpubl. MA diss. McMaster 1996, 132.
[72] Laynesmith, *Last medieval queens*, 230.

fifteenth century, who did not experience the factional politics of England, also maintained continuity in their households. For instance, some servants from the household of Joan Beaufort, wife of James I, went on to serve the next queen, Mary of Guelders, wife of James II.[73] Later, chamber servants from the household of Margaret Tudor's Scottish predecessor, Margaret of Denmark, went on to serve in the chamber of her son, James IV.[74] Sparse records make it difficult to trace the rest of Margaret of Denmark's household, including her ladies and gentlewomen.[75] However, there is a chance that one of Margaret Tudor's Scottish ushers of her chamber, Lucas Taillefeir, was a relative of Margaret of Denmark's porter of Stirling Castle, Thomas Taillefeir.[76] Both the lack of records and the fifteen-year gap between Margaret of Denmark's death and Margaret Tudor's arrival in Scotland makes it difficult to draw further conclusions. It is possible, for instance, that there was a wholesale changeover of Scottish staff between the two queens, or that there was a generational change, with younger members of the same families like the Taillefeirs taking positions in the new queen's household.

Often continuity between household staff has been seen as a burden for both kings and queens, who might be forced to accept servants from previous monarchs despite their own personal preferences.[77] In eighteenth-century France, for example, Marie Leszczynska, consort of Louis XV, had to accommodate the relatives, friends and allies of the former regent and his mistress in her household, despite her own personal dislike for their loose morals. Her successor, Marie Antoinette, subsequently inherited some attendants from Marie Leszczynska's household. This situation, created by the factional politics of the French court during the reign of Louis XV and the weak position of Marie Leszczynska, reflected the 'ossification of Court structures', that occurred in the later decades of the *ancien régime*.[78] Such factionalism certainly occurred in the sixteenth century as well, but the continuity exhibited by Catherine's and Margaret's households was different and potentially useful to them as foreign queen consorts.[79]

---

[73] Downie, *She is but a woman*, 116-17.

[74] William Hepburn, 'The household of James IV, 1488-1513', unpubl. PhD diss. Glasgow 2013, 119.

[75] For example, in 1473 Margaret of Denmark had six ladies who received royal livery, but neither their names nor their national origins were recorded: *LHTA*, i. 29.

[76] NRS, MS E34/2, fo. 6r; *ERS* ix. 249-50.

[77] For more on the potential problems caused by 'legacy personnel' see Caroline Hibbard, 'The role of a queen consort: the household and court of Henrietta Maria, 1625-1642', in Ronald G. Asch and Adolf M. Birke (eds), *Princes, patronage, and the nobility: the court at the beginning of the modern age, c. 1450-1650*, New York 1991, 400-1.

[78] John Rogister, 'Queen Marie Leszczynska and faction at the French court', in Clarissa Campbell Orr (ed), *Queenship in Europe, 1660-1815: the role of the consort*, New York 2004, 197.

[79] Unsurprisingly, given the acrimonious transition between Catherine and her successor as queen, Anne Boleyn, there was less continuity between the households of Henry's

There were several reasons for including members of the previous queen's household in the new queen's staff. Firstly, members of any queen's household would have expected to be supported by the king upon the death of his wife, and given annuities, corrodies or supernumerary positions. Employing these 'legacy personnel' was a way of minimising expenses and making use of servants who would in any case have been supported by the king. Secondly, for many posts, such as the queen's Lord Chamberlain or her Master of Horse, the noble incumbent would have expected and had the right to be reappointed to the queen's household. One such was Catherine's first Lord Chamberlain, Thomas Butler, the elderly earl of Ormond, who nominally served Catherine for three years before relinquishing the position to his stepson, William Blount, Lord Mountjoy.[80] Continuity was thus both a practical use of resources and an expected court practice.

Although most of the household connections between Elizabeth of York and her daughter and daughter-in-law occurred after her death, there is also evidence that Elizabeth and Catherine's households were administratively close from an early date. A list drawn up for Margaret Beaufort in 1502 shows both the queen's officers and servants and the servants of the new princess of Wales.[81] The household lists of both Elizabeth and Catherine are incomplete, suggesting that Margaret Beaufort and Elizabeth were still making staffing decisions.[82] The inclusion of both Elizabeth and Catherine's households in this list indicates that Elizabeth and Margaret Beaufort expected there to be connections, transfers or even overlap between the queen's household and that of her daughter-in-law.

Elizabeth's death in 1503 probably altered any existing plans for staffing Margaret's household in Scotland. Instead of placing new servants with the queen of Scots, many of Elizabeth of York's servants and staff began serving her daughter upon the death of their mistress.[83] In particular, many of Elizabeth's waiting women went on to accompany her daughter to Scotland, in part because there were few positions for women at Henry VII's court without the queen. Lady Eleanor Verney, the wife of Margaret's Lord Chamberlain Sir Ralph Verney and the head of her ladies-in-waiting, had served her mother as a noble attendant and had frequently travelled with Elizabeth of York.[84]

---

wives than might have been expected under different circumstances, though this was not a universal trend and some members of Catherine's household made the transition: Harris, *English aristocratic women*, 217. Margaret also, as the queen regent in Scotland for her infant son, did not have an immediate successor in Scotland.

[80] TNA, MS LC9/50, fo. 203r. See also *LP* i/1, 82; i/1, 1221, p. 29.
[81] SJC, MS D102.11.
[82] Jones and Underwood speculate that the list represents Margaret's involvement or possible interference in staffing Elizabeth's household: *King's mother*, 161.
[83] A few of those who did not journey to Scotland found positions in the household of Margaret Beaufort. Many of Elizabeth's officers had been servants of Margaret Beaufort or her kinsmen, so their return to her service was unsurprising: ibid. 161.
[84] Neal, 'The queen's grace', 190.

Mistress Eleanor Jones, one of Elizabeth's gentlewomen, accompanied the young Margaret to Scotland and stayed with her for at least four years, receiving fees and gifts from James IV at New Year.[85] Additionally, Margaret Beaufort may have also stepped in to organise her granddaughter's household.[86] Elizabeth Denton, another gentlewoman to Elizabeth of York, was also lady mistress of the royal nursery and accompanied Margaret on the wedding journey to Scotland, for which she was paid by Margaret Beaufort some years later.[87]

Not all of Elizabeth's ladies went to Scotland with Margaret; many of those noble ladies who remained in England eventually joined Catherine's household, six years after the death of Elizabeth of York. For example, two of Catherine's chamberers in 1509, Mistress Mary Redding and Mistress Anne Luke, had also served as gentlewomen to Elizabeth of York.[88] Anne Weston, Elizabeth Saxby and Alice Davy all served first Elizabeth of York and then Catherine of Aragon.[89] Later, the king's grant of an annuity for Elizabeth Saxby specifically cites her service to Henry VIII's parents, Catherine of Aragon and Mary Tudor, the king's sister.[90] In addition to these gentlewomen, Catherine's household also included ladies from Elizabeth of York's family, who had played a prominent role in focusing Yorkist support for the Tudor dynasty.[91] Elizabeth's household and extended family was therefore a natural source of English support for Catherine when she became queen.

Catherine probably found it entirely acceptable to welcome her predecessor's waiting women into her household because she had already experienced a similar form of continuity with her early Spanish household. Catherine's first group of gentlewomen and ladies had been handpicked by her mother Isabella before she left Spain.[92] Many of her ladies or their families had served Isabella in the past, and Catherine was well-aware of her ladies' past relationship with her mother. She specifically refers to the connection between her Spanish ladies and her mother in her letters to her father Ferdinand when requesting his help in arranging marriages and dowries for them.[93] Somewhat unusually, Catherine's lengthy stay in England during her widowhood meant that her own Spanish servants and ladies, who naturally would have formed the core of her queenly household, had gradually left her service. Moreover, she was eager to dismiss some who had remained for various failings. Only a handful of Spanish

---

[85] NRS, MS E21/6, pp. 197-9, 313. See also *LHTA* ii. 337, 442; *Privy Purse expenses*, 5, 100.
[86] Margaret Beaufort hosted part of Margaret Tudor's farewell journey in 1503 at her residence of Collyweston: Jones and Underwood, *King's mother*, 84.
[87] Ibid. 272.
[88] TNA, MS LC9/50, fo. 192v. See also *LP* i/2, 82, and Neal, 'The queen's grace', 192.
[89] *LP* iii/1, 8; *Privy Purse expenses*, 11, 64, 99; Neal, 'The queen's grace', 192, 193.
[90] TNA, MS E404/90. See also *LP* ii/1, 470.
[91] See p. 33 above and Figures 2, 3; Laynesmith, *Last medieval queens*, 228.
[92] *CSP Spanish*, i. 288. See also Earenfight, 'Raising infanta Catalina', 422-3.
[93] *Letters of royal and illustrious ladies*, i. 129.

servants, including a few gentlewomen and chamberers, served her as queen. Nevertheless, a legacy of service to her mother and father was so important to Catherine that she cited it many years later when pensioning off her former servants and sending them home to Spain.

Male members of the households of Catherine and Margaret also show continuity with other female royal households, despite the fact that there were more opportunities at court for male household officers and servants, since they could potentially find employment with the king's household after the death of the queen. Indeed, some of the male household officers and servants of Elizabeth of York did move to the household of the king or appear in the household of Henry VIII in 1509. However, when Margaret Tudor left for Scotland in 1503, she brought male servants from her mother's household with her, indicating the importance of loyalty, experience and familiarity in the selection of her household. Margaret brought with her men who seem to have been specialists in serving royal women, including wardrobe staff who obtained, cleaned and repaired the queen's clothing, as well as chaplains and yeomen who had served in her mother's chapel and chambers.[94] Margaret would have known many of these men by sight, as her mother had often used her chamber and wardrobe servants to send clothing and goods to her daughter.[95] This familiarity would have extended to Margaret's household officials, including the head of her early household Sir Ralph Verney. Verney was a fast-rising courtier who had connections to prominent noble families and the Tudors through his wife, Eleanor Pole Verney, who became Margaret's chief gentlewoman.[96] Both Eleanor and her husband were members of Elizabeth of York's household and were the thus an experienced, trustworthy couple to oversee Margaret's household in Scotland. Verney was familiar with the Scottish marriage and the Scottish court, having participated in some of the negotiations for Margaret's marriage and acted as a witness to the Scottish estates' confirmation of her dower.[97]

Many of Catherine's early male servants also came from Elizabeth of York's household, and they reflect the ongoing patronage that brought stability to the new queen's household. A few had even spent time in Margaret Beaufort's establishment, thus transitioning from one royal woman to the next. Of the 122 men listed as part of Catherine's household for the coronation in 1509, thirty-two were part of Elizabeth of York's household in the funeral accounts

---

[94] *Privy Purse expenses*: Richard Justice, 7, 15, 46; Henry Roper, 10, 19, 36; Christopher Plomer, 37, 62; Edmund Levisay (Levesey), 35, 36; John Bricht, 36, 49, 56, 58, 71, 72, 74, 95; Hamnet Clegg, 21, 62.

[95] Ibid. 19, 33-4.

[96] Eleanor Pole was the sister of Richard Pole (see p. 32 above for his marriage to Margaret Plantagenet), and thus the daughter of Geoffrey Pole and Edith St John, Margaret Beaufort's half-sister on her mother's side: Pierce, 'The king's cousin', 188.

[97] *Privy Purse expenses*, 99; *Letters and papers of the Verney family down to the year 1639*, ed. John Bruce (Camden o.s. lvi, 1853), 29-30, 33.

of 1503, and nineteen more had been listed as part of Elizabeth's household in the 1501 list, bringing the total to fifty-one men who served both queens.[98] While it comes as no surprise that highly coveted positions would be claimed as a matter of right by influential courtiers like the Butlers or the Blounts, the pattern of resumption of offices (and even promotion) continued down the social scale. All of the grooms of the Chamber listed as part of Elizabeth of York's household in 1501 appear in Catherine's household beginning in 1509, and they continued to serve Catherine for many years.[99] Griffith Richards, one of Catherine's busiest servants, was originally a clerk of the signet to both Elizabeth of York and Margaret Beaufort.[100] Richards served Catherine in that capacity and eventually became receiver-general of Catherine's lands and knight of the body to Henry VIII.[101]

Many of these servants would continue to serve royal women in England after Catherine's death. Both Catherine's daughter Mary and Katherine Parr actively sought to place members of the former queen's household in their own households or to find places for them elsewhere. Princess Mary probably had intimate knowledge of her mother's servants from her infancy and this contributed to her familiarity with her mother's servants after the divorce.[102] Service to the queen had far-reaching implications and could continue through multiple generations of both servant and mistress: Katherine Parr, the future queen, was the daughter of Maud Parr, one of Catherine's ladies, and she initially had found a place in Princess Mary's household as a result of her mother's service. Katherine Parr would continue to promote her mother's connections from Catherine's household when she became Henry's sixth queen by finding a place for Lady Mary Kingston, who had served Catherine since 1509.

This chapter has shown that connections between Elizabeth of York and her daughter Margaret and daughter-in-law Catherine can be found throughout the early Tudor court, in the queen's household, family and courtly activity. Elizabeth's queenship was certainly a model for Catherine and Margaret to emulate, but the first Tudor queen consort also shaped the court through her own familial and household connections, leaving behind a legacy of noble allies, servants and family members. After Elizabeth's death in 1503, they accompanied her daughter into Scotland and later introduced her daughter-in-law, England's first foreign consort in over fifty years, to the structures and traditions of the English court. Thus, in multiple ways, the queenships of Catherine of Aragon and Margaret Tudor were significantly influenced by Elizabeth's legacy as queen.

---

[98] *LP* i/1, 82; TNA, MS LC2/1; SJC, MS D102.11; Neal, 'The queen's grace', appendix VI.
[99] SJC, MS D102.11; *LP* i/1, 82.
[100] Jones and Underwood, *King's mother*, 161.
[101] TNA, MS E101/417/2; *LP* iv/2, 2972.
[102] McIntosh, *Heads of household*, 20.

2

Material Magnificence, Royal Identity and the Queen's Body

'[the Queen] was very richly attired, and had with her 25 damsels mounted on white palfreys, with housings all of one fashion, most beautifully embroidered with gold; and all these damsels wore dresses slashed with gold lama in very costly trim, and were attended by a number of footmen in excellent order'.[1]

'After the joust the ambassadors visited the Queen ... She is rather ugly than otherwise, and supposed to be pregnant; but the damsels of her court are handsome, and make a sumptuous appearance.'[2]

These two assessments of Catherine of Aragon, made by Nicolo Sagudino, secretary to the Venetian ambassador at the English court, emphasise the importance of clothing to the assertion of magnificence and royal identity. In his description of Catherine's appearance at a major court ceremony, Sagudino does not focus solely on the queen's physical looks; instead, he links together the queen's own presence with her clothing and the clothing of her attendants. Although Catherine herself is 'rather ugly than otherwise', the ladies of her court and her own rich attire supersede her physical form. Her body, which was 'supposed' to be pregnant, was one part of her presence as queen, but it was figuratively and literally obscured by the 'rich attire' of her own clothing and the dresses of her ladies. Sagudino's focus on Catherine's attire, and the attire of her ladies, is not unusual; nearly every detailed description of Catherine discusses her personal appearance and the fabric, cut or style of her clothing, and many sources include descriptions of her ladies. Ambassadors like Sagudino focused on the queen's appearance because Renaissance monarchs used sumptuous, rare clothing to reinforce their status and authority, as the idea of magnificence became a crucial political and social concept and humanist virtue for kings and queens.[3] Catherine's identity as queen was thus formed not only through her actions, but through her appearance, dress and company as well.

Catherine and Margaret used clothing to emphasise their agency and superior social status compared to the men around them in order to maintain royal dignity and their own authority, which was especially crucial at moments

---

[1] CSP Venetian, ii. 624, p. 247.
[2] Ibid. ii. 624, p. 248.
[3] Hayward, Dress, 9–11.

when they faced challenges at court. Because their marriages placed them above all other men in their kingdoms, save their husbands, their identities, honour and status as queens had to be asserted and re-asserted. Material culture and clothing was one of the most visible ways for Margaret and Catherine to do this during times of tension or crisis. This chapter presents a close analysis of three difficult moments during their queenship: their first pregnancies, Margaret's return to England in 1515 and the Anglo-French diplomatic summit of 1520 known as the Field of Cloth of Gold. These moments were periods of personal or political crisis for Catherine or Margaret, and clothing and material culture allowed them to assert their honour and status in the face of isolation or opposition. By focusing on their clothing and material culture, it is possible to understand how they harnessed visible symbols of their status in order to overcome threats to their authority. The importance of clothing to the creation of early modern social and political status meant that dressing as the queen cemented their identities as queens, not only for themselves, but also for their households, courtiers and kingdoms.

Catherine's and Margaret's use of clothing to embody their queenships during moments of isolation and tension was effective because of the close relationship between the body of the queen, the king and the governance of the realm. Their honour and identities as queens were closely tied to their appearance, their bodies and the material culture that clothed and surrounded those bodies. Becoming the queen invested their bodies with enormous political potential as their physical sexuality led to intimacy and influence with the king and their potential role as mothers of the heir to the throne. Theories of kingship in the pre-modern period equated the king's control and command of his queen's body with his ability to govern his kingdom.[4] This connection gave additional symbolic power and cultural capital to the body of the queen and how she dressed and appeared in public. Catherine's and Margaret's clothing reflected the honour and status of their husbands, and they could use this relationship to deploy the language of clothing in support of their own goals. The same connection between the queen's clothing and the king's power made Catherine's and Margaret's clothing an important means to negotiate their queenship during moments of tension or isolation.

In the pre-modern period, clothing was crucial in the creation of identity and subjectivity because of its interaction with the body. Clothing influenced the way others saw the queen's body and as such was a representation of her identity.[5] Clothing and material culture allowed Catherine and Margaret

---

[4] John Carmi Parsons, 'Violence, the queen's body, and the medieval body politic', in Mark D. Meyerson, Daniel Thiery and Oren Falk (eds), *A great effusion of blood? Interpreting medieval violence*, Toronto 2004, 251-2; Joanna L. Laynesmith, 'Telling tales of adulterous queens in medieval England: from Olympias of Macedonia to Elizabeth Woodville', in C. P. Melville and Lynette G. Mitchell (eds), *Every inch a king: comparative studies on kings and kingship in the ancient and medieval worlds*, Leiden 2013, 199-203.

[5] Catherine Richardson, 'Introduction', to Catherine Richardson (ed.), *Clothing culture*,

to embody queenship, which gave them the agency to assert their queenly identities in moments of political crisis, setbacks or isolation. Becoming a queen was an ongoing, discursive process, and because clothing was both changeable and materially present, Catherine and Margaret could use their royal wardrobes to negotiate moments of tension by deploying their clothes as outward signs of their identities, their honour and their dignity.

The queen's clothing and material surroundings separated and distanced her from her subjects, establishing her identity as royalty and her sanctity as an anointed queen. Queens and their bodies were sanctified and joined with their husbands through the sacrament of marriage and their coronations. The outward sign of the monarch's sanctity was her magnificent clothing, which honoured and exalted her body even as it obscured her physical form. Like a holy relic encased in gold and jewels, the queen's body was glorified and protected by her clothing. In the pre-modern period, the clothing of the elite was markedly different from the clothing of the masses in both substance and style. Clothing and dress served to embody social rank and distance the wearer materially and visually from non-elites.[6] Only members of the royal family could afford to wear the fabrics, furs and jewels that comprised a queen's wardrobe. Additionally, due to sumptuary laws, only members of the royal family were permitted to wear certain fabrics and colours, such as cloth of gold or ermine fur.[7] So, both physically and legally, the wardrobes of the royal family and the elite were distinguishing markers of social and cultural identity.

The layers of magnificent clothing, made of silks and velvets in royal purple and scarlet, shot through with threads of gold and silver, and sewn with pearls and rubies worn by the queen might appear to hide her body and thus obscure the connection between her clothing and her body. In the sixteenth century, however, elites frequently used exterior coverings to represent hidden, interior treasures. Just as a reliquary might both celebrate and hide a holy relic of a saint's body, the queen's magnificent exterior clothing emphasised her body's preciousness and exclusivity, in part because it was covered or partially hidden.[8] Moreover, the queen's physical presence was closely controlled

---

1350-1650, Aldershot 2004, 8-9; Ann Rosalind Jones and Peter Stallybrass, *Renaissance clothing and the materials of memory*, Cambridge 2000, 2-5. Despite its obvious connection with the body, few works consider the interaction between the body and clothing in history: Susan J. Vincent, *Dressing the elite: clothes in early modern England*, New York 2003, 2-4; Ulinka Rublack, *Dressing up: cultural identity in Renaissance Europe*, New York 2010, 17-19, 37-8.

[6] Jane Stevenson, 'Texts and textiles: self-presentation among the elite in Renaissance England', *Journal of the Northern Renaissance* iii (2011), 48.

[7] Maria Hayward, *Rich apparel: clothing and the law in Henry VIII's England*, Burlington, VT 2009, 29, 46-8; Maria Giuseppina Muzzarelli, 'Reconciling the privilege of a few with the common good: sumptuary laws in medieval and early modern Europe', *JMEMS* xxxix (2009), 599-600.

[8] I would like to thank Carol Symes for first suggesting this comparison to me. Glyn Redworth has noted that the seventeenth-century Spanish monarchy treated the king

and managed through access to her chambers, which both proclaimed her majesty while obscuring her physical presence from all but the most deserving courtiers. Kings and queens alike attended various public ceremonies – such as mass at the Royal Chapel – only to repair behind a screen (usually made of sumptuous material such as velvet) for lengthy periods, which did not lessen the importance of their presence at these events. Catherine's and Margaret's embodiment of queenship was bound to their clothing and the material culture of their surroundings, regardless of their physical presence, even during moments of tension or queenly ceremony, such as the ritual process of royal childbirth.

Catherine's and Margaret's first pregnancies

The connection between the material culture of magnificence and the legitimation of the queen and her body as perpetuator of the dynasty came to the forefront of royal ritual during the ceremonies associated with royal childbirth, lying-in and churching. These rituals focused exclusively on the queen and celebrated her condition through church ceremony, court banquets and the conspicuous display of material objects. Of course, childbirth rituals promoted the king's lordship and the child's legitimacy, but pre-birth preparations, lying-in and churching were also signs of the importance of the queen's condition and her role within the monarchy. Childbirth rituals sanctified a process that was hidden, uncertain and beyond the control of the king, yet necessary to the political survival of the realm.[9] These rituals also reflected the pre-Reformation Catholic understanding of childbirth, which held the female body's role in reproduction and childbirth as sacred. Childbirth was positively associated with the holy motherhood of the Virgin Mary and thus worthy of special religious protection, such as the relics used to help women, including queens, in labour.[10] In practice, pregnancy and childbirth were uncertain and tense experiences for early modern women and had the potential to go very wrong for a variety of reasons. Childbirth rituals, such as confinements that limited access to the mother, were in part attempts to control the experience as much as humanly possible in an effort to protect the mother and child.[11]

'almost as if he were himself a precious relic', though this was in a much more sustained and systematic fashion than what was practised in the sixteenth century: *The prince and the infanta: the cultural politics of the Spanish match*, New Haven 2003, 63.

[9] For more on the relationship between pregnancy, the queen's body and the governance of the realm see John Carmi Parsons, 'The pregnant queen as councilor and the medieval construction of motherhood', in John Carmi Parsons and Bonnie Wheeler (eds), *Medieval mothering*, New York 1996, 9–40.

[10] Mary Elizabeth Fissell, *Vernacular bodies: the politics of reproduction in early modern England*, Oxford 2006, 14.

[11] Catherine and Margaret would have been well aware of the dangers of pregnancy:

Catherine and Margaret both experienced the perils of childbirth and the uncertainty of their children's survival. They each experienced especially difficult first pregnancies, and the material culture of lying-in and churching helped to affirm their status as queens even as they faced questions about their ability to bear children. Honourable ceremony and the display of royal magnificence acknowledged Catherine's and Margaret's position as queens and legitimated their pregnancies, regardless of their final outcome. Magnificent clothing and material furnishings affirmed the authority of the queen's pregnancy by asserting her right to participate in all the privileges of monarchy.

Material culture was especially important during Catherine's and Margaret's pregnancies because of the close connection between the pregnant body and clothing during the pre-modern period. When a queen became pregnant, her clothing naturally had to change, thereby announcing her condition to the world.[12] The ordering of new garments and the changes to a woman's wardrobe established her pregnancy; effectively, it was a signal to the world that her body was, indeed, pregnant.[13] Beyond clothing, the elaborate rituals of lying-in and churching meant that elite women acquired new furnishings specifically for pregnancy and childbirth. Thus, changes to the material furnishings of the queen's household, including curtains, beds, pallets, canopies and screens, reflected and established her body's pregnancy. For queens such as Catherine and Margaret, their first pregnancies provoked a flurry of activity for their Wardrobe staff, who were tasked with acquiring or making a number of new furnishings for the queen's chamber.

Both Catherine and Margaret experienced difficult first pregnancies in which the material culture of royal childbirth helped to strengthen their positions after periods of uncertainty. Catherine's first two pregnancies were in fact a year-long ordeal that involved a miscarriage, a phantom pregnancy, and finally the birth of a young prince, who lived only fifty-two days. Catherine's maternal career began conventionally enough; after five months of marriage, Henry VIII wrote to Catherine's father in November 1509 to inform him that his daughter was pregnant, and by December the news was announced publicly.[14] The young couple's happiness was short-lived, however, when in January 1510 Catherine had a sudden miscarriage that was kept secret from everyone except the king, her confessor, two waiting women and her physician. Shockingly, Catherine's physician believed that the queen still remained pregnant with another child, and so Catherine continued to prepare for her lying-in.

Lying-in, or confinement, began when a queen retired to her chambers about a month to six weeks before the anticipated birth in a highly ritualised process

---

Margaret's mother, Elizabeth of York, died in childbirth in 1503, and Catherine's eldest sister, Isabella, died in childbirth in 1498, when Catherine was twelve.

[12] Jones and Stallybrass, *Renaissance clothing*, 2–3.

[13] Catherine Mann, 'Clothing bodies, dressing rooms: fashioning fecundity in the Lisle letters', *Parergon* xxii (2005), 149.

[14] *CSP Spanish*, i. 24; *CSP Venetian*, ii. 25.

dominated by the women of the court. Within her chambers, a queen would live in seclusion, waited on only by the women of her household.[15] The ritual enclosure of the queen emphasised her value and importance to the monarchy, even as it isolated her from the rest of the court.[16] Catherine probably began her confinement in March 1510, but weeks passed and there was no birth announcement. It became increasingly clear that there would be no Tudor heir that spring, but observers were uncertain as to what had happened in the queen's chambers.[17] Had she miscarried? Was there a stillbirth? Or, most worryingly, had she never been pregnant at all? This confusion put the queen in an especially vulnerable position, and rumours began to fly that the queen could not conceive at all. Because Catherine's pregnancy had continued to be recognised in public even after her miscarriage, it had developed, essentially, into a phantom pregnancy. Moreover, the king and his councillors were embarrassed and confused over the dilemma of the queen's confinement, which had stretched out much longer than the usual thirty to forty days. According to the Spanish ambassador, the privy councillors to the king were 'very vexed and angry at this mistake'.[18] Once it became clear that Catherine was not with child, it became a public necessity to negotiate the queen's return to court with as little loss of face as possible.[19] In June news was released that the queen had miscarried, and she re-emerged from her confinement soon after.[20]

The story of the queen's miscarriage conveniently skirted the true events, conflating the earlier January miscarriage with Catherine's later confinement and phantom pregnancy.[21] Catherine, who conveniently elided these two events in a letter to her father in May 1510, has been accused of 'deceiving' or, at the very least, acquiescing in the deception of her husband, her father and the realm of England in the matter of her phantom pregnancy.[22] However, it is entirely possible that Catherine was misled by her physicians and genuinely believed herself to be pregnant right up to May 1510. If this was the case, Catherine's ignorance about her own body and human reproduction is

---

[15] English and Scottish royal childbirth rituals were closely related to each other and to traditions in Burgundy and France. See also Downie, *She is but a woman*, 128-30; Kay Staniland, 'Royal entry into the world', in Daniel Williams (ed.), *England in the fifteenth century: proceedings of the 1986 Harlaxton symposium*, Woodbridge 1987, 297-313; and L'Estrange, *Holy motherhood*, 83-7.

[16] Laynesmith, *Last medieval queens*, 115.

[17] Both Catherine's confessor and the Spanish ambassador relate the entire confusing tale in their dispatches to Spain in May 1510: *CSP Spanish*, supplement i. 7, 8.

[18] Ibid. i. 8.

[19] Ibid.

[20] *CSP Venetian*, ii. 73.

[21] It was not until the release by the Spanish archives of the letters of Catherine's confessor and the ambassador that historians understood the confusing truth of the matter.

[22] *CSP Spanish*, ii. 43; Starkey, *Six wives*, 118.

disturbing, as her menses had returned sometime after the miscarriage.[23] It is perhaps more plausible to consider that Catherine may have only realised weeks or months after her sudden and probably traumatic miscarriage that her physicians were wrong. Catherine may have been reluctant to admit to the phantom pregnancy publicly and thus continued with the rituals of royal confinement in an effort to save face. This does not mean that her husband was unaware of her condition. At some point, Catherine and Henry must have both realised that she was no longer pregnant after her miscarriage in January 1510, because Catherine conceived again sometime in March of 1510, indicating that Henry likely slept with her shortly before her first confinement. Since it was highly unlikely that the king would have slept with his supposedly eight-months pregnant wife, we can speculate that Catherine had not 'deceived' her husband in any meaningful way.[24]

Although Henry may not have been deceived, Catherine may have used the queenly ritual of confinement to contain the truth of her phantom pregnancy and mitigate her embarrassment, as it seems that no one outside of the inner circles at court understood the extent of the confusion surrounding the phantom pregnancy. Miscarriages or phantom pregnancies were not unheard of in the sixteenth century, but the public nature of royal pregnancy made Catherine's situation vulnerable to rumours that she could not conceive.[25] Catherine's situation in 1510 was sadly echoed decades later when her daughter Mary's phantom pregnancy in 1554 was the subject of widespread domestic and foreign gossip.[26] Like that of her daughter, Catherine's miscarriage and phantom pregnancy was a personal and political loss for the queen, and she returned to court life amid speculation about her ability to provide the longed-for Tudor heir.[27]

The embarrassing events of early 1510 meant that it was especially important to Catherine that her second confinement be recognised as a legitimate pregnancy. Although Catherine had been furnished with all the necessities for her confinement in early 1510, including blue sarcenet curtains for the cradle in the nursery, in December 1510 the queen's Wardrobe of the Beds worked to prepare the queen's chambers anew.[28] Once more, yards of blue cloth and

---

[23] CSP Spanish, supplement i. 8.

[24] Non-generative sexual activity, such as sex with a pregnant woman, was condemned by the Church and considered sinful, even if the participants were married: Katherine Crawford, European sexualities, 1400–1800, Cambridge 2007, 29.

[25] Judith M. Richards, Mary Tudor, New York 2008, 178.

[26] Ibid. 174–8.

[27] CSP Spanish, supplement i. 8. The Spanish ambassador believed that although Catherine was healthy, her irregular eating habits made her menstrual cycles erratic, which made conception more difficult and probably contributed to the confirmation of a false pregnancy: Patricia Crawford, 'Attitudes to menstruation in seventeenth-century England', P&P (May 1981), 47–73, and European sexualities, 1400–1800, 111–14.

[28] Hayward, Dress, 198.

lace for curtains, screens and canopies were provided to Catherine's yeomen of the beds to prepare her chamber for her lying-in at Richmond.[29] These preparations would have been widely known, as they required the participation of the king's Great Wardrobe staff as well as the queen's Wardrobe of the Beds staff, one of the primary ways in which male household staff contributed to the queen's childbirth preparations.[30] Even before Catherine took to her chamber, the entire royal household was aware of the arrangements for the queen's lying in, which allowed Catherine to link her second pregnancy with the magnificence of royal childbirth, while also dispelling rumours and fears about her ability to conceive. In December 1510 she entered confinement, and she gave birth to a boy on New Year's Day 1511, to great rejoicing at court. Henry ordered preparations for a great tournament to celebrate the birth of his son, and ambassadors from the pope, France, Spain and Venice offered the queen their congratulations in person.[31] After a difficult beginning, Catherine's first successful pregnancy was clearly greeted as a joyous occasion that legitimated her position as queen.

Margaret's first pregnancy was also an ordeal for the young queen. Margaret had been married for three years before she conceived in late 1506, which probably indicates that James had waited to consummate the marriage out of consideration for Margaret's youth. While it was fairly common for very young elite brides to wait before consummating their marriages in the pre-modern era, Margaret must have felt some relief when she did conceive.[32] Margaret's first confinement, like that of her sister-in-law, produced a burst of activity in preparation for the first legitimate royal birth in Scotland in decades.[33] Margaret's yeomen of the beds received new bedding for the young queen, including a crimson satin canopy and red and green taffeta curtains for her bed of estate, alongside assorted pallets, couches, featherbeds and stools.[34] The queen's pregnancy appeared to be progressing normally. During her confinement she was even entertained by a female singer, sent especially to her chamber by the king on 16 February.[35] On 21 February she gave birth to a young prince named, inevitably, James. Although the king was overjoyed and gave the lady who brought him the news £40 Scots and a gilt cup, all was not well with the queen, who had become gravely ill with some sort of childbed fever.[36] Margaret remained

[29] TNA, MS E101/417/4; *LP* i/1, 647.
[30] Mann, 'Fashioning fecundity', 140–1.
[31] *CSP Venetian*, ii. 95. The infant Prince Henry died at the age of six weeks.
[32] Parsons, 'Mothers, daughters, marriage, power', 66.
[33] James IV had had numerous illegitimate children with several mistresses before he married Margaret in 1503: Trevor Chalmers, 'James IV (1473–1513)', *ODNB*.
[34] NRS, MS E21/8, fo. 27r–v. See also *LHTA* iii. 266–8.
[35] *LHTA* iii. 369.
[36] NRS, MS E21/8, fo. 90r. See also *LHTA* iii. 369. In the early sixteenth century £1 sterling was equal to £3 Scots: Alexander Grant, *Independence and nationhood: Scotland, 1306–1469*, London 1984, 240.

confined for over a month. In mid-March the king, distressed over Margaret's illness, journeyed to his favourite shrine of St Ninian's in Whithorn to pray for her recovery.[37] Margaret eventually made a full recovery and would subsequently join her husband on a joint pilgrimage to Whithorn later that summer.

Although there is no mention of Margaret's emergence from her chambers, it is more than likely that both she and Catherine observed the ritual of churching. When a woman was ready to leave her confinement, she would officially re-enter normal life through the ceremony of churching. Churching was a ritual of purification and thanksgiving that celebrated a woman's return to public life after childbirth. Churching was a uniquely female-centred public ritual that was practised by nearly all new mothers in the pre-Reformation period, including queens. Gale McMurray Gibson has argued that churching was 'woman's theatre' that celebrated women's bodies, as the centre of the ritual was the woman's body, and men (even priests) were very much on the margins. Additionally, only women who bore legitimate children could be churched, and thus it became a symbol of legitimacy and acceptance by the community of the validity of the birth itself.[38] For queens, churching was not only a female rite of purification, but also an important political ceremony that confirmed the legitimacy and the rights of their children.

A queen's churching was significantly more elaborate than that of other elite or common women, and Margaret's churching was probably similar to the rituals observed by her English ancestors and relatives.[39] In England the queen's churching would begin with the queen lying on her state bed behind the rich curtains that the king had furnished for her a few months before. Two high-ranking noblewomen would approach the bed and draw back the curtains, revealing the queen in her material splendour. The queen was then ceremonially raised from the bed by two dukes or earls. The court would then process to hear mass in the royal chapel, followed by feasting in the queen's chamber.[40] Significantly, both male and female courtiers contributed to the ceremony and witnessed the queen's emergence from her confinement. For queens, churching not only celebrated their return to court life but also marked the fulfilment of one of their most important duties, providing royal heirs.

The queen's churching welcomed her back to society by reincorporating her body into the normal rhythms of the court, and the importance of the queen's body at this juncture was emphasised through the rich clothing usually worn by queens when they were churched. In England in the fourteenth century Queen Philippa of Hainault ordered several lavish suits of clothes for her first churching after the birth of her son, Edward of Woodstock. These clothes

---

[37] NRS, MS E21/8, fo. 41r. See also *LHTA* iii. 287.
[38] Paula Rieder, *On the purification of women: churching in northern France, 1100–1500*, New York 2006, 147.
[39] Downie, *She is but a woman*, 132.
[40] Staniland, 'Royal entry', 308.

included a luxurious purple velvet set of robes embroidered with golden squirrels and a second suit of red velvet.[41] Because of her illness, Margaret seems to have remained confined for longer than usual, and she probably did not emerge from her chambers until late March or early April. Although there is no explicit mention of Margaret's churching gown in Scottish sources, an entry in the royal accounts shows that, in late March, Margaret's Wardrobe received cloth of gold and velvet to be turned into a gown for the queen.[42] These were especially costly materials, given to the queen from the king's own storehouse, and thus the gown was probably intended to be worn at a major ceremony. Significantly, Margaret had no other new gowns made until June, when her household began preparing for her pilgrimage to Whithorn.[43] It seems likely then that the March cloth of gold gown was intended for her churching ceremony, and the unusually rich fabrics indicate the importance of welcoming Margaret back into court life after a difficult and dangerous pregnancy.

Margaret's first pregnancy, while not as politically precarious as Catherine's first, was a difficult period for the sixteen-year-old queen. After three childless years of marriage, her first pregnancy must have seemed like a joyous occasion, and the material and ritual preparations for her confinement would have established her position as a queen who had fulfilled one of her most important duties. However, the illness that she suffered after birth evidently brought her very near death. Childbed fever had killed her mother when Margaret was eleven, so she would have known first-hand how real the dangers of childbirth were. When Margaret was healthy enough to re-join court life, her churching would have been a solemn rite of thanksgiving that affirmed her importance in the eyes of the court and re-established her identity as queen after a long confinement.

The material culture of royal childbirth provided both Catherine and Margaret with legitimacy and support during very difficult first pregnancies, and Catherine, at least, understood the importance of material culture in establishing her authority as a mother. After her death in 1535 numerous goods relating to her confinements were found in storage, including purple cloth of tissue coverings lined with ermine, shirts and smocks, and mattresses for a cradle. One of the most precious items was a fine linen covering fringed with gold, which was probably a christening cloth.[44] Catherine's last confinement

---

[41] Caroline Shenton, 'Philippa of Hainault's churchings: the politics of motherhood at the court of Edward III', in R. G. Eales (ed.), *Family and dynasty in late medieval England: proceedings of the 1997 Harlaxton symposium*, Donington 2003, 107–8.

[42] NRS, MS E21/8, fo. 29v. See also *LHTA* iii. 269.

[43] NRS, MS E21/8, fos 29v–30r. See also *LHTA* iii. 269–70.

[44] BL, MS Royal 7 F XIV, fo. 136v. See also 'Inventories of the wardrobes, plate, chapel stuff, &c. of Henry Fitzroy, duke of Richmond and Katherine, princess dowager', ed. John Gough Nichols (Camden o.s. lxi, 1854), 30, 36, 40. Cloth of tissue was the most expensive form of cloth of gold, incorporating gold and silver thread woven on a ground of fine fabrics

had occurred in 1518, so these items had been kept and treasured for years after they were needed. As in so many areas of Tudor court life during the divorce, the material culture of childbirth had become a battleground between Catherine and Anne Boleyn. A few years before Catherine's death, Henry VIII had attempted to force Catherine to give Anne a christening cloth that she had brought with her from Spain. Catherine had flatly refused to give any support, material or otherwise, to the new queen's pregnancy.[45] She sought to deny Anne and her future offspring the legitimacy that an object such as a royal Spanish christening robe would have conferred at this critical juncture.[46] After numerous pregnancies, many of which ended in miscarriages, Catherine understood the importance of the material culture of childbirth and how it could confer legitimacy and honour upon the queen and her children.

Margaret's return to England

Margaret Tudor returned to England under significantly less triumphal circumstances than when she had left it twelve years before. Margaret's reign as queen consort of Scotland had ended in 1513 with the death of her husband James IV at the Battle of Flodden, where a Scottish invading army was devastated by a smaller English force. Margaret's son, barely a year old, succeeded his father as James V. James IV had appointed Margaret guardian and regent for her son, but her relations with the Scottish nobility quickly soured. After a disastrous second marriage to Archibald Douglas earl of Angus in 1514, Margaret lost her guardianship and eventually had to flee Scotland for her English homeland. Heavily pregnant with her child by Angus, she arrived at Harbottle Castle in the north of England in September 1515.[47] After a difficult birth and subsequent illness, she remained in the north of England for several months before journeying south to London. While Margaret was recovering, her brother Henry VIII sent envoys to ensure that his sister was being treated honourably and to provide her with clothing. Margaret had fled Scotland in secret, arriving in England with only the clothes on her back and accompanied by two attendants, having been forced to leave all of her wardrobe goods in Scotland.[48] Henry was obliged to provide his sister with a number of gowns so that she did not lose her honour.

During this difficult period, when Margaret was isolated from her family and had lost her position as regent, the queen turned to clothing in an effort

such as velvet or silk: Lisa Monnas, 'Cloth of gold', in Gale R. Owen-Crocker, Elizabeth Coatsworth and Maria Hayward (eds), *Encyclopedia of dress and textiles in the British Isles* c. 450–1450, Leiden 2012, 132–3.

[45] *CSP Spanish*, iv/2, 1107.
[46] In the end Catherine failed, as some of the goods relating to childbirth were taken away by Anne after Catherine's death: BL, MS Royal 7 F XIV, fo. 136v.
[47] See Figure 4 above.
[48] *LP* ii/1, 929.

to regain her honour and authority. Margaret's use of clothing to assert her status has contributed to her historical reputation as a frivolous and vain queen, an assertion which has been commonly made by Scottish and English historians since at least the nineteenth century.[49] However, belittling Margaret's desire for appropriate clothing reveals a fundamental misunderstanding of the importance of material culture in the assertion of honour and authority for isolated or vulnerable queens such as Margaret. Traditional, nationalistic histories, relying on records that emphasise 'statist ideologies and political practices',[50] not only disapprove of Margaret's potentially disruptive political career but also ignore or dismiss one of her chief expressions of royal identity and claims to power, her clothing. When we take into account the importance that pre-modern society placed on clothing as a marker of honour and status, Margaret's so-called vain behaviour – including her delight in clothes and her repeated requests for money to buy new clothes – becomes understandable as a necessary assertion of her honour and statement of her royal identity during periods when she faced political opposition or isolation.[51]

It was not only Margaret's dignity that was implicated in her clothing; her appearance was a reflection on her brother's honour as well. Pre-modern women, including royal women, were expected to uphold male honour by dressing as befitted their social status.[52] For queens, dressing appropriately potentially benefitted the entire monarchy; Isabeau of Bavaria, queen of France from 1385 to 1422, used luxurious clothing to maintain the dignity of the French monarchy when her husband Charles VI suffered from bouts of insanity.[53] Margaret's clothing reflected not only her own status, but also the status of her royal male relatives, including her brother Henry VIII, her son James V and her bloodline as a whole. In her letters to her brother and his advisors, Margaret drew upon this concept to justify her requests for money and clothes. For example, in a letter to Cardinal Wolsey she explicitly connected her request for money to her brother's honour and her own. Margaret needed the money so that she could distribute gifts and largesse at the New Year, 'both for the kyng my brothers honour and myne'.[54]

[49] Fradenburg, 'Margaret Tudor and the historians', 42.

[50] Ibid. 45.

[51] Margaret was nearly always short of money: *Letters of royal and illustrious ladies*, i. 220–1, 223–5. For a reconsideration of accusations of vanity and wardrobe extravagance against one of Margaret's successors, Anne of Denmark, wife of James VI, see Maureen M. Meikle, '"Holde her at the oeconomicke rule of the house": Anna of Denmark and Scottish court finances, 1589–1603', in Maureen M. Meikle and Elizabeth Ewan (eds), *Women in Scotland, c.1100–c.1750*, East Linton 1999, 105–11, and Stevenson, 'Texts and textiles'.

[52] Dyan Elliott, 'Dress as mediator between inner and outer self: the pious matron of the high and later Middle Ages', *Mediaeval Studies* liii (1991), 279–308.

[53] Rachel C. Gibbons, 'The queen as "social mannequin": consumerism and expenditure at the court of Isabeau of Bavaria, 1393–1422', *Journal of Medieval History* xxvi (2000), 393.

[54] *Original letters, illustrative of English history; including numerous royal letters; from autographs in the British Museum, and one or two other collections*, ed. Henry Ellis, London 1824, i. 130.

After her flight to England in 1515, Margaret remained in the north while recovering from childbirth and awaiting an invitation to London. At Morpeth Castle, when she could barely rise from her bed due to illness, Margaret not only enjoyed and appreciated the new clothing her brother had sent, but she also used the clothes themselves to reassert her status as queen and demonstrate her close relationship with her brother. Henry's envoy, Christopher Garneys, described Margaret's reaction to the cloth he had brought north from London:

> Nevertheless she has a wonderful love for apparel. She has caused the gown of cloth of gold, and the gown of cloth of tynsen [tinsel] sent by Henry, to be made against this time, and likes the fashion so well, that she will send for them, and have them held before her once or twice a day to look at.[55]

Upon first reading, Garneys's letter might give the impression that Margaret was vain and frivolous. The letter goes on relate how Margaret 'is going to have in all haste a gown of purple velvet lined with cloth of gold, a gown of right crimson velvet furred with ermine ... These five or six days she has had no other mind than to look at her apparel'.[56] The implication one could draw from this description is that Margaret placed more value on her wardrobe than on the serious business of politics. However, Margaret's desire to have her new gowns brought before her was a method of reasserting her dignity as queen, even as she was unable to leave her bed. Undoubtedly, she took pleasure in the beautiful fabrics and colours of her new gowns. However, the fabrics and furs of the gowns themselves were significant: only those of royal blood could wear purple cloth of gold, and ermine was a costly imported fur associated with royalty.[57] Colours such as purple and crimson were restricted to the upper ranks of the elite.[58]

Garneys's description of Margaret's behaviour was part of a larger account that focused on assuring the king that his sister was being treated well and in accordance with her royal dignity, and his keen eye as an experienced courtier knew how to read the material culture of hospitality. He discussed the preparations of Margaret's host, Lord Dacre, for the Christmas season at Morpeth, stating that he 'never saw a baron's house better trimmed in all his life'.[59] Garneys described the tapestries, gilt and silver plate, and rich food that Dacre provided in glowing terms, all of which reflected on Margaret's honour as the royal guest, and, by extension, Henry's own honour. Garneys made a point of noting the Scottish and English nobles who came to pay their respects to

---

[55] *LP* ii/1, 1350. Tinsel was an expensive silk cloth that incorporated gold or silver into the brocade: Hayward, *Dress*, 435.
[56] *LP* ii/1, 1350.
[57] Hayward, *Rich apparel*, 29, 102-3.
[58] Idem, 'Crimson, scarlet, murrey and carnation: red at the court of Henry VIII', *Textile History* xxxviii (2007), 140-2; Hayward, *Dress*, 121.
[59] *LP* ii/1, 1350.

Margaret, including the disaffected Lord Chamberlain of Scotland and Scottish and English border lords. He interpreted the preparations at Morpeth as the appropriate response to the visit of the king's sister and dowager queen of Scots.

Margaret's concern about her apparel during her visit to England becomes more understandable when we consider the costly goods that she was forced to leave behind in Scotland. These included articles of clothing such as sleeves and partlets (a panel insert for the front of a gown) made of expensive materials such as satin, velvet, and cloth of gold, decorated with pearls, rubies and diamonds.[60] She also left a number of hats and headdresses, decorated with gold chains and jewels. One particularly stunning-sounding item was a red hat with the 'King of France's great diamond' set upon it.[61] All of these items would have cost a great deal to replace, and they represent the legacy of Margaret's career as queen consort and later, queen regent. For Margaret, these richly decorated clothes were important in facilitating the display of royal magnificence in Scotland and were sorely missed when she fled to England.

As soon as she was able, Margaret began making efforts to recover her possessions from Scotland, sending commissioners to obtain her goods and carry them to her in England. They were successful in obtaining a number of items for Margaret, including the wardrobe pieces listed above, and other precious objects.[62] Some of these objects were devotional, such as a shield of gold with the image of the Virgin, or five sets of rosary beads made of carnelian, coral or pearl.[63] A large number of Margaret's headdresses were sent to her in England, and some of them were quite elaborate, one featuring a bird wrought in gold decorated with eighty-one pearls, and another with leaves of gold and eight rubies.[64] Scottish fashion seems to have favoured very elaborate headdresses, as noted by observers in the late fifteenth century, so the appearance of these items in Margaret's wardrobe probably reflect a continuing fashion in Scotland that may have been different from what was popular in England.[65] The effort expended to recover these items indicates not only their material worth but also their symbolic importance in recovering Margaret's dignity after a series of political setbacks.

The goods that Margaret was able to recover from Scotland indicate that although she was frequently short of ready money, she was still able to dress

---

[60] NRS, MS SP13/23; *LP* ii/1, 2398. Partlets were a decorative in-fill for a low neckline or a chest covering.

[61] Ibid.

[62] The indenture shows that Margaret's servants received these items in September 1516: NRS, MS SP13/23.

[63] Thomas Thomson (ed.), *A collection of inventories and other records of the Royal Wardrobe and Jewelhouse; and of the artillery and munitioun in some of the royal castles*, Edinburgh 1815, 26-7.

[64] *LP* ii/1, 2398

[65] Margaret Scott, 'A Burgundian visit to Scotland in 1449', *Costume* xxi (1987), 17.

as befitted her station. This suggests that she may have been receiving some income in Scotland, although it was not uncommon in the sixteenth century for the elite frequently to run up debts in order to dress appropriately, so her expensive clothing is not a true indication of her financial situation.[66] Margaret's efforts to recover her Scottish wardrobe, and the willingness of her brother Henry to provide her with a new one, indicates that dressing appropriately for her station was not merely a luxury for Margaret; rather, it was a political necessity, as it was for all Renaissance monarchs.[67]

Henry VIII's gifts of clothing to his sister were also a public confirmation of the king's support for her, and they carried a political message to her attendants and, more broadly, the Scottish regency administration led by the duke of Albany. Henry's generous and public gifts of clothing to Margaret were an implicit criticism of the Scots' behaviour towards the mother of their sovereign. When Garneys first presented Margaret with the gifts from Henry, she called in a group of visiting Scottish lords to see her gifts, reportedly saying '[s]o, my Lord, here ye may see that the King my brother hath not forgotten me, and he would not I should die for lack of clothes'.[68] Margaret asserted that the clothing sent by Henry represented their close relationship and her importance as the king's sister. At the same time, her need for clothing reflected badly on the Scottish regime, particularly because news of Margaret's treatment by Albany's administration and her subsequent flight to England had spread across Europe through the Venetian ambassador in England.[69]

Henry's gifts to Margaret would have indicated her importance not only as the king's sister, but also as the Scottish queen dowager and former regent. Gifts were an important marker of esteem and intimacy between sovereigns, and sixteenth-century diplomacy frequently included the exchange of gifts between sovereigns and their ambassadors.[70] Gifts were exchanged between sovereigns for a variety of reasons as part of their usual communications and diplomatic relations, or they could mark the opening of negotiations, the conclusion of an alliance, or dynastic occasions such as marriage or childbirth. Monarchs used gifts to repair diplomatic relationships and resume alliances, as when Ferdinand of Aragon sent Henry VIII a jewelled collar, two horses, and a sword in an effort to gain his help against the French.[71] According to Catherine of Aragon, those gifts were important, not because of their material

---

[66] For a discussion of Margaret's financial status at this juncture see William Kevin Emond, 'The minority of King James V, 1513-1528', unpubl. PhD diss. St Andrews 1988, 121. Later, Anne of Denmark would have to borrow money to maintain the dignity of her court in Scotland: Meikle, '"Holde her at the oeconomicke rule of the house"', 106.

[67] Stevenson, 'Texts and textiles', 39-40.

[68] LP ii/1, 1350.

[69] LP ii/1, 929.

[70] Tracey A. Sowerby, '"A memorial and a pledge of faith": portraiture and early modern diplomatic culture', EHR cxxix (2014), 315.

[71] CSP Venetian, ii. 653.

value, but because they reminded Henry of Ferdinand whenever he looked at them.[72]

When Margaret arrived in the north of England in 1515, her political position was precarious and uncertain. Her flight from Scotland had isolated her from her young sons, James V and Alexander, duke of Ross (who died suddenly in 1515), and from political life in Scotland. She needed to overcome this isolation in order to have any chance of being reunited with her sons or regaining power in Scotland. While Margaret was lying ill in bed after childbirth in England, one of the few ways in which she could assert her status and her close relationship with her brother Henry was by drawing attention to the cloth and clothing that Henry had sent north as gifts. Margaret's display of her gowns would have served to remind her servants, attendants and the men around her that she was a queen and the sister of the king of England. Margaret's delight in her new clothes was in part because they were a manifestation of her identity as queen and her connections to those in power.

Material diplomacy: Catherine of Aragon at the Field of Cloth of Gold

In the summer of 1520 Catherine of Aragon had to navigate one of the most difficult ceremonial events of her political career, the Field of Cloth of Gold. This famous meeting of the English and French monarchs and their royal courts in a field in northern France was designed by Cardinal Wolsey, Henry VIII's chief minister, to cement the Anglo-French alliance that formed the heart of his plan for a European-wide peace.[73] Catherine, however, viewed the meeting with the French as a threat to English friendship with her own dynasty, headed by her nephew, Charles V, king of Spain and Holy Roman Emperor.[74] As queen, she could not publicly oppose her husband's intentions to meet the French, so she had to work within the ritual framework of court spectacle in order to express her opposition and propose an alternative alliance. First, Catherine worked to ensure that her nephew Charles V would visit England before the French meeting, thus presenting to both Henry and his courtiers an alternative to friendship with Francis I. Then, using her clothing and the liveries of her household, Catherine inserted symbols of her dynasty and of Spain into the Anglo-French spectacle, thus publicly offering the English an alternative to the alliance with France. Although Catherine's efforts did not ultimately prevent the Anglo-French alliance, they kept the possibility of a closer alliance with Charles V available, such that in 1521 Henry would turn away from France towards Catherine's nephew once again.

---

[72] *CSP Spanish*, ii. 231.
[73] Glenn Richardson, *The Field of Cloth of Gold*, New Haven 2014, 6.
[74] See Figure 1 above.

The Field of Cloth of Gold, with its emphasis on the rituals of hospitality, magnificent display and royal spectacle, provides an excellent opportunity to discuss how Catherine could use her clothed body to express her political views during a tense diplomatic moment. While Catherine was required to participate in rituals of hospitality welcoming the French court, she could attempt to improvise within the expectations of queenship in order to signal her own goals and concerns.[75] Clothing and appearance took on a heightened importance during this event, especially as the French and English courts sought to outdo each other by displaying their taste, wealth and ingenuity. The extravagant and expensive clothing of the French nobility alone led one observer to comment that many nobles 'wore their mills, forests and fields on their backs'.[76] Because of this emphasis on display, Catherine's clothing was even more symbolically powerful than usual. Catherine was at the centre of these celebrations, and her clothing not only displayed the wealth and pomp of majesty, but it also proclaimed her own heritage and diplomatic views.

The changeable nature of clothing made it an ideal vehicle for Catherine's dual identities as queen of England and Spanish princess. Because the events of 1520 presented a challenge to the Anglo-Spanish alliance that her marriage had cemented, Catherine had to navigate her conflicting loyalties to both her husband and her Spanish dynasty. Clothing could be used to make a statement of dynastic identity and loyalty, but the mutable nature of clothing meant that this identity was potentially fluid, a useful trait for a queen consort at the centre of multiple dynastic allegiances.[77] Catherine used her clothing, and the liveries of her household, to emphasise both her Spanish heritage and her loyalty to her English husband, thus avoiding the accusations of disloyalty or interference that often plagued foreign-born queens. As plans for the meeting with France went forward, Catherine's opposition did not prevent her from equipping her own wardrobe and her household with the clothes and goods needed to make her argument against the alliance, even as she maintained her honour as queen. Putting on a magnificent display was expected of her as England's queen and was a significant political calculation that allowed Catherine to assert both her loyalties to England and her investment in the continuing alliance with Spain.

Catherine's opposition to the French meeting was well-known in court circles, but the queen was careful to voice her objections without directly challenging her husband. Instead of publicly opposing the meeting, Catherine

---

[75] For ritual improvisation by early modern actors see Anthony B. Cashman III, 'Performance anxiety: Federico Gonzaga at the court of Francis I and the uncertainty of ritual action', *SCJ* xxxiii (2002), 340-1.

[76] *Mémoires de Martin et Guillaume Du Bellay*, ed. V. L. Bourilly and F. Vindry, Paris 1908, i. 102.

[77] Richardson, 'Introduction', 20-1; Roze Hentschell, 'A question of nation: foreign clothes on the English subjects', in Richardson, *Clothing culture*, 49-50. For Catherine's dual identities and her wardrobe see Hayward, 'Spanish princess'.

made her argument against the alliance to her counsellors, who then relayed to Henry that the queen 'had made such representations, and shown such reasons against the voyage, as one would not have supposed she would have dared to do, or even to imagine'. Catherine's stratagem worked, because it was reported that after her outburst, she was then 'held in greater esteem ... than ever she was', by Henry and his court.[78] News of Catherine's opposition had even made its way back to France, where the French king's mother Louise of Savoy interrogated the English ambassador about Catherine's intentions at the Field of Cloth of Gold.[79] Catherine's actions were seen as influential and potentially popular, even as they seemed to skirt the bounds of propriety. Because France was the hereditary enemy of the English and the site of the kingdom's most famous and lucrative victories, Henry and some of his nobles were ambivalent about Wolsey's peace plan.[80] Catherine's opposition, then, voiced what many at the English court were probably already thinking.

Catherine's dynastic loyalties were complemented by her concern for the position of her daughter Princess Mary, the four-year-old heir presumptive to the English throne. The prospect of a French marriage for Mary, which was a component of the Anglo-French alliance, would have united England and France dynastically. Not only would this marriage prevent Mary from forming a dynastic alliance with Catherine's family, but it would also potentially permanently join England and France together, if Mary were to inherit the throne. With the example of her mother Isabella, queen in her own right of Castile, Catherine saw no reason why Mary could not become queen of England. Her future husband would therefore influence England's alliances into at least the next generation. Thus, it was vitally important that the young princess be protected from a French marriage that would potentially permanently inhibit Spain's interests.

Catherine hoped to lessen the impact of the Field of Cloth of Gold by pursuing a meeting between Henry VIII and Charles V, which would take place before the meeting in France. Believing that her nephew's personal presence would help to counteract French influence, Catherine worked with Marguerite of Austria, Charles's paternal aunt and regent of the Netherlands, to ensure that the emperor visited England before the Field of Cloth of Gold.[81] Catherine used her familial connection to Charles to justify her desire for the meeting to her husband, claiming that it was 'her greatest desire in the world' to see Charles, her dear nephew.[82] She could draw upon the emotional

---

[78] *LP* iii/1, 728. This report was written by the French ambassador to England, who was understandably worried about Catherine's opposition to the meeting, so his assessment of her actions must be treated carefully.

[79] *LP* iii/1, 721.

[80] Peter Gwyn, 'Wolsey's foreign policy: the conferences at Calais and Bruges reconsidered', *HJ* xxiii (1980), 756-7.

[81] *LP* iii/1, 776.

[82] *LP* iii/1, 689.

and familial connection between herself and Charles as an excuse for urging the meeting, which provided a cover for both Catherine and Charles's more political motivations.[83] Before arriving in England, Charles wrote to his aunt Catherine to thank her for all her efforts in organising the meeting, saying that 'the arrangements ... have given him the greatest satisfaction'.[84] In this instance, Catherine hoped that the rituals of hospitality that governed such events would work towards her goal of drawing Henry closer to Charles. In May 1520 Catherine and Henry at last hosted Charles for a brief visit at Canterbury.

Once she had brought together Henry and Charles, Catherine chose to emphasise her loyalty to her husband through her dress. This was consistent with Catherine's history of diplomatic interventions in England, where she emphasised the need for England and Spain to pursue mutually beneficial relationships. Thus, Catherine used her clothing to remind Henry and the English court that she was a dutiful, loyal wife even as she embraced her nephew. On the second day of her nephew's visit, Catherine wore a gown of cloth of gold embroidered with Tudor roses. The next day, Catherine combined a necklace of five strings of pearls featuring a pendant of the patron saint of England, St George, wrought in diamonds, with a Flemish headdress. The Flemish headdress may have been meant to be an allusion to Charles's Flemish upbringing, while the pendant was very similar to the 'Lesser George' badges worn by members of the Order of the Garter, Europe's oldest and most honourable chivalric order. Founded by Edward III (Catherine's great-great-great-grandfather), the Order of the Garter was closely associated with English nationalism, and the pendant could have been a powerful symbol of Catherine's loyalty to England.[85] Catherine's clothing demonstrated her loyalty to her husband and England, while also paying respect to her dynasty and lineage. Despite Catherine's efforts, the meeting with Charles did not prevent the English alliance with France; however, it did serve to begin a new round of 'serious relations' between Charles and Henry VIII, which would eventually lead to closer relations when the French alliance finally fell apart.[86]

After the meeting with Charles, Catherine and Henry set off for Calais and their meeting with Francis I and the French court. As the name implies, the Field of Cloth of Gold was above all about display: of military prowess in the jousts, of bountiful and rich food at the feasts, of clever and witty entertainment at

---

[83] Catherine was not the only woman to use the language of love, devotion and familial loyalty to pursue diplomatic aims: Lorraine Attreed, 'Gender, patronage, and diplomacy in the early career of Margaret of Austria (1480–1530)', *Mediterranean Studies* xx (2012), 3–27, and Natalie Mears, 'Love-making and diplomacy: Elizabeth I and the Anjou marriage negotiations, c. 1578–1582', *History* lxxxvi (2001), 442.
[84] *LP* iii/1, 776.
[85] *CSP Venetian*, iii. 50; Hayward, *Dress*, 227. Catherine was descended from Edward III through his son John of Gaunt, whose daughter was Catherine's great-grandmother and her namesake: Peggy K. Liss, *Isabel the queen: life and times*, Philadelphia 2004, 383.
[86] Richardson, *Field*, 183.

the masques, and of gorgeous and expensive clothes and jewels at every opportunity. Although chroniclers and observers pay far less attention to her than to the lances broken and the figures in masques, Catherine was in full view of the English and French courts as a spectator to her husband in the jousts, sitting with her ladies on a dais At times, she was seen dining and conversing with her counterpart Queen Claude, and with the French king's mother, Louise of Savoy. In fact, she was probably more recognisable and easily viewed on her dais by the majority of the French and English courts than the king, who would have been occupied preparing for the joust and frequently off-stage.[87] Catherine's appearance and the clothing of her attendants were frequently in full view of the courts, and she used her clothing and the clothing of her household to make political statements about her dynasty and her connection to the English monarchy.

The men and women of Catherine's household had spent months preparing for this voyage, and their participation was crucial in Catherine's display of magnificence and honour at the festivities, both behind the scenes and as attendants in full view of the French and English courts. For an extraordinary event like the Field of Cloth of Gold, the liveries worn by the queen's servants took on a special importance in scale, cost and significance. Ordinarily, when Catherine's yeoman of the robes, Elis Hilton, ordered liveries for the queen's servants, about ninety men received cloth or clothing in black worth around £90 total.[88] When he began preparing for the Field of Cloth of Gold, Hilton's orders became larger and much more complex. In one account leading up to the great meeting, Hilton ordered clothing for fifty-five men of the queen's guard, seven henchmen, thirteen grooms and pages of the chamber, six footmen, and many others, amounting to over 150 people. The total outlay for Hilton in one account book, from April and May 1520, was £710 3s. 1½d.[89] This sum was close to Catherine's Wardrobe expenses for an entire year and demonstrates the importance that Catherine attached to outfitting her household appropriately for the occasion.[90]

The liveries and clothing provided by Catherine to her servants reflected her loyalties to both her marital and natal dynasties in England and Spain. Catherine took a close interest in the liveries of her household: she was well-aware of the connection between her own honour and the appearance of her

---

[87] Hall details Henry's and Francis's triumphs at the joust, but they are visible only when they enter the lists, whereas Catherine and her French counterpart Queen Claude remained on their dais throughout the competition: Janette Dillon, *Performance and spectacle in Hall's Chronicle*, London 2002, 85–8.

[88] JRL, MS Latin 239, fos 2r–3v.

[89] TNA, MS E315/242/3, fo. 31r. See also *LP* iii/1, 852. Most of the costs appear to have been paid out from Catherine's income, as her receiver Griffith Richards reimbursed Hilton for £549 3s. 3d.

[90] For 1525 (the first year of available data), Catherine's Wardrobe of the Robes spending was around £866: BL, MS Cotton appendix LXV, fo. 11v. See also *LP* iv/3, 6121.

household. For the Field of Cloth of Gold, she kept an especially close eye on outfitting her servants. In one instance, Catherine ordered Hilton to give away coats originally made for her guard because she did not like the green cloth that Hilton had purchased.[91] The misstep with the guard's coats notwithstanding, Catherine's most visible servants, those attending to her in public, including her guards, footmen and henchmen (young noble pages), put on a magnificent display. Each group wore different combinations of colours and fabrics, all denoting an association with the queen. Her fifty-five guardsmen and twelve yeomen and grooms of the Stables wore the Tudor livery colours of green and white, as did her litter-carriers.[92] Catherine's henchmen were by far the most colourful and fashionable of her male retinue: these young pages were outfitted with coats and doublets made of green and russet velvets, with cloth of gold and silver placards, and black velvet bonnets.

Livery clothing for Catherine's servants also included symbolic badges that celebrated her marital and natal dynasties. Catherine's footmen had doublets of red velvet upon which were embroidered cloth of gold sheaves of arrows, one of Catherine's personal badges.[93] Catherine's sheaf of arrows badge was based on her mother Isabella's emblem from Spain, which had been used extensively by her mother and her mother and father together during their joint rule.[94] Catherine's emblems for her servants' liveries had often combined her own dynastic badge with the Tudor rose, and a combination badge was most likely in use at the Field of Cloth of Gold as well.[95] Catherine's badges and colours would identify specifically her servants and the dynastic alliances that her queenship represented – alliances that in 1520 encompassed the Spanish, Burgundian and Austrian dynasty of Habsburg and reminded viewers of Catherine's illustrious heritage as the daughter of the formidable Isabella of Castile. The marked clothing of her servants – wearing Tudor colours and the queen's badges – proclaimed her loyalty to her marital and natal families.[96]

---

[91] TNA, MS E315/242/3, fo. 26r. See also *LP* iii/1, 852.

[92] TNA, MS E315/242/3, fos 25v–26v. See also *LP* iii/1, 852.

[93] TNA, MS E315/242/3, fos 22v–23r. See also *LP* iii/1, 852.

[94] It is important to note that Catherine's emblems were specifically symbols of her natal dynasty, and in particular her illustrious parents Ferdinand and Isabella, but they were not necessarily nationalistic emblems associated with the kingdom of Spain: TNA, MS E315/242/3, fos 22v, 23r. See also *LP* iii/1, 852, and Barbara S. Weissberger, 'Tanto monta: the Catholic monarchs' nuptial fiction and the power of Isabel I of Castile', in Anne J. Cruz and Mihoko Suzuki (eds), *The rule of women in early modern Europe*, Urbana 2009, 43–63. Catherine also used her father's symbol of the yoke from time to time, although this could cause some confusion in England: David Starkey, 'Ightham Mote: politics and architecture in early Tudor England', *Archaeologia* cvii (1982), 155.

[95] BL, MS Royal 7 F XIV, fo. 134v. This comes from an inventory of Catherine's Wardrobe taken after her death, and thus the items themselves cannot be dated. However, the quantity – 35 coats of red and green stripes – would indicate that they were intended for an important ceremonial occasion, and possibly the Field of Cloth of Gold.

[96] Occasionally some members of Margaret's household in Scotland wore the livery

To an even greater degree than her male servants, the clothes worn by Catherine's gentlewomen and lady attendants, members of the nobility and gentry of England, were also reflections of the queen's own beauty, style and wealth.[97] The ambassadors who observed the events of the Field of Cloth of Gold did not hesitate to link the queen with her ladies and servants, and the English were well aware of the potential scrutiny. The English ambassador wrote shortly after his arrival at the French court in early 1520 that

> the Queen here, with the King's mother [Louise of Savoy], make all the search possible to bring at the assembly the fairest ladies and demoiselles that may be found ... I hope at the least, Sir, that the Queen's Grace shall bring such in her band, that the visage of England, which hath always had the praise, shall not at this time lose the same.[98]

As with all the elements of display at the Field of Cloth of Gold, the physical beauty and wardrobes of the ladies became a competition between the English and French courts.

Catherine's ladies excited comment for their appearance and dress as they accompanied the queen to the jousts held by Henry and Francis. The Mantuan ambassador to France observed that when Catherine ascended the gallery to watch the jousts, she was accompanied by a 'great retinue of ladies, who were neither very handsome nor very graceful; they were ornamented in the English fashion, and not richly clad'. In comparison, the same ambassador favoured the French queen, whose ladies were 'richly dressed and with jewels', clearly more to his taste.[99] As the Mantuan rulers were allies of the French king in 1520, their ambassador's criticism is not surprising and is almost certainly partial.[100] Other Italian ambassadors did not find such fault with Catherine's ladies, describing them as 'handsome and well-arrayed', and in one case of faint praise, 'well-dressed but ugly'.[101] The English chroniclers claimed that '[t]o tell you the apparel of the ladies, their riche attyres, their sumptuous Iuelles, their diuersities of beauties, and the goodly behauior from day to day sithe the fyrst metyng, I assure you ten mennes wittes can scarce declare it'.[102] Regardless of

---

colours of her husband's house, red and yellow, as when they accompanied the queen on a pilgrimage to Whithorn in 1507: NRS, MS E21/8, fo. 64v. See also *LHTA* iii. 321.

[97] For a more general discussion on the political importance of the appearance of the queen's ladies at court see Harris, *English aristocratic women*, 231-2.

[98] *State papers of Henry VIII*, vi. 56, quoted in Ives, *Anne Boleyn*, 31.

[99] *CSP Venetian*, iii. 81. Early modern beauty consisted of a fairly consistent set of features: red lips, white skin, blond hair and black eyebrows: Edith Snook, *Women, beauty and power in early modern England: a feminist literary history*, Basingstoke 2011, 2-3. In their youth, Catherine and Margaret were praised for their beauty, although this was an expected compliment for young princesses. Both would have had the requisite pale skin and fair hair.

[100] Cashman, 'Performance anxiety', 337.

[101] *CSP Venetian*, iii. 68, 50.

[102] Dillon, *Hall's Chronicle*, 93.

their assessments, it is clear from observers' comments that the appearance of Catherine's ladies was an important component of her of display at the Field of Cloth of Gold, and their dress was yet another arena in which the French and English courts sought to assert their superiority.

Catherine's ladies and her servants accompanied the queen to the Field of Cloth of Gold to enhance her royal dignity and the political message that Catherine wished to convey with her own physical presence, that England's long relationship with Catherine's dynasty was still an attractive and important element of their foreign policy. In order to be effective, Catherine's message had to be presented as a part of a display of royal magnificence through sumptuous dress, for both the queen and her servants. Catherine's clothing had to be made of the most expensive materials that would reflect her royal status and assert her position as equal to the French sovereigns. There is no direct Wardrobe account specifically for the queen's clothes for the Field of Cloth of Gold. However, at the beginning of 1520, Catherine's wardrobe received orders for clothing that may have been in preparation for the meeting and would have been suitable for the magnificence and spectacle of the Field of Cloth of Gold. Catherine ordered three gowns to be altered 'after the devising of Sir Thomas Boleyn, when he came out of France', which is an indication that Catherine wished to keep current on the latest European fashion.[103] Around the same time, Catherine also ordered a gown of cloth of tissue lined with crimson velvet, a gown of crimson velvet with gold embroidery, and in what must have been a striking combination, a gown of yellow damask of gold, edged with purple velvet and pearls.[104] Though it is not explicitly stated that these gowns were for the meeting in France, they do correspond to the types of gowns some observers describe Catherine as wearing when she met both Francis I and Charles V. By using predominately royal colours such as purple, crimson and gold, and luxurious materials, these gowns were material manifestations of Catherine's royal status and a powerful expression of royal magnificence.

Catherine worked to ensure that her appearance maintained the values of magnificence and majesty that were expected of a queen, but she also worked to adapt royal magnificence to her own political ends. She could use her own wardrobe to make a subtle, political statement, which was amplified by the clothing of her ladies and the servants who surrounded her. During the Field of Cloth of Gold, Catherine used national styles of dress and coiffure to draw attention to her Spanish lineage and insert a Spanish presence into the Anglo-French event. When attending one of the jousts held between the French and English knights, Catherine wore her hair

---

[103] France was the acknowledged leader of fashion in northern Europe: Hayward, *Dress*, 12.
[104] JRL, MS Latin 239, fos 15v–16r. Justice's account, though not consistently dated throughout, clearly included the period for the Field of Cloth of Gold, as it includes an entry (fo. 17r.) for allowances for Justice and his two servants 'with the Queen's grace at Calais'.

in the Spanish fashion, with the tress of hair over her shoulders and gown, which last was all cloth of gold; and round her neck were most beautiful jewels and pearls. She was in a litter, covered completely with cloth of gold, embroidered with crimson satin foliage, which was wraught with gold ... The horses and pages were all covered in like manner, as also the 40 hackneys [sic] of her ladies and the six waggons [sic].[105]

Her Spanish coif involved a long braid of hair encased in gold and jewels that hung down her back, and usually this hairstyle was worn with a Spanish bonnet.[106] The French and English women at court usually wore their hair pinned up and covered by gold nets, ribbons or linen coifs, so Catherine's long braid and bonnet would have clearly differentiated her from other national styles.[107] In wearing her hair in 'the Spanish fashion' Catherine emphasised her dynastic allegiance during an event that threatened the Anglo-Spanish alliance with an Anglo-French one. Catherine increased the effect of her statement by dressing her household in a similar manner, extending the statement made by her clothing, and turning her personal body and its clothing into a public, corporate one.

The Field of Cloth of Gold was not the first occasion on which Catherine had used her clothing to make political points, nor was she the only monarch to use national styles of dress to draw attention to diplomatic or dynastic loyalties. Henry VIII was known for adopting foreign styles of dress to make gestures of friendship and alliance, or to simply display his worldly taste in clothing.[108] Ten years after the Field of Cloth of Gold, Catherine's niece Eleanor of Austria, second queen of Francis I, used her Spanish fashions as a political tool to indicate her allegiance to Spain.[109] Eleanor's marriage to Francis was arranged in the face of the French defeat at the hands of her brother Charles, and thus began (and continued) with diplomatic and political distrust and tension between the married couple. Eleanor dressed in Spanish fashions at the French court for several years, until Francis sent away her Spanish ladies and likely pressured her into adopting French fashions.[110] Like Catherine at the Field of Cloth of Gold, Eleanor used clothing to express her familial loyalties in the face of political isolation and tension at the French court.

---

[105] *CSP Venetian*, iii. 85.

[106] For more on Spanish hairstyles for women see Janet Cox-Rearick, 'Power-dressing at the courts of Cosimo de' Medici and François I: the "moda alla spagnola" of Spanish consorts Eléonore d'Autriche and Eleonora di Toledo', *Artibus et Historiae* xxx (2009), 40, 47, and Hayward, 'Spanish princess', 30.

[107] Hayward, *Dress*, 171.

[108] Ibid. 12.

[109] Cox-Rearick, 'Power-dressing', 39–40. See Figure 1 above.

[110] Cox-Rearick, 'Power-dressing', 49. As far as is known Catherine of Aragon and Margaret Tudor were never pressured into adopting specific styles, although local tailors and materials likely dictated to some extent the style of clothing that they wore: Hayward, 'Spanish princess', 25.

Catherine also chose to wear Spanish styles of dress or Spanish elements in her clothing on other occasions during her queenship, and Spanish fashion in England became specifically linked with the queen. Catherine owned numerous gowns with sleeves cut in the 'Spanish fashion', which meant that the sleeves were elaborately slashed to reveal white undersleeves and banded with jewels and gold embroidery; Catherine also owned gowns more generally described as in the Spanish fashion or style.[111] Often, she would wear Spanish dress on days of high court ceremony or church liturgy, when her style of dress would be displayed widely before a large court audience. For instance, she dressed in Spanish fashion for visiting Spanish ambassadors on May Day of 1515.[112] The long-standing association between Catherine and Spanish fashion was not lost on her husband, and during the divorce crisis Henry declared that he hated the Spanish style of dress, even when worn by other women.[113]

As Henry's reaction to Spanish fashion makes clear, Catherine's clothing was a powerful component of her identity as queen, and she used material culture to support her political and diplomatic goals during moments of isolation or tension. Clothing was a vital aspect in the negotiation and creation of queenly identities for both Catherine and Margaret. Their identities as queens were a complex amalgamation of multiple roles and relationships, and their clothing could, at different times, be used to emphasise or assert certain aspects of queenly identity over others. Pre-modern women deployed clothing to uphold their honour and status, and at difficult moments in their queenships Catherine's and Margaret's clothing in particular made political claims for them. Clothing was a self-performance that could carry multiple types of meaning – legitimacy, political relevance, dynastic loyalty – that could support and enhance Catherine's or Margaret's claims to honour and status as queens. By focusing on specific moments of tension, isolation or political difficulties during the lives of Catherine and Margaret, it is possible to begin to understand how clothes could literally make a queen.

---

[111] TNA, MS E101/418/6, fos 9v, 11r, 21v. For detailed descriptions of Spanish sleeves see Cox-Rearick, 'Power-dressing', 40, and Hayward, 'Spanish princess', 18.
[112] *LP* ii/1, 411; Hayward, *Dress*, 178.
[113] *LP* v. 1187, p. 521.

3

The Social Queen

'[O]n the .iii. day of May she [Margaret] made her entry into London, riding on a white palfreye (which ye quene of England had sent to her) behynde syr Thomas par richely besene, & wt great company of lordes & ladyes, she roade thoroughe the citie to Baynardes Castel, & from thence she was conueyghed to Grenewiche, & there receaued ioyously of the kyng, the quene, the Frenche quene her syster, and highly was she feasted.'[1]

In 1516 Margaret returned to London for the first time in thirteen years, where her brother Henry VIII greeted her in magnificent Renaissance style. Her arrival in London began with lavish celebrations which included two days of jousting, banquets and a play. These celebrations not only honoured Margaret, but also featured Catherine of Aragon and occasionally Margaret's younger sister, Mary Tudor Brandon, the dowager queen of France, as spectators of the tournaments and hostesses of the entertainments and banquets. The three queens at the court of Henry VIII provided the king with an opportunity to celebrate his dynasty and participate in the chivalric displays and courtly entertainments that the young Tudor monarch enjoyed. The queens' presence added prestige and magnificence to these dynastic celebrations, and the events were deemed important enough to commemorate with a musical manuscript illuminated with the personal badges of the three queens – Catherine's pomegranates, Margaret's daisies and Mary's marigolds – surrounding the Tudor rose.[2] The Venetian ambassador noted the occasion, remarking on the presence of three queens in England, and more specifically on the confluence of pregnancies that resulted in the birth of three royal cousins within the span of a year.[3]

The presence of Catherine, Margaret and Mary at these entertainments show how important the queen (or queens) were to the social world of the Renaissance court, and in turn, how public spectacle and entertainment could incorporate, or in Margaret's case re-incorporate, queens into the political, dynastic and symbolic structures of the realm. While Margaret's visit was

---

[1] Edward Hall, *Hall's chronicle: containing the history of England, during the reign of Henry the Fourth, and the succeeding monarchs, to the end of the reign of Henry the Eighth, in which are particularly described the manners and customs of those periods.*, London 1809, 584.

[2] BL, MS Royal 11 E XI, fo. 2r (see cover image); Theodor Dumitrescu, *The early Tudor court and international musical relations*, Aldershot 2007, 130.

[3] *CSP Venetian*, ii. 661; Margaret's daughter Margaret Douglas, born October 1515; Catherine's daughter Princess Mary, born February 1516; Mary Tudor Brandon's son Henry, born March 1516. See also Sadlack, *French queen's letters*, 134.

unusual, her presence emphasised the importance of women, including the queen and her ladies, to the Renaissance courts of Europe. Catherine's and Margaret's predecessor and nearest role model, Elizabeth of York, provided them with an example of how queens could participate in the pageantry and ceremonies of the court.[4] Elizabeth's chamber became a site for court ceremony, and her household contributed to the spectacles that proclaimed the prestige of the new Tudor monarchy. Following their predecessor's example, Catherine's and Margaret's participation in court sociability gave them access to power and influence through their visual and physical association with their husbands.

At the princely courts of Europe in the pre-modern period, queens helped to establish international prestige and magnificence through the exclusivity of their royal blood, yet it is often difficult to understand how Catherine and Margaret fitted into the dazzling courts of their flamboyant husbands. Unlike some of their successors, they did not (as far as we know) commission masques or pageants. After they became queens, they did not appear to perform in the courtly dancing and disguisings that their husbands spent a great deal of time and money devising. How did Catherine or Margaret participate and benefit from the social world of the Renaissance court? They seem to have remained in the audience, either because of court protocol or personal inclination, and yet their presence at court entertainments greatly enhanced their queenship. As the audience for their husbands' chivalrous exploits, Catherine and Margaret were associated with the power and prestige of their husbands, emphasising the importance of the marital relationship and subsequently their political and dynastic identities. Additionally, as the chief hostesses for the royal court, their chambers became the centre not only of relaxing courtly pastimes, but also of diplomatic discussions and the exchange of information, news or gossip, which led to the creation of a host of connections amongst the elite. These social roles emphasised their relationship with the king, and Catherine and Margaret, although seemingly retiring or passive in the social world of the court, benefited a great deal from these traditional queenly roles.

The duties of Catherine and Margaret at court were rooted in their functions as wives as well as queens and thus were born out of sixteenth-century gender roles. Princely courts can often appear to be all-male arenas, as traditional sources for court life, such as ambassadors' accounts, chronicles and pageant accounts, tend to focus on the activity of the king and his household.[5] Yet, these courts were considered incomplete without women, and the queen and her household established the necessary gendered balance to Renaissance kingships.[6] These gendered social roles allowed Catherine and Margaret to assert their identity as queens by publicly enacting their

---

[4] See chapter 1 above.
[5] Ives, *Anne Boleyn*, 205–6.
[6] Olwen Hufton, 'Reflections on the role of women in the early modern court', *TCH* v (2000), 1–2.

relationship with their husbands and their social responsibilities as hostesses and audience for the royal court. The queen's role as hostess was rooted in the medieval responsibilities of the lady as mistress of the household, whose duties included welcoming guests and providing hospitality. The queen's role as audience originated in the ideals of chivalry, in which the lady was a source of inspiration for valorous deeds and the principal witness and authenticator of knightly renown.[7]

Participation in the social life of court by Catherine and Margaret required the consistent support of the queen's ladies, who were in constant attendance on the queen and represented the only large group of women permanently present at the royal court. As Olwen Hufton has observed, 'a court without women is like a body without a nervous system', and most of the ladies at court were part of the queen's household.[8] Throughout Europe, elite courts required the presence of women, even in the Vatican.[9] In France, the royal court was only deemed truly a court when men and women were socialising together, and this more often than not occurred in the household of the queen or the queen mother.[10] The social world of the Renaissance court, with its opportunities for elite mixed-sex gatherings that were almost unique in the pre-modern world, were possible because of the important roles that queens like Catherine and Margaret fulfilled.[11] When Catherine or Margaret watched a court spectacle or entertained in their chambers, they did so surrounded by a group of noble ladies who extended the queen's presence and at times acted as her proxies. Like their mistress, the ladies of the queen's household were audiences for court spectacle. They also actively participated in court entertainment as performers.

The first section of this chapter considers how Catherine and Margaret and their ladies participated in court spectacles, specifically their husbands' tournaments. Tudor court spectacles incorporated the audience as part of the spectacle itself, and the relationship between the audience and performers gave

---

[7] Maurice Keen, *Chivalry*, New Haven 1984, 116-17; Joachim Bumke, *Courtly culture: literature and society in the high Middle Ages*, trans. Thomas Dunlap, Berkeley 1991, 335; Roy C. Strong, *Splendor at court: Renaissance spectacle and the theater of power*, Boston 1973, 38; Kipling, *Triumph of honour*; Stevenson, *Chivalry and knighthood*, 82-3.

[8] Hufton, 'Role of women', 1.

[9] Renate Ago, 'Maria Spada Veralli, la buona moglie', in Giulia Calvi (ed.), *Barocco al femminile*, Rome 1992, 53-70; Hufton, 'Role of women', 1-2.

[10] Caroline zum Kolk, 'Catherine de Médicis et l'espace: résidences, voyages et séjours', in Giulia Calvi and Isabelle Chabot (eds), *Moving elites: women and cultural transfers in the European court system*, San Domenico di Fiesole 2010, 54.

[11] Jeroen Duindam, *Dynasties: a global history of power, 1300-1800*, Cambridge 2016, 126, and 'The politics of female households: afterthoughts', in Nadine Akkerman and Birgit Houben (eds), *The politics of female households: ladies-in-waiting across early modern Europe*, Boston 2014, 368-9.

political and social meaning to the entertainments.[12] As the audience for their husbands' exploits, especially at tournaments that highlighted the relationship between the king and queen, Catherine and Margaret demonstrated before the court their honour and influence with the king. The second section of this chapter shows how the smaller, more intimate pastimes of the queen's chamber were an important point of access for the queen to those who had power and influence at court. These pastimes, including music and dance, were part of Catherine's and Margaret's duties as hostesses, and their hospitality facilitated the political and cultural interactions at court and provided them with opportunities to assert their identities as queens.

The queen as audience: spectacles, tournaments and the queen's ladies

Henry VIII and James IV were masters of royal spectacle, and their reigns were a high point for the participation of women in court entertainments and sociability.[13] While both men promoted royal power through magnificence, spectacle and pageantry, their most successful expressions of majesty required the queen to be by their side. From the earliest weeks of Henry's reign, for example, Catherine wrote to her father of the celebrations at court, informing him with evident delight that '[o]ur time is ever passed in continual feasts'.[14] These entertainments were lavish and costly, and they were designed to ensure that the English and Scottish courts were culturally competitive on a European stage.[15] As young, active monarchs, both kings were frequently at the centre of these entertainments, often featuring in pageants, dances and tournaments designed to exhibit the kings' own skill as well as entertain ambassadors and noble visitors at their court.[16] Catherine and Margaret participated in these revels as the honoured audience for their husbands' exploits, and the revels were important in forming a strong royal partnership. Their role as audience for their husbands' spectacles not only fulfilled contemporary gender expectations

---

[12] Sarah Carpenter, 'The sixteenth-century court audience: performers and spectators', *MET* xix (1997), 4-6.

[13] Barbara Harris argues that after 1530 revels and entertainments at the English court declined. Women were subsequently on the margins of court activities, so Catherine's queenship may have been a high point for female influence at court during Henry's lifetime: *English aristocratic women*, 237.

[14] *Letters of royal and illustrious ladies*, i. 159.

[15] For example, David Starkey (ed.), *Henry VIII: a European court in England*, London 1991, and Anglo, *Spectacle, pageantry*, and 'The evolution of the early Tudor disguising, pageant, and mask', *Renaissance Drama* i (1968), 3-44. Henry VIII expanded his father's Revels establishment, employing William Cornish to supervise and devise entertainments that were the precursors of early seventeenth-century masques: W. R. Streitberger, 'The development of Henry VIII's revel's establishment', *MET* vii (1985), 87; Fradenburg, *City, marriage, tournament*; MacDonald, 'Princely culture in Scotland'.

[16] Streitberger, 'Revel's establishment', 87; Stevenson, *Chivalry and knighthood*, 90-3.

but also associated their own identities with the power and magnificence of their husbands' courts.

Although sitting in the audience may appear to be a passive role to modern eyes, in doing so Catherine and Margaret fulfilled the ideal gender roles for monarchy: the active, virile king and the passive, beautiful queen. This relationship between queen and king, audience and performer, is important because Renaissance court entertainments did not conform to modern theatrical notions of performer and audience. Court spectacles were a dynamic interaction between different types of participants, some of whom presented an entertainment while others served as witnesses to the splendour, valour or magnificence of the occasion, giving legitimacy and meaning to those presenters.[17] Before the courts of James IV and Henry VIII, Catherine and Margaret provided the symbolic or narrative focus for the dance, tournament or pageant, which in turn demonstrated the strength of their relationship with the king and their access to power and influence.[18] While accounts of performances at court naturally draw our historical gaze towards the dancing or drama unfolding in the narrative, the gaze of the court itself would have been directed towards the royal audience sitting in chairs of estate.[19]

The adoption of these seemingly passive roles was certainly not an unthinking posture for either queen, but a deliberate choice based on their own relationship with the king and the gender and social expectations of the royal court. This meant that that Catherine and Margaret could use their relationship with the king to intervene, sometimes publicly, in the ceremonies themselves. For instance, in May 1517 Catherine and Margaret performed a public and deliberately staged intercession before Henry VIII when they pleaded for the lives of a group of London apprentice boys who were about to be executed for their part in the Evil May Day riots.[20] This act may have earned Catherine lasting fame as a champion of London's poor, and it was certainly a calculated decision by Catherine and Margaret to adopt a more active role on this occasion.[21] Years earlier, Margaret had reputedly tried to intervene with her husband before the

---

[17] For the complex interaction between court performers and audiences see Carpenter, 'Audience'.

[18] Literary depictions of Catherine reflect her role as audience. In the Robin Hood pageants and ballads of the sixteenth century, Catherine's role was as the 'passive' partner to the king, becoming a stimulus to Henry's entertainments but not initiating action on her own: Victor I. Scherb, '"I'de have a shooting": Catherine of Aragon's receptions of Robin Hood', *Research Opportunities in Renaissance Drama* xlii (2003), 128. Other authors have commented on Catherine's passive role: Jansen, *Monstrous regiment*, 117, 120.

[19] Fradenburg, *City, marriage, tournament*, 254. For a discussion of the monarch as audience in the seventeenth century see Roy C. Strong, *Art and power: Renaissance festivals, 1450–1650*, Woodbridge 1984, 5.

[20] *CSP Venetian*, ii. 887.

[21] Catherine's actions were praised in a ballad still popular fifty years later, which may indicate her lasting personal popularity: Mattingly, *Catherine of Aragon*, 172.

battle of Flodden, pleading with him not to lead his forces in person.[22] Both queens understood how to modulate their public roles – active and passive – to suit their own agenda.

Catherine's and Margaret's passive roles as spectators for the splendid entertainments of their husbands' courts gave them power and authority because their behaviour publicly linked them to their husbands. By fulfilling the expectations of the court and sixteenth-century social and gender roles, these queens' passivity intertwined with the active knightly roles of the tournament, linking their role as lady with the honour and value of their husbands' exploits. These public appearances established Catherine's and Margaret's identities as the devoted partners of their husbands, whose favour and association gave them authority and legitimacy. For example, tournaments began with the queen's permission or in her honour, usually with the king and his knights doing reverence to the queen and her ladies. Henry VIII and Francis I did so at the Field of Cloth of Gold: '[th]us with honour and noble courage these two noble kynges with their compaignies entered into the feld, and them presented unto the Quenes, and after reverence dooen to theim, thei roade round about the tilte'.[23] Thus, Henry and Francis were able to fulfil one of the chivalric ideals of the tournament by revering their queens consort, and their queens were able to fulfil an important and powerful queenly duty that established their closeness to their king.[24]

The adoption of Burgundian-style tournaments in England and Scotland in the later years of the fifteenth century then became important opportunities for queens like Catherine or Margaret to contribute to the magnificence of their husband's monarchy. In particular, the fashion for elaborately staged tournaments required a new degree of participation by the queen and her ladies. Developed at the courts of Réné of Anjou and the dukes of Burgundy in the fifteenth century, tournaments featuring a dramatic plot and elaborate costumes were favoured by monarchs across Europe, including Henry VII, Henry VIII and James IV.[25] Above all, these productions required the presence of a lady (the queen) in order to fulfil their dramatic plots, which were 'a predetermined romantic saga which was always to find its hero and heroine in the king and his consort'.[26] The logic of the tournament required the presence of the queen in the audience to have meaning for the knights and the spectators.

---

[22] John Pinkerton, *The history of Scotland from the accession of the house of Stuart to that of Mary*, London 1797, ii. 96.

[23] Dillon, *Hall's Chronicle*, 84.

[24] For the idea of early modern women finding power within a patriarchal system see Barbara J. Harris, 'The view from my lady's chamber: new perspectives on the early Tudor monarchy', *HLQ* lx (1997), 215–47, and Sadlack, *French queen's letters*.

[25] For Burgundian influences on the Tudor court see chapter 1 above and Kipling, *Triumph of honour*.

[26] Strong, *Splendor at court*, 38.

In France, Savoy, the Low Countries and elsewhere, tournaments celebrating queenly beauty, love and magnificence gave women access to influence and power '[w]ithin the rhetoric of politics and chivalry'.[27] Indeed, Elizabeth I's success in harnessing romantic chivalry to her own personal cult of monarchy suggests that the presence of a strong warrior-king in the tiltyard was not required for chivalric display to be effective.[28] Rather, it was the presence of Elizabeth in the audience that gave meaning to the feats of arms of her knights. The entertainments of the first half of Henry VIII's reign in particular were notable not only for their political and diplomatic importance, but also for the inclusion and participation of the women of the court.[29] The incorporation of women into Burgundian-style tournaments, coupled with the enthusiasm of both James and Henry for this style of tournament, meant that Catherine's and Margaret's reigns featured unprecedented opportunities for the queen and her women to participate in court entertainments and thus share in the honour and favour often reserved for male courtiers.

Catherine's important role as the inspiration and validation of her husband's chivalric prowess was publicly noted and celebrated at the English court. A Tudor carol written in Catherine's voice proclaims the king's prowess in the tournament and demonstrates the relationship between the queen and her lord in the chivalric tradition: 'my soverayne lorde for my poure sake/Six coursys at the ryng dyd make,/Of which four tymes he dyd it take;/Wherfor my hart I hym bequest,/And of all other for to love best/My soverayne lorde'.[30] Although the author of the lyrics and the circumstances of its performance is unknown, the addressee of the poem is the king and the speaker is Catherine.[31] The song may have been performed as part of the festivities after the tournaments, perhaps even by Catherine or, more likely, one of her ladies. Regardless of whether it was actually sung by the queen, the poem's voice makes clear the important relationship between the queen and her king, and Catherine's role as inspiration and audience for Henry's triumphs.

Scottish tournament tradition has, until recently, been relatively neglected by historians, and the scarcity of sources makes it difficult to construct a detailed picture of any one Scottish tournament. The role of women in Scottish

---

[27] Sadlack, *French queen's letters*, 86.

[28] For the Tudor use of chivalry to encourage political loyalty see Steven J. Gunn, 'Chivalry and the politics of the early Tudor court', in Sydney Anglo (ed.), *Chivalry in the Renaissance*, Woodbridge 1990, 120-4.

[29] Harris, *English aristocratic women*, 237; Streitberger, *Court revels*, 94.

[30] This is transcribed in John E. Stevens, *Music and poetry in the early Tudor court*, London 1961, 405, H50, verse 1.

[31] William Cornish set the poem to music: ibid. 241. It is possible, although unlikely, that Catherine wrote the lyrics herself. Paula Higgins has argued that anonymous poems in a women's voice written in similar French manuscripts were not necessarily written by men: 'The "other Minervas": creative women at the court of Margaret of Scotland', in Kimberly Marshall (ed.), *Rediscovering the muses: women's musical traditions*, Boston 1993, 179.

tournaments is even more difficult to discover. Because the only surviving sources for Scottish tournaments are financial records that have little information about the events of the tournaments themselves, there are few details about women's roles.[32] This does not mean that women were absent entirely from the Scottish tournament tradition. Katie Stevenson notes that '[a]s courtly literature was popular in Scotland, we can assume that some tournaments, if not all, were held with women in the audience, in the name of a lady, to win a lady's honour or other such gesture'.[33] The personalities of the monarchs in question probably slowed the growth of the romantic tournament tradition in Scotland. James III, James IV's father, was uninterested in tournaments, and he was at odds with his queen for most of his reign, a combination that did not favour the development of women's participation in Scottish chivalric spectacle during his lifetime.[34] It is possible that the arrival of a young English princess sparked a trend for tournaments with a courtly love theme, as both Margaret's wedding celebrations and the tournaments in 1507 and 1508 incorporated themes of courtly love and female participants (including Margaret's ladies) into the festivities.[35]

From the beginning of her marriage, Margaret and her women were crucial participants in James's court spectacles. During her wedding celebrations, Margaret was entertained in a variety of ways, most famously through elaborate entry pageants that greeted her in Edinburgh. Historians have focused on these pageants because they consisted of complex imagery and allegories that were part of the European tradition of royal entry and pageant ceremony.[36] But the civic pageants, staged by Edinburgh burgesses along the procession route through the town to Holyrood Palace, were not characteristic of most of the spectacles of James's reign. Rather, it was the entertainments and jousts held after the wedding at Holyrood that were indicative of the courtly tournament spectacles favoured by James. James had held tournaments throughout his reign, at Shrovetide, at midsummer, and to celebrate embassies or marriages, and they became significantly more elaborate after his marriage in 1503.[37]

Margaret's first encounter with the tournament tradition of Scottish chivalry came as she rode to Edinburgh with James; the journey established Margaret's role as James's chivalric partner and, more specifically, the inspiration for the king's mercy. Riding pillion behind the king, Margaret and James encountered a pageant representing a tournament between two Scottish knights. The knights were fighting over the love and loyalty of a lady, who was also a performer in the pageant: 'wherof cam owt a Knyght on Horsbak, armed at all Peces, having

---

[32] Stevenson, *Chivalry and knighthood*, 91–3.
[33] Ibid.
[34] Fradenburg, *City, marriage, tournament*, 335 n. 59.
[35] Stevenson, *Chivalry and knighthood*, 80–1.
[36] See, for example, Gray, 'Royal entry', and Fradenburg, 'Sovereign love'.
[37] Stevenson, *Chivalry and knighthood*, 83–90; Fradenburg, *City, marriage, tournament*, 175.

hys Lady Paramour that barre his Horne. And by Avantur, ther cam an other also armed, that cam to hym, and robbed from hym hys sayd Lady, and at the absenting blew the said Horne'.[38] The performer-knights were two members of James's court, Sir Patrick Hamilton and Patrick Sinclair, so it is likely that the lady was also from the royal court or a court family.[39] After the knights fought both with spears and swords, Margaret and James called a halt to the fighting (it is unclear from the account who actually spoke out). After learning the reasons behind the duel, James consented to arrange another day to finish their dispute, taking upon himself the role of judge and arbiter of honour.[40] Margaret is quite passive during this exchange (it is not even clear if she was the one who called out for the combat to stop), but her role is nevertheless crucial: it is her presence (and her wedding) that causes James to postpone the duel for another day. As the entire performance was likely staged for the benefit of Margaret and her entourage, her presence was also the indirect catalyst for the chivalric display, and its themes of love and faithfulness reflected a message directly aimed at Margaret's upcoming nuptials.[41]

After she entered Edinburgh and witnessed the civic pageants, Margaret's chamber at Holyrood became the focus of socialisation for the wedding celebrations, and James continued to incorporate his young queen into his expression of chivalry. The wedding jousts were performed in the lower court of the palace, while the queen with her ladies watched from the windows of her great chamber and the king watched from his chamber.[42] Though separate, the chambers were both richly arrayed, Margaret's even more so than the king's, according her honour and respect equal to, if not greater than, the king's. As both James and Margaret were the audiences for the joust, the chivalric display was intended to prove the skills and honour of the Scottish knights at the tilt and to reaffirm their loyalty to their king and their new queen.[43] Margaret and her ladies also served as the chivalric inspiration for James, prompting him to create knights in her honour: 'the Kynge, for the luffe of the present Qwene and hyr Ladyes, did make XLI Knyghts ... This doone, he sayed to the Qwene, and Lady – These are your Knyghts, and taking hyr by the Haund, led hyr to the Doore of hyr Chammer, and when they war well and honnestly served, as was also all the Felischip with Plenty of Ypocras'.[44] Later in the narrative, Margaret's absence delays the creation of yet more knights, which was 'put off to the

---

[38] Young, 'The fyancells of Margaret', 288.
[39] Ibid. Although Young names the knights, he does not mention the identity of the lady.
[40] Ibid.
[41] For the importance of the audience in assigning meaning to sixteenth-century entertainments see Carpenter, 'Audience', 4–6.
[42] Young, 'The fyancells of Margaret', 298.
[43] Ibid. 297.
[44] Ibid. 298. Ypocras, or hippocras, was a type of spiced mulled wine.

next Day for the Luffe of hyr'.⁴⁵ The delay indicates Margaret's absence was unplanned (likely she was fatigued from the festivities) and suggests that there was some degree of flexibility and adaptation during these ceremonies.⁴⁶ The delay also demonstrates Margaret's importance to the proceedings; without the queen to witness them, James's actions had no chivalric value and must thus be postponed until she is present.

Margaret's wedding celebrations are unusual for a tournament account in that she features prominently (for obvious reasons) in the narrative of the events surrounding her marriage. It was more common for chroniclers and ambassadors recounting tournaments to focus on the king's exploits and the overtly masculine and martial nature of the tournament itself, which makes it easy to underestimate the importance of the female audience in the elaborate tournaments of the sixteenth century. However, the account books for Henry or James's revels reveal how the queen as audience was incorporated into the fabric of the tournament through symbolic gestures and material culture. In Henry VIII's November tournament of 1510, a heavily-pregnant Catherine was given a dozen silk roses when the jousts began and was presented with a garland later on in the celebrations.⁴⁷ These gifts were most likely presented by the knights to Catherine as part of the narrative of the tournament. Often these tournaments involved symbolic plots that incorporated the queen and her ladies into the dramatic action.⁴⁸ Visual symbols of the queen that connected her dynastic identity with the king pervaded Henry's tournaments as well. A gift of horse armour from Emperor Maximilian in 1509 was embossed with pomegranates, Catherine's personal badge.⁴⁹ Henry and his knights would often ride wearing H and K as part of their emblems, and Henry famously would ride as the knight 'Coeur Loyale' or Loyal Heart in the 1511 jousts celebrating the birth of his son.⁵⁰ Catherine also awarded prizes at Henry's tournaments, including the one celebrating the birth of Prince Henry in 1511 and at the Field of Cloth of Gold in 1520.⁵¹

The visual closeness of the king and queen at the tournament, through badges and emblems, stressed Catherine's personal and political closeness to Henry, and hence to the heart of political power at court. Henry VIII's enthusiasm for tournaments, and particularly his personal participation in the joust,

---

⁴⁵ Ibid. 300.
⁴⁶ English queens' coronations also featured the creation of knights (of the Order of the Bath), and this aspect of the ceremony was also adaptable, varying in number and sometimes honouring men who had close connections to the new queen: Laynesmith, *Last medieval queens*, 91.
⁴⁷ *LP* ii/2, 12.2.
⁴⁸ Strong, *Splendor at court*, 37-8.
⁴⁹ Karen Watts, 'Henry VIII and the founding of the Greenwich armouries', in Starkey, *Henry VIII: a European court*, 42-3.
⁵⁰ Dillon, *Hall's Chronicle*, 37.
⁵¹ *LP* i/1, 1491; *CSP Venetian*, iii. 50.

gave political significance to these entertainments. Those courtiers who were close to the king were visually associated with him at the tournament as well. Henry's knights were dressed in a similar manner to the king, emphasising their closeness to the monarch. The knights chosen to accompany the king were his closest companions, and many men advanced their court careers through their skill in the lists.[52] Although Catherine may have been seated in the stands, her symbols and emblems visually connected her role as audience with the king's role as knight in an unmistakable way.

Catherine and Margaret had important roles to play after the feats of arms were over. As the highest ranking ladies at their respective tournaments, they were responsible for distributing prizes to the winners of the jousts, and often this took place while they were hosting a banquet in their own chambers at the end of the day's activities. In this way the participation of Catherine and Margaret in their husbands' tournaments marked their status as the public partner of the king and the first hostess of the kingdom. The preparations for the tournament welcoming Margaret back to England in 1516 were lavish and featured both Henry and his brother-in-law Charles Brandon, duke of Suffolk, in the lists.[53] Margaret would have observed the jousts from the stands, probably with her sister Mary and with Catherine. As the tournament was in her honour, she would in all likelihood have awarded the prizes. After the second tournament day, the knights went to a banquet in honour of the queen of Scots in Catherine's chamber, further emphasising Catherine's role as hostess for her sister-in-law and the royal court as a whole.[54]

Amplifying the queen's presence at these spectacles were her ladies and gentlewomen, and both Catherine's and Margaret's ladies were a reflection and extension of their own identities as queens.[55] Drawn from networks of court families and the nobility of Scotland, England and Spain, these ladies were expected to appear alongside their queen in public, dressed in magnificent clothes and representing the beauty of the kingdom. Entertainments at court gave these women an opportunity to interact with male courtiers, forming friendships and finding potential marriage partners along the way. For Catherine and Margaret, their ladies supported them as part of the audience for the king's exploits, much as the king's companions supported him in the lists. Catherine's and Margaret's households offered the highest and most prestigious

---

[52] Steven J. Gunn, 'The early Tudor tournament', in Starkey, *Henry VIII: a European court*, 48.

[53] W. R. Streitberger, 'Henry VIII's entertainment for the queen of Scots, 1516: a new revels account and Cornish's play', *Medieval and Renaissance Drama in England* i (1984), 31. Brandon married Henry's sister Mary in 1515.

[54] Dillon, *Hall's Chronicle*, 59.

[55] Elizabeth Brown discusses this important role of the queen's ladies for Elizabeth I in '"Companion me with my mistress": Cleopatra, Elizabeth I, and their waiting women', in Susan Frye and Karen Robertson (eds), *Maids and mistresses, cousins and queens: women's alliances in early modern England*, New York 1998, 132.

posts for women in the kingdom, comparable to the king's closest companions. While Henry VIII's Privy Chamber was staffed by twenty men in the 1520s, Catherine was served by a staff of sixteen women in analogous positions.[56] Because these ladies and gentlewomen attended the queen throughout the day and at court gatherings and ceremonies, they became part of Catherine's and Margaret's identities as queens. Their appearance was commented upon by foreign ambassadors and observers, and they were constantly seen in the public spaces of the court with their mistresses.

These ladies became an extension of the queen's presence, reflecting the queen's own magnificence and honour through their behaviour and dress, especially at court ceremonies and entertainments. Catherine's ladies were supplied with sumptuous livery clothes reflecting their important position as close companions to the queen.[57] Catherine's Wardrobe provided her ladies with gowns of tawny chamlet, sleeves in crimson satin, and kirtles of yellow satin.[58] Margaret's ladies received livery gowns at New Year in tawny damask, black satin or tawny velvet.[59] Liveries visually linked the queen with her attendants and her servants. This visual connection would then be displayed before the court when the queen formed part of the audience for the jousts or disguisings. The queen's ladies created a glittering impression not only of the queen's magnificence, but also of her own wealth and discrimination in outfitting her ladies.

As the audience for the king's exploits, the queen and her ladies were also the centre of attention, the axis around which chivalric events revolved, and it was crucial that they understood how to participate in games of courtly love and chivalric play. One morning in January 1510 Henry and a few companions burst into Catherine's chambers, disguised as outlaws or Robin Hood's men.[60] The queen and her ladies reacted suitably to this intrusion, possibly because they were forewarned. Despite the fact that they were 'abashed' and surprised at the suddenness of the king's arrival, dances and 'pastime' were made before the king and his companions left.[61] Their appropriate reaction – both surprise at the intrusion and a recognition that the king was amongst the outlaws – flattered Henry's desire for courtly games. The interlude demonstrates how important Catherine and her ladies were to the role that Henry was playing, as the king had cast himself in the role of courtly lover to his new bride. For Catherine, participating in the king's revels drew her closer to the king, forming a stronger relationship and consequently greater access and influence at court.

[56] Harris, 'View', 237.
[57] Idem, *English aristocratic women*, 228–9.
[58] JRL, MS Latin 289, fos 8v, 9.
[59] NRS, MSS E21/12, fo. 55r; E21/10, fos 46v–47r. See also *LHTA* iv. 430, 228–30.
[60] *LP* ii/2, 1490.
[61] Dillon, *Hall's Chronicle*, 31.

Lack of participation in such events, either through disinterest or misunderstanding, could seriously damage the relationship between the king and his wife. Henry's fourth marriage to Anne of Cleves got off to a rocky start when he visited her in disguise before the wedding, and she ignored him.[62] During his marriage to Catherine, Henry frequently wore a mask to hide his identity while participating in court entertainments, and Catherine's correct identification of him as the king proved his natural superiority.[63] Anne's failure to understand Henry's intrusion as a courtly love-game and thus recognise the king seems to have hurt their relationship, contributing to their quick divorce a few months later.

The queen's ladies could also actively participate in such court events as the pageants, disguisings and dances that comprised the court entertainments of the early sixteenth century. Although Catherine was not an active performer in these entertainments, she continued in her role as an audience member. Her ladies, however, frequently danced with the king and his companions, as the conceit of many court entertainments revolved around the courtship of a group of ladies. Catherine's ladies represented the queen because they were part of her household and an extension of her presence and status at court. When Catherine was confined to her chambers because of pregnancy, her ladies continued to participate in court revels as representations and reminders of the queen. For the New Year's pageants of 1511 Catherine was confined to her chambers, preparing for birth of her first son. The court, however, did not forget the queen, and the New Year's pageants celebrated Catherine through her women, who danced 'appareled in garmentes of Crymosyn Satyn enbroudered and trauessed with cloth of gold, cut in Pomegranettes and yokes, strynged after the facion of Spaygne'.[64] The pomegranate was famously Catherine's personal symbol taken from her parents' arms, and the yokes were also another symbol usually associated with her father Ferdinand.[65] The queen may not have been participating, or even present, during these pageants, but her presence was clearly felt through the appearance of her ladies.

Margaret's ladies also participated in the entertainments of James's court, although the limitations of Scottish sources mean that their roles are less easily discerned than those of Catherine's ladies. They certainly had a major role to play in one of James's most famous tournaments, the tournament of the Wild Knight and the Black Lady in June 1507, a celebration of the birth of his son.[66] This was the most elaborate tournament of his reign, and it was such a success that it was restaged in May 1508 for visiting French knights. While there is no

[62] Retha M. Warnicke, 'Henry VIII's greeting of Anne of Cleves and early modern court protocol', *Albion* xxviii (1996), 570; Starkey, *Six wives*, 627-8.
[63] Carpenter, 'Audience', 10.
[64] Dillon, *Hall's Chronicle*, 36-7.
[65] Weissberger, 'The power of Isabel I of Castile'.
[66] Stevenson, *Chivalry and knighthood*, 95-6.

contemporary narrative account for either tournament and thus no indication of what role Margaret may have played in the festivities in 1507, it seems highly likely that Margaret was an honoured audience at this celebration, given her recent successful fulfilment of one of the key roles for a queen, the birth of an heir. Moreover, it is clear from surviving sources that her ladies contributed to the pageantry of the tournament in significant ways.[67]

The tournament of the Wild Knight and the Black Lady was one of the few tournaments during James's reign with an overtly courtly theme that specifically incorporated a woman in to the plot of the tournament, and Margaret's ladies contributed to the spectacle of the tournament and the subsequent banquet.[68] While there is no record of the Black Lady's identity, she and her maiden attendants were more than likely members of Margaret's household.[69] Their wardrobes indicate that they were members of the elite and were meant to be revered within the narrative of the tournament. The Black Lady wore a damask gown covered in gold flowers with green and yellow taffeta borders, and her ladies wore matching taffeta gowns. The Black Lady's epithet may have come from her specially designed black sleeves and gloves made of fine, chamois leather with an upper layer of gauze. She also wore a matching handkerchief or favour made of the same fine gauze tied around her arm, and this favour was probably granted to her chosen knight during the tournament.[70] The Black Lady's squire attendants, William Ogilvy and Alexander Elphinstone, also connected her to the court elite and Margaret's household. Ogilvy and Elphinstone were favoured members of the king's household, and both men would be closely connected to Margaret's ladies. Alexander Elphinstone would marry her favourite English gentlewoman, Elizabeth Barlow, in August 1507, only a few months after the first Wild Knight tournament. William Ogilvy was already married to Alison Roule, one of Margaret's gentlewomen.[71] These

---

[67] When James repeated the tournament in 1508, Margaret's participation in that event would have been limited simply because the queen was again pregnant and was probably unable or unwilling to join in any of the more physical activities, such as dancing. Margaret gave birth to an unnamed daughter in July 1508 who died a few days later: John Leslie: *The history of Scotland, from the death of King James I, in the year M.CCCC.XXXVI, to the year M.D.LXI*, trans. James Dalrymple, Edinburgh 1895, ii. 129.

[68] Stevenson, *Chivalry and knighthood*, 91–2. The other tournament with courtly themes was Margaret's wedding jousts.

[69] Who the Black Lady actually was or her ethnic background is nearly impossible to determine. While Margaret was served by several 'Moorish' women at court, including a lady named Ellen More who was particularly favoured, the preparations for the tournament give no indication of the identity or ethnicity of the Lady or her maidens. Fradenburg even speculates that Margaret could have been the Black Lady, though given the complete lack of reference to the queen in connection with the Black Lady, this seems highly unlikely: *City, marriage, tournament*, 255–9. See also M. E. Robins, 'Black Africans at the court of James IV', *Review of Scottish Culture* xii (2000), 34–45.

[70] NRS, MS E21/9, fo. 57v. See also *LHTA* iii. 259; iv. 64.

[71] *LHTA* iii. 258; *RMS* i. 3105, 3171, 3269.

connections indicate that Margaret's ladies could have been participants in the tournament and that one of them was likely the Black Lady herself.

The Black Lady's close associations with Margaret's household emphasises the close connection between the king and queen in the creation of the Scottish tournaments in 1507 and later in 1508. Even if Margaret did not actually participate in the entertainments (and in the case of the 1508 tournament she probably could not due to her pregnancy), her ladies certainly did, both as participants in the chivalric spectacle and later at the banquet held after the joust, which also featured an appearance by the Black Lady.[72] Behind the scenes, Margaret and her women were also involved in preparing for the festivities. Lady Musgrove, Margaret's English mistress of the wardrobe, was sent 'certain stuff' by Sir John Ramsay for the banquet and the dance in June 1508.[73] This banquet also featured an entertainment, including a choreographed dance by the king's companions, who were outfitted with five dancing coats of red and yellow satin, the royal livery colours.[74] The Black Lady may have also featured in the banquet celebrations, as at least one later chronicler mentions her making a dramatic exit, as if she had disappeared into the sky.[75] The tournament of the Wild Knight and the Black Lady as a whole thus provided many opportunities for the queen's ladies to participate and contribute to the spectacle at court, building a stronger connection between the queen, her ladies and the king.

With their ladies supporting or participating in court entertainments, Catherine's and Margaret's involvement in the spectacular and ceremonial social world of the court was clearly greater than their mere presence in the audience. The chivalric values that James and Henry embraced included the importance of performing acts of valour before a lady, making the female audience an integral and necessary part of tournament tradition embraced by both the Scottish and English courts in the early sixteenth century.[76] While James or Henry were jousting in a tournament, their queens, as both the king's public partner and the object of his chivalrous attention, formed the audience. The courts of Henry VIII and James IV featured active monarchs who were participants in tournaments, masks, disguisings and plays at court. These spectacles, although placing Catherine and Margaret in a passive role as audience, in fact required their participation as the appropriately magnificent, royal and appreciative audience in order to fulfil the ideals of courtly chivalry and in turn they were able to establish their political and symbolic identities as their husbands' partners and queens.

---

[72] *LHTA* iv. 129.

[73] She was sent items by Sir John Ramsay for the banquet hosted by the king during the tournament: NRS, MS E21/9, fo. 93v. See also *LHTA* iv. 125.

[74] NRS, MS E21/9, fo. 57v. See also *LHTA* iv. 64.

[75] Fradenburg, *City, marriage, tournament*, 255.

[76] Sadlack, *French queen's letters*, 132–3; Keen, *Chivalry*, 116–17; Stevenson, *Chivalry and knighthood*, 91–2.

The queen as hostess: dancing, music and socialisation

When Margaret returned to England in May 1516, she entered London at the head of a grand procession. She passed through the city before arriving at Baynard's Castle, a small royal palace close to St Paul's Cathedral. Margaret would use Baynard's Castle as her primary residence while in London, staying there with her own household, which included a number of Scots who had served her while she was queen consort.[77] For the next year Margaret was a guest at the English court, and during this period Catherine incorporated her sister-queen into court life as England's foremost hostess. Margaret, in turn, participated in impromptu social gatherings in Catherine's chambers, helping her sister-in-law fulfil her traditional queenly duty of hospitality by entertaining visiting ambassadors or foreign noble guests. Margaret would have been familiar with these types of informal entertainments, as she had presided over similar gatherings at the Scottish court.

Catherine's important role in courtly hospitality can be seen throughout Margaret's visit to London. From the beginning of Margaret's stay, Catherine acted as her sister-in-law's hostess through both symbolic gestures and material support. Baynard's Castle was the official London residence of Tudor queens consort, and thus Margaret was physically staying under Catherine's roof.[78] Baynard's Castle had both symbolic and mundane associations with Catherine as queen of England, and Margaret's time there was tied to Catherine's own hospitality. Moreover, Margaret entered London riding on a white palfrey given to her by Catherine.[79] This gift of a horse was commensurate with other gifts that Catherine gave to royal women, such as her gift of two palfreys to Queen Claude of France at the Field of Cloth of Gold.[80] A small saddle horse for female riders, the palfrey was specifically associated with women as riders, givers and recipients. Additionally, the palfrey was prominently displayed as Margaret entered the city and the gift was seen by many observers, including the ambassadors who reported it to the rest of courtly Europe, as establishing Catherine's reputation as a hostess.[81] As queen, sister-in-law and lady of Baynard's Castle, Catherine was

---

[77] TNA, MS E36/215, fo. 516v. See also *LP* ii/2, 1475. English accounts for 1516 show payments to Margaret's household, including a number of servants from Scotland, including Luke Taylford (Lucas Taillefeir), her yeoman usher who had served in Scotland since 1506, Jammy Dogge (James Dog) her keeper of the wardrobe in Scotland since 1511, and Edward Benestede, an Englishman who had been her treasurer in Scotland until 1508 or possibly longer.

[78] Simon Thurley, *The royal palaces of Tudor England: architecture and court life, 1460–1547*, New Haven, CT 1993, 78.

[79] Felicity Heal, *Hospitality in early modern England*, Oxford 1990, 21.

[80] *CSP Venetian*, iii. 94.

[81] Giustiniani, *Four years*, i. 222.

Margaret's hostess on both a ceremonial and a mundane level while she was in England.[82]

As Margaret experienced during her visit, most of the court's entertainments were not the large and costly spectacles discussed in the previous section; instead, they were smaller pastimes that frequently occurred in the queen's outer chambers, her Great Chamber or Presence Chamber. The queen's apartments in the sixteenth century mirrored the organisation of the king's apartments, which were divided into a series of rooms with increasingly restricted access, thus providing layers of security and privacy. Typically, the queen's apartments in Scotland were comprised of three tiers of rooms: the Hall, Great Chamber and Chamber.[83] In England, Catherine's lodgings were composed of three chambers as well, her Great Chamber, her Presence Chamber and her Privy Chamber. The Privy Chamber or Chamber was actually a suite of rooms, to which only the queen's ladies and a very restricted number of male servants were allowed access. The Privy Chamber was where the queen prayed, slept, ate (except for formal banquets), dressed and relaxed.[84] Margaret's Great Chamber or Catherine's Presence Chamber was where they hosted their mixed social gatherings and entertainments for visitors.[85]

James and Henry were both social monarchs, who were known for their approachable style of kingship and love of good company, which meant that the informal social events in the queen's chambers were important opportunities for Catherine and Margaret to foster their relationships with their husbands.[86] Historians have argued that the socialisation of the king with his courtiers were important to the development of personal and political relationships at the English and Scottish courts, but the pastimes of the queen's chamber are

---

[82] *LP* ii/1, 1861; Dillon, *Hall's Chronicle*, 58, Hall states that Sir Thomas Parr escorted Margaret into London. Parr was married to Maud Parr, who would eventually become gentlewoman to Catherine and the mother of Henry VIII's last wife Katherine Parr. It is possible that Parr's service to Margaret during this visit brought Maud to the notice of Catherine.

[83] Dunbar, *Scottish royal palaces*, 151.

[84] It is difficult to know exactly who had access to the queen's Privy Chamber. For reasons of modesty and privacy, it would have been mostly women, so probably only the queen's chamberers, gentlewomen and ladies-in-waiting: Harris, *English aristocratic women*, 214–15. Of course, the king and certain specified members of the queen's household were granted access to the queen's Privy Chamber. In 1509 Catherine had two gentlemen ushers whose rank indicates that they may have been permitted access to the Privy Chamber: *LP* i/1, 82. According to a later addition to the 1526 Eltham Ordinances, the queen's household included a gentleman usher of the Privy Chamber, whose title suggests that he had access to the queen's Privy Chamber: 'Ordinances for the household made at Eltham in the XVIIth year of King Henry VIII A.D. 1526', in *A collection of ordinances and regulations for the government of the royal household, made in divers reigns*, London 1790, 167.

[85] Dunbar, *Scottish royal palaces*, 133; Harris, *English aristocratic women*, 215.

[86] David Starkey, 'Intimacy and innovation: the rise of the Privy Chamber, 1485–1547', in David Starkey (ed.), *The English court: from the Wars of the Roses to the Civil War*, London 1987, 77–80; Hepburn, 'Household', 61.

often forgotten in this discussion.[87] Before his marriage to Margaret, James's social pastimes in his chambers included music-making and gambling, often in the company of his latest mistress.[88] James's easy rapport with his household servitors can be glimpsed in one memorable royal payment to William Sinclair, when the king lost 28s. Scots on a bet that Sinclair's baby would be a boy.[89] Sinclair was one of James's jousting companions and usher of the king's outer chamber, and thus was a close companion to the king.[90] Henry VIII also had an active, even intimate social relationship with his young companions early in his reign.[91] Both James and Henry would continue their social pastimes in the chambers of their wives, which allowed Catherine and Margaret to build strong relationships with their husbands and cultivate access to influence and patronage.

The social entertainments in the queen's outer chambers, which featured smaller, mixed-sex gatherings and informal pastimes such as music-making and dancing, were a frequent feature of the vibrant social world of the English and Scottish courts. The chambers of Catherine and Margaret thus became important spaces for members of the court to pass along news and gossip, request favours or win distinction for their beauty, wit or accomplishments. This informal business of the court, which women were skilled in conducting, often evades written sources because of its undocumented nature.[92] As the primary legitimate site for mixed-sex socialising at court, the queen's chambers were an important site for women's activities. Furthermore, the queen's lodgings were frequently used for court ceremony and spectacle, even for events that were not specifically 'female'. Catherine and Margaret played hostess for the king's male guests, which allowed them to form relationships and gather information from important political and diplomatic figures at court.[93] These social gatherings gave Catherine and Margaret access to the social spaces at court where they could engage in the informal exchanges that were at the heart of sixteenth-century court life and pursue their own agenda, patronage and connections.

The queen's chamber was a focus for courtly activities in part because of royal traditions of hospitality. The queen's position as hostess had evolved from the

---

[87] Norman Macdougall, *James IV*, East Linton 1998, 61; Hepburn, 'Household', 148; Starkey, 'Intimacy and innovation', 77.

[88] See, for example, *LHTA* i. 124–5, 128, 130.

[89] Ibid. i. 140.

[90] Sinclair would later become Margaret's usher of the outer chamber: NRS, MS E34/2, fo. 6r; Hepburn, 'Household', 123; Stevenson, *Chivalry and knighthood*, 84.

[91] Starkey, 'Intimacy and innovation', 80.

[92] For the informal role of women at court and the opportunities that they had see Hufton, 'Role of women'.

[93] Laynesmith, *Last medieval queens*, 245–6. Historians have noted this important duty for other queens: Erica Veevers, *Images of love and religion: Queen Henrietta Maria and court entertainments*, Cambridge 1989, 7.

older medieval tradition of the king's household as a domestic establishment, in which the wife of the king, like many elite women, managed the provisioning of the household and welcomed guests and visitors. By the sixteenth century Catherine and Margaret had very little to do with the practical management of the royal household, but the idea of the queen as symbolic mistress of the household and royal hostess remained.[94] Hospitality, which was closely related to notions of good lordship, patronage and largesse, was important to the reputation of any great household, and women in particular were expected to provide hospitality to guests.[95] Christine de Pizan, in her conduct book *The treasure of the city of ladies*, recommended that the noble lady in particular should provide welcome and hospitality to her husband's friends and courtiers.[96] Courtly and chivalric literature also praised ladies for their hospitality when they welcomed knights to the court and provided them with opportunities to gain honour through chivalric acts.[97] Hospitality was a humanist virtue as well, and the female patrons of Renaissance Italy presided over humanist courts known for both their hospitality and their learning. One of the most popular works of courtly literature of the sixteenth century, Baldesar Castiglione's *The book of the courtier* (1528), was set at the gracious court of Elisabetta Gonzaga, duchess of Urbino, whose hospitality encourages the courtiers to refined and witty conversation.[98] Queenly hospitality was an expected form of social participation in sixteenth-century court life that presented opportunities for the queen and her household to mix with the most influential and powerful men of the kingdom.

Hospitality was an important component of early modern diplomacy, and both formal ambassadors and foreign visitors to court were welcomed by Catherine and Margaret as part of their queenly duties.[99] In an era when domestic politics and foreign diplomacy were conducted in settings of household hospitality, the queen's role as mistress of the household meant that she was well-placed to aid the king in achieving his political goals. She could also pursue her own agenda at these gatherings by providing a relaxed atmosphere of conviviality that could soothe the tension of negotiations.[100] For instance, Catherine and her ladies would often entertain ambassadors alongside the king in her chambers. Henry liked to invite ambassadors to her chamber for an evening's entertainment, which featured music and dancing by

---

[94] Pizan, *Treasure*, 40-1; Laynesmith, *Last medieval queens*, 246; Michalove, 'Equal in opportunity', 53, 58.

[95] Heal, *Hospitality*, 12-13, 22, 182.

[96] Pizan, *Treasure*, 40-1.

[97] Helen Fulton, 'A woman's place: Guinevere in the Welsh and French romances', *Quondam et Futurus* ii (1993), 14-15.

[98] Baldesar Castiglione, *The book of the courtier*, trans. George Bull, New York 1978.

[99] Catherine Fletcher, '"Furnished with gentlemen": the ambassador's house in sixteenth-century Italy', *RS* xxiv (2010), 520, 522.

[100] Harris, *English aristocratic women*, 234.

THE SOCIAL QUEEN

her ladies. In October 1516 the Venetian ambassador Sebastiano Giustiniani visited Henry's court and stayed for dinner. After dinner he was sent for by the king, whom he found in Catherine's chamber with Margaret, listening to music and dancing with her ladies. Even an informal entertainment at court required the participation of ladies, and the presence of two queens together would have impressed upon the ambassador the strength and connections of Henry's dynasty.[101] Catherine and her ladies also entertained and occupied members of foreign delegations while the king and his ministers negotiated with the envoy alone.[102]

Music and dance performances displayed the talent and sophistication of the court before foreign audiences, and even the intimate pastimes in the queen's chamber could help to establish magnificence and further the conduct of diplomacy.[103] After a banquet for newly arrived French ambassadors, the king took one of the ambassadors to the Catherine's chamber, where she and her ladies amused the company with dancing and music, including one memorable performance by the keyboardist Dionysius Memo, which lasted for four hours.[104] Memo's performances before foreign diplomats were opportunities for Henry to show off his virtuoso musician, whom he had hired with the help of the Venetian ambassador.[105] When Catherine, her ladies and Memo, acted as impromptu entertainers for the ambassadors, Henry was able to demonstrate the sophistication of his court and offer a compliment to the Venetian ambassadors who had helped him entice the musician to England.

Catherine's diplomatic hospitality included hosting foreign guests, even when she did not agree with their diplomatic goals or support her husband's foreign policy. While the most spectacular example of the division between Catherine's own wishes and Henry's policy might be the celebration of the French alliance at the Field of Cloth of Gold, Catherine entertained diplomatic rivals on a more intimate scale as well. She entertained Henry VIII and his French guests at her personal country estate of Havering-at-Bower during the summer progress of 1519, and her hospitality was particularly praised by later chroniclers.[106] Despite Catherine's private opposition to France, the king sought to impress noble French hostages who were staying at the English

---

[101] Giustiniani, *Four years*, i. 301.

[102] Dillon, *Hall's Chronicle*, 64.

[103] For the importance of dance and entertainments in large-scale diplomatic spectacles see Dumitrescu, *International musical relations*, 21–4.

[104] Giustiniani, *Four years*, ii. 97. Memo was an Italian friar who was the organist at San Marco, Venice, working for the Doge before being introduced to Henry by the Venetian ambassador. He had close access to the king at court, and keyboardists in general were highly regarded and much sought after in this period: Dumitrescu, *International musical relations*, 86, 95.

[105] *CSP Venetian*, ii. 783; Andrew Ashbee, 'Groomed for service: musicians in the Privy Chamber at the English court, c. 1495–1558', *EM* xxv (1997), 190.

[106] *LP* iii/2, 1537.

court in fulfilment of the Anglo-French peace treaty of 1518.[107] Catherine's hospitality was part of Henry's programme to entertain the hostages in high style, and she did not neglect her duty as the kingdom's foremost hostess: '[f]or their welcomyng she purveyed all thynges in the moste liberallest maner: and especially she made to the kyng suche a sumpteous banket that the kyng thanked her hartely, and the straungers [the French hostages] gaue it greate prayse'.[108] Despite the fact that the French alliance threatened Spain, Catherine understood that politically it was in her interest to maintain her role as the kingdom's hostess.

Whether or not she agreed with Henry's policies, Catherine's involvement in hosting ambassadors gave her an opportunity to discuss foreign policy and present her own concerns about English diplomacy. These personal interactions usually went unrecorded (unlike, for example, written orders from the king or his ministers), and therefore it has been difficult to gauge the extent of Catherine's involvement in Henrician diplomacy. Nevertheless, Catherine's hospitality clearly gave her access to key diplomatic actors, and occasionally there is evidence that she used this to discuss diplomacy. In 1527 the English court hosted a large French delegation with the aim of negotiating a new Anglo-French alliance, which included plans for the marriage of Catherine's daughter Mary to the second son of Francis I. Catherine hosted Henry and the French ambassadors in her chamber several times during this visit, and she took the opportunity to express her concerns about the alliance's impact on her nephew the emperor.[109] Ultimately the alliance went forward, but the exchange reveals how intimately connected Catherine and her hospitality was to her diplomatic interventions, and that conversations about policy were not an uncommon occurrence in her chambers.

One of the unique ways in which Catherine and Margaret could contribute to the social world of the court was through the mixed-sex gatherings held in their chambers. Male and female courtiers gathered in Catherine's and Margaret's chambers to talk, play cards, dance and enjoy music from the queen's musicians. Unlike most of the sixteenth-century world, in northern Europe elite women frequently socialised with men, and at the royal court the queen's outer chambers, staffed by her male officers and female attendants, were never strictly gender segregated.[110] The queen's ladies played an important and unique role in contributing to hospitality at court, because they were the only group of women consistently at court. These ladies were featured in all

---

[107] Glenn Richardson, '"Most highly to be regarded": the Privy Chamber of Henry VIII and Anglo-French relations, 1515-1520', *TCH* iv (1999), 130-1.

[108] Dillon, *Hall's Chronicle*, 68.

[109] *LP* iv/2, 3105.

[110] Duindam, *Dynasties*, 126. The exception being when the queen was confined for childbirth, in which case all household duties within her chambers were taken over by her ladies and gentlewomen: see chapter 2 above.

the ceremonial and social occasions in the queen's chamber, where they would have interacted with male courtiers.[111]

Casual social gatherings in the queen's chamber included games and pastimes that could bring together the queen, her ladies and the king's courtiers. Catherine herself enjoyed playing games and owned a chess set carved in ivory and a clever case to hold a chessboard.[112] Chess and other games often included wagers, and payments for gambling debts leave a record of the informal pastimes of the court. For instance, in February 1519 Henry Courtenay, earl of Devon paid out 40s. in 'playing money' at a game in Catherine's chamber.[113] Courtenay was Henry VIII's cousin and a prominent courtier, but he was not a member of Catherine's household. Six months after Courtenay gambled in the queen's chamber, he would marry Gertrude Blount, daughter of Catherine's Lord Chamberlain and one of Catherine's closest ladies-in-waiting.[114] It is entirely possible that the match was made over a game in the queen's chambers.

Margaret often played cards with James and some of his companions, especially during the winter holiday season. On New Year's Eve 1503 James lost £70 Scots playing cards in Margaret's chamber, and on other occasions the royal couple played cards with James's illegitimate son, Alexander Stewart, archbishop of St Andrews, and with Andrew Forman, bishop of Moray and a career diplomat.[115] Both men seem to have had a particular relationship with Margaret. Born in 1493, Alexander Stewart was only four years younger than the queen, and they may have become friends over the years. Helen Newsome has argued that the young archbishop was the most likely recipient of a gift of a Book of Hours from Margaret, and that Margaret may have named her posthumous son by James IV after Alexander, who had perished at Flodden alongside his father.[116] Stewart had been educated on the Continent and upon his return in 1510 had become one of the king's most important administrators, so on both a personal and political level it was useful for Margaret to befriend her husband's son. Margaret's other gambling companion, the

---

[111] Historians have only recently begun to analyse the historical significance of the queen's ladies and the importance of the queen's chamber to the success of the court: J. L. Laynesmith and Barbara Harris have argued that the queen's chamber was an empowering arena that featured the unique ways in which the queen could contribute to her husband's court: Laynesmith, *Last medieval queens*, 250; Harris, *English aristocratic women*, 234-7. See also Akkerman and Houben, *The politics of female households*.

[112] BL, MS Royal 7 F XIV, fo. 136r.

[113] *LP* iii/1, 152.

[114] J. P. D. Cooper, 'Courtenay, Gertrude, marchioness of Exeter (d. 1558)', *ODNB*. See Figure 2 above.

[115] NRS, MSS E21/6, p. 281; E21/7, fo. 125r; E21/9, fo. 78v; E21/12, fo. 21r. See also *LHTA* ii. 412; iii. 181; iv. 99, 402. Alexander Stewart was James IV's illegitimate son by his mistress Marion Boyd: Trevor Chalmers, 'Stewart, Alexander (c.1493-1513)', *ODNB*.

[116] Helen Newsome, 'Reconsidering the provenance of the Henry VII and Margaret Tudor Book of Hours', *Notes and Queries* lxiv (2017), 233-4.

bishop of Moray, had helped to negotiate Margaret's marriage and had escorted the young queen to Scotland.[117] These gambling debts show how Margaret's chamber became a space for socialisation, and how it was useful in helping the queen to build relationships with important members of her husband's court.

These entertainments also gave Catherine and Margaret opportunities to observe courtly interactions and collect information in the form of gossip and news. The circulation of information at court was crucial to the queen's ability to stay abreast of political developments, and her ladies could also pass along the most up to date information to their families and kin networks.[118] The news and gossip gathered by the queen's ladies, and facilitated through socialisation in her chambers, is yet another example of an informal, oral interaction that leaves few traces in surviving sources of the period. Often it is only the outbreak of a court scandal that reveals the role of the queen's ladies in passing along information. In 1510 several of Catherine's ladies were dismissed from court by the king for spreading rumours about his own romantic interest in Lady Anne Stafford Hastings.[119] As Lady Hastings was the sister of the duke of Buckingham, the most powerful peer in the kingdom, the gossip was not only personally embarrassing for the king but also had the potential to cause political trouble. In the Renaissance courts of England and Scotland, where the personal was political, the queen and her ladies had a level of access and exposure to the king and his advisors that made it possible for them to become influential conduits and brokers of information.

Entertainments in the queen's chamber were opportunities to display the talents of the queen, her ladies and her musicians. Music and dancing featured heavily, and her ladies and her gentlemen would have been expected to perform dances for the amusement of the company, which they would have learned as part of their courtly education.[120] Some of Catherine's ladies played or sang and could entertain the queen in her chambers, and their talents often received positive notice by others at court, including the queen.[121] In 1525 Catherine inquired after one of her former ladies, Katherine Stafford Neville, countess of Westmorland, asking 'whether the good lady Neffyll did use to play so much as she was wont to do'.[122] Even after she had left the court, presumably upon her marriage, Lady Neville's talents earned her the notice

---

[117] Young, 'The fyancells of Margaret', 258, 261, 267. See also C. A. McGladdery, 'Forman, Andrew (c.1465-1521)', *ODNB*.

[118] Daybell, 'Gender, politics and diplomacy', 109-11.

[119] *LP* i/1, 474.

[120] Jennifer Nevile, 'Dance in Europe, 1250-1750', in Jennifer Nevile (ed), *Dance, spectacle, and the body politick, 1250-1750*, Bloomington 2008, 34-5, 38; Stevens, *Music and poetry*, 244.

[121] Harris, *English aristocratic women*, 231.

[122] *LP* Add. i/1, 467. This inquiry was directed towards Sir Arthur Darcy, the earl of Westmorland's step-brother, who had delivered a token to the queen from Lady Neville. See Figure 3 above.

and remembrance of the queen, useful in maintaining their relationship at a distance.

Margaret's chambers in Scotland certainly became a space for courtly amusement and mixed-sex socialising amongst Scottish and English courtiers. The Scottish poet William Dunbar celebrated the social gatherings in Margaret's chamber in verse, providing a comical literary record of the world of the Scottish court. Dunbar was intimately connected to the court of James IV and seems in particular to have spent a great deal of time with Margaret, writing not only a poem for her wedding, but also an occasional poem recording her 1511 visit to Aberdeen. He wrote three poems about or addressing members of her household specifically.[123] His poem 'Ane Dance in the Quenis Chamber' features a series of teasing descriptions of members of the Scottish court dancing in Margaret's rooms.[124] The poem shows how socialisation between men and women, Scottish and English, might have occurred in the queen's chambers through music and dance. Dunbar describes a wide social range of courtiers, from Sir John Sinclair, a Scottish knight newly returned from France, to the fool John Bute. The poet himself, as well as the queen's English almoner and two of her ladies, also join in. The dancing is mixed, two women and four men, and each dancer is hoping to impress the others. Only Lady Musgrove, Margaret's English mistress of the wardrobe and the object of Dunbar's affections, is successful in impressing the poet.[125] The poem remains silent as to whether the queen witnessed these dances, but it is clearly situated within her chambers as a social space for the Scottish court. Moreover, it is the presence of the queen's ladies at court, and in particular the English Lady Musgrove praised by Dunbar, that makes such a pastime possible. Dunbar's poem reveals how different members of the court would have congregated and socialised in the queen's chamber using informal dance as a pastime and social tool.

The importance of music and dancing to Catherine's and Margaret's hospitality meant that they needed to patronise musicians whose skills supported their entertainments. The musicians who played in the queen's chamber were usually a mixed consort of two or three whose instruments were suited to playing music for dancing. The queen's minstrels were a fixture at Henry VIII's court from the very beginning, receiving gifts at New Year starting in 1510.[126] In 1516 Catherine's accounts show that two minstrels, including a tabret or

---

[123] Dunbar, *Poems*, 100-4, 135, 141; Priscilla Bawcutt, *Dunbar the makar*, Oxford 1992, 51, 82, 87, 90-3. For Dunbar as a source for the court of James IV see Hepburn, 'William Dunbar'. More generally, Margaret was the focus for poetic activity at the Scottish court, including works by Sir David Lindsay, William Stewart and Dunbar: Priscilla Bawcutt, '"My bright buke": women and their books in medieval and Renaissance Scotland', in Jocelyn Wogan-Browne and Felicity Riddy (eds), *Medieval women: texts and contexts in late medieval Britain: essays for Felicity Riddy*, Turnhout 2000, 20.

[124] Bawcutt, *Dunbar*, 51.

[125] Dunbar, *Poems*, 100-1.

[126] *LP* ii/2, 1444.

small drum player, were part of the queen's musical establishment.[127] By 1519 Catherine had a mixed band of three minstrels including a tabret and rebec or early violin player. This ensemble of tabrets and rebec would have been able to perform many types of dance music for the queen and her ladies.[128] Dance music, including the popular French *basse dance* and the Italian *bassadanza*, could be played in intimate settings by a tabret keeping the beat and the rebec or pipe improvising a melody or tenor line.[129] Less formal dancing, including rounds and English or Scottish folk dances, could also have been performed with this fairly simple instrumental grouping.

In March 1520 two of Catherine's regular minstrels and Giles Duwes, a lutenist and the clerk of the queen's library, were all issued tawny gowns and black doublets by Richard Justice, possibly indicating that these three were meant to play together at the Field of Cloth of Gold in the summer.[130] Liveries defined the musicians as members of the queen's household and usually featured her personal emblems. Catherine's musicians would have thus been marked as the queen's minstrels whenever they performed in livery, and these performances served to remind anyone watching of the queen's hospitality, and, of course, her patronage. Margaret also had musicians for her dancing, specifically a tabret player, Jakes, who was probably accompanied by some of the many other musicians of the court, such as Guilliam the tabret player who was paid three times in 1512 to play for the king and queen.[131]

Catherine and Margaret relied on their international connections to expand their musical patronage and enhance their hospitality. They both brought musicians with them to their new kingdoms as part of their wedding parties. In 1502 one of the Spanish trumpeters in Catherine's wedding party, John de Cecil, was hired by Henry VII immediately after the rest of Catherine's escort had left, and stayed at the English court until 1514.[132] The musicians of Catherine's chamber were primarily French or English, but Henry VIII relied

---

[127] TNA, MS E101/418/6, fos 32r, 34v.

[128] Dumitrescu, *International musical relations*, 100. Dumitrescu adds that there was a close connection between tabret players and the households of queens, which possibly indicates that dance music had a specifically feminine association. Significantly, all three musicians were referred to as minstrels 'of the queen's chamber' in 1519, indicating that their primary music function was to play music in the queen's chamber: TNA, MS E36/216, fo. 58v. See also *LP* iii/2, 1533.

[129] Anthony Rooley, 'Dance and dance music of the 16th century', *EM* ii (1974), 79–81.

[130] JRL, MS Latin 289, fos 13v, 14r.

[131] NRS, MS E21/10, fos 98v, 105r, 116v. See also *LHTA* iv. 316, 331, 339, 356. It is important to keep in mind that these musicians would have likely played multiple instruments, and thus several different combinations of groupings could be produced from a limited number of players: Dumitrescu, *International musical relations*, 101.

[132] Cecil's name has been Anglicised by English sources. He is mentioned as a Spanish trumpeter for Catherine's brother-in-law, Philip of Burgundy, and later accompanied the English ambassador to the Spanish court in 1511: Dumitrescu, *International musical relations*, 67–8, A.3, 231.

on her Spanish connections to bring in musicians from abroad. In 1519 her servant Francisco Felipez brought eight Spanish minstrels back to England.[133] When Margaret journeyed to Scotland in August 1503, she took along an assortment of trumpeters, minstrels and one lutenist. Most of the minstrels stayed only a few months, departing in October 1503, but at least two of these musicians stayed on at the court of James IV for some time.[134] Bountas the trumpeter stayed from August 1503 to February 1504, and is recorded as playing in the queen's chamber.[135] James Camner, an English lutenist, stayed for even longer, and he was especially favoured by James IV, who gave him wages, livery and New Year's gifts. Camner's fees were significantly higher than those of the other minstrels at court, indicating how highly his skills were valued.[136] James and Margaret were unable to hold on to him, however, and Camner left for England in April 1505.

Music-making, dancing, gambling and a host of other activities made Catherine's and Margaret's chambers both attractive and important spaces for courtly gatherings and the business of the court. The successful performance of queenly duties and queenly roles at court was necessary for queens like Catherine and Margaret to create and maintain social and political relationships with their husbands and their courts as a whole. At court, their chambers were centres of sociability because as queens they were the king's public partner, hostess and audience. In providing a convivial atmosphere through music and dance, Catherine and Margaret performed their expected role as hostess and in return ensured that they and their ladies maintained connections and influence with courtiers, ambassadors and the king.

Margaret's visit to the English court ended in May 1517, when she returned to Scotland after lengthy negotiations with the regency government there. She was evidently sad to leave her brother's court, as one member of her escort reported back to Cardinal Wolsey: 'Her grace considereth now the honour of England, and the poverty and wretchedness of Scotland, which she did not affore, but in her opinion esteemed Scotland equal with England.'[137] Margaret's reluctance to leave was a testament to the hospitality that she had experienced at the court of her brother and the consideration shown by her sister-in-law in hosting her at court. Margaret probably exchanged parting gifts with Catherine, which may have included a Flemish Book of Hours that had originally been a gift to Margaret from her husband James IV. According to the inscription in

---

[133] *LP* iii/1, 202. After Catherine's death, Felipez petitioned Cromwell for payment of debts incurred while in the queen's service, including money lost when he was robbed in France while escorting the eight Spanish minstrels to England. The minstrels were escorted by Felipez to Windsor, but they are not mentioned thereafter.

[134] NRS, MS E21/6, p. 268. See also *LHTA* ii. 399.

[135] NRS, MS E21/6, pp. 266, 288. See also *LHTA* ii. 398, 418.

[136] NRS, MS E21/6, 344. See also *LHTA* ii. 472.

[137] *LP* ii/2, 3365.

her own hand, Margaret gave the book to someone whom she considered a sister, which could be either Catherine or Mary Tudor Brandon. Considering the role Catherine played in hosting Margaret and the time that they spent together while Margaret was in England, it seems likely that Margaret gave her hostess the book as a farewell gift.[138] Like the palfrey given to Margaret at the beginning of her visit, the gift of a Book of Hours to Catherine would have been a material reminder of their relationship and of Margaret's visit. It would have acknowledged Margaret's own role as guest and Catherine's as hostess.

When Catherine and Margaret met in 1516, they had experience as queens consort who understood that the duties of hospitality and sociability were important elements in their queenship. Although Margaret was no longer queen consort, her welcome at the Tudor court by her sister-in-law ensured her participation as an honoured guest in similar activities – tournaments, banquets, informal music and dancing – to those that she had presided over as hostess during her reign as queen consort in Scotland. Catherine and Margaret were often audiences for grand spectacles and entertainments at court. Their participation in their husbands' tournaments as favoured audience and spectators proclaimed their honour and their relationship with the king before the entire court. These important queenly roles could not be carried out without the support of the queen's household, especially the queen's ladies. Even when Catherine or Margaret were not present at courtly ceremonies, such as when they were confined for their lyings-in, their presence was felt through the performances of their ladies. In tournaments and disguisings, grand ceremonies and evening gatherings in the queen's chambers, the queen's ladies were crucial to the extension and support of the queen's own identity as a welcoming hostess and social leader of the court. These were, of course, the expected social and gender roles of a queen consort, but it is also important to recognise that successfully fulfilling these duties – as audience or hostess – also built upon and displayed the queen's relationship to the centres of power in the kingdom, the king and his household. The next chapter will consider how Catherine and Margaret used this relationship to reward the men and women of their households, thus fulfilling their duties as heads of households and patrons.

---

[138] Janet Backhouse, 'Illuminated manuscripts associated with Henry VII and members of his immediate family', in Thompson, *Reign of Henry VII*, 184. Erin Sadlack believes that this book was a gift to Mary Tudor, but Mary, Catherine and Margaret all addressed each other as sisters in their letters, so the language is not definitive: *French queen's letters*, 156. For letters where Margaret refers to Catherine as her sister see *Letters of royal and illustrious ladies*, i. 231; TNA, MS SP 1/32, fo. 179.

4

Patronage in Partnership

'Sir as for newys I have none to send, but that my lorde of Surrey ys yn great favor with the Kyng her that he cannott forber the companey off hym no tyme off the day. He and the bichopp off Murrey orderth every thyng as nyght [near] as they can to the Kyngs pleasure. I pray God it may be for my por [poor] hartts ease in tyme to come. They calnot my Chamberlayne to them, whych I am sur wull speke better for my part than any off them that ben off that consell. And iff he speke any thyng for my cause my lord of Surrey hath such wordds unto hym that he dar speke no furder.'[1]

A few days after her marriage to James IV of Scotland, Margaret Tudor, the thirteen-year-old queen of Scots, dictated these words in a letter to her father. At first glance, this letter seems to be little more than an expression of the homesickness that she experienced in marrying a strange man sixteen years her senior. Scholars have noted the unhappiness of the young queen and commented on the difficulties faced by royal brides in the sixteenth century.[2] While Margaret certainly had a difficult time adjusting to her new life at first, she was not merely homesick. Instead, it was the behaviour of the English envoy the earl of Surrey that was causing her great distress. During the delicate first days of her marriage, Margaret's attempts at creating a relationship with the king and her household officers were hampered by Surrey's special relationship with the king. Surrey had become so friendly with the king of Scots that James 'cannott forber the companey off hym no tyme off the day'. This situation worried Margaret because Surrey's relationship with the king usurped the proper role of her chamberlain, Sir Ralph Verney. Margaret claimed that Surrey would not allow Verney to speak for her, even though, as chamberlain, Verney was responsible for overseeing the queen's household and representing her interests to the wider court. Margaret's access to the king was thus restricted, and her ability to compensate those who had accompanied her to England limited. She was forced to ask her father to reward her footman Thomas because 'I am not able to recumpence hym, except the favor off your Grace.'[3] Margaret would later become successful in fulfilling her social duties at

---

[1] *Original letters*, i. 42.
[2] Buchanan, *Margaret Tudor*, 34-5; Barrow, 'Marriage, gift exchange, and politics', 79-80; Pamela Tudor-Craig, 'Margaret, queen of Scotland, in Grantham, 8-9 July 1503', in Thompson, *Reign of Henry VII*, 278. For a more nuanced consideration of Margaret's letter see Perry, *Sisters to the king*, 29-30.
[3] *Original letters*, i. 42.

court and rewarding her servants, but her letter reveals that she had to develop her relationship with the king gradually and with the help of her household.

Even at such a young age Margaret was well aware of the relationships and responsibilities that were part of her new role as queen and head of household. Her most important relationship as a young queen was the one with her husband, and this too Surrey was putting in jeopardy by monopolising the king's attention and preventing Margaret's chamberlain from establishing himself as her representative. It must have been an especially frustrating situation for Margaret and her household, as Surrey was due to leave within days and would be little help to them in Scotland in the years to come.[4] Margaret knew that her success as a patron and a queen depended on her relationship with the king, and that she could not rely on her father's courtiers once they left for England.

After Surrey's departure Margaret was able to forge a strong relationship with her husband, in part through the social pastimes and chivalric games of the Scottish court, and she was able to work with her husband to reward members of her household and gain access to royal patronage. Over the years James evidently came to trust his young wife, to the extent that in his testament he named her guardian of their young son and Scotland's first official female regent, roles she assumed after the disastrous battle of Flodden in 1513.[5] During their marriage James and Margaret worked together, rewarding staff, arranging marriages and forming a partnership that was at the heart of a successful pre-modern monarchy. For both Catherine and Margaret, their relationships with their husbands granted them access and influence at the royal court, which yielded political power and patronage.

Access to patronage was one tangible outcome of the queen's relationship with the king. Catherine's and Margaret's courtly roles as audience and hostess gave them access and influence with their husbands and his courtiers through the connections formed by their participation in courtly spectacle and the social world of the court. This relationship enabled Catherine and Margaret to work with their husbands to reward members of both royal households with material gifts. Catherine's and Margaret's patronage also included the arrangement of marriages for their ladies. These marriages secured connections between the native nobility and their households and were often the happy outcome of the socialisation that Catherine and Margaret fostered in their own chambers. Catherine and Margaret supported these marriages by arranging marriage contracts, jointures and wedding gifts: they were another form of patronage and reward. Furthermore the marriages themselves acted as demonstrations of the queen's own relationship and influence with the king.

---

[4] The tragic irony of this episode is that this was the same earl of Surrey who would command the English army that defeated the Scots and killed James IV at the battle of Flodden in 1513.

[5] For more on Margaret's legal position as regent see Blakeway, *Regency*, 24.

Rewards and gifts from the king and queen

The cooperative nature of a royal couple's patronage during this period often obscures the queen's agency in distributing patronage, and so it is important to understand that James and Margaret, or Catherine and Henry, distributed rewards together in a partnership similar to other elite marriages. For aristocrats the family was the key political unit through which they competed for resources, and wives as well as husbands used their kinship networks in pursuit of their goals.[6] Operating on a much larger scale, the king used his wife's household to foster patronage in order to distribute rewards and create important connections with the political elite, particularly through the marriages of her ladies to noblemen. The queen was not a passive partner in this process. Instead, she was actively involved in maintaining relationships and alliances in furtherance of not only her own status, but also for the greater political security and benefit of her husband and the dynasty of which her children were a part.

This is not to say that there were no conflicts between Catherine and Henry or Margaret and James. As in any relationship, there were moments of tension and disagreement, when the king would assert his superior position over the queen, her household and patronage. For instance, if the king felt that the queen's household was meddling in his own affairs, he could dismiss some of its members. In early 1510 Henry VIII dismissed one of Catherine of Aragon's ladies, Elizabeth Stafford Radcliffe, Lady Fitzwalter, sister of the duke of Buckingham, after she interfered in an affair between Sir William Compton and her younger sister, Lady Anne Stafford Hastings.[7] The affair between Compton and Lady Hastings was believed to be a smokescreen for Henry's own pursuit of the lady, and when her sister Elizabeth informed Catherine and the duke of Buckingham of these goings-on, scandal erupted and the king was furious. The king, according to the Spanish ambassador, would have dismissed more of Catherine's ladies, but he feared to create an even greater scandal.[8] In this instance, Catherine's household interfered with, and even jeopardised, her relationship with the king, but these events were scandalous in part because they were so unusual.

Despite some minor disagreements, Catherine and Margaret were able to capitalise on their proximity and access to their husbands' patronage in order to reward their own followers at court. Throughout Europe royal consorts expanded their patronage opportunities by petitioning the king for rewards or favours for their servants and others outside their household who came to them for mediation.[9] The ideals of good government and princely virtue

---

[6] Harris, 'View', 221-2.
[7] See Figure 3 above.
[8] *LP* i/1, 474.
[9] Some scholars have argued that the early sixteenth century saw a redefinition of the

encouraged princes to be liberal in their generosity and to spend lavishly, both at court and through the distribution of lands, titles, offices and privileges, and their consorts were encouraged to do the same.[10] Patronage bestowed by Catherine and Margaret benefited their queenship by forming bonds of obligation and enhancing their own reputation and renown as virtuous queens, for, as Christine de Pizan wrote in 1405, 'munificence is one of things that most magnifies the reputation of great lords and ladies'.[11] Catherine's and Margaret's patronage connected them with the wider political nation and helped to establish bonds of obligation with native nobility and servants when they were foreigners in a strange land. It also demonstrated the good relationship that they had with their husbands, which expanded their access to rewards and gifts.[12]

In pre-modern Europe queens had access to patronage available through their own not insubstantial resources and through their relationship with their husbands. For instance, Anne of Brittany, independent ruler of Brittany and queen consort of France, is an extreme example of the dual opportunities available to queens as patrons, as her patronage could be accomplished through her independent resources as duchess of Brittany or her royal access as queen of France.[13] Other types of queenly patronage could be pursued by working with the king. In ducal Italy, where a duchess might not have had access to independent resources, her relationship with her husband was critical for exercising patronage.[14] English medieval queens had also acted as intermediaries to obtain patronage for their servants.[15] In the seventeenth century Henrietta Maria, consort of Charles I of England, collaborated with her husband over the artistic patronage for which he is famous.[16] Like these consorts, Catherine and Margaret worked with their husbands to recognise members of their households deserving of reward. In turn, they sought to reward members of their

queen's role as a patronage broker as opposed to an independent patron. Nicole Hochner argues that Anne of Brittany established French queens as negotiators of royal authority and intercessors during the reign of Louis XII: 'Revisiting Anne de Bretagne', 150-2. See also Sarah Bercusson, 'The duchess' court in sixteenth-century Italy: a comparison of female experience', in Calvi and Chabot, Moving elites, 132-3.

[10] Linda Levy Peck, '"For a king not to be bountiful were a fault": perspectives on court patronage in early Stuart England', JBS xv (1986), 36; Quentin Skinner, *The foundations of modern political thought*, I: *Renaissance*, Cambridge 1978, 127.

[11] Pizan, *Treasure*, 54.

[12] Harris, 'View', and *English aristocratic women*, 61-75.

[13] Hochner, 'Revisiting Anne de Bretagne', 150, 153.

[14] Bercusson, 'Duchess' court', 132-3.

[15] Lisa St. John's work on English medieval queens has looked at queens as intermediaries in the pursuit of reward and patronage: *Three medieval queens: queenship and the crown in fourteenth-century England*, Basingstoke 2012, 3.

[16] Caroline Hibbard, 'Henrietta Maria in the 1630s: perspectives on the role of consort queens in *ancien régime* courts', in Ian Atherton and Julie Sanders (eds), *The 1630s: interdisciplinary essays on culture and politics in the Caroline era*, Manchester 2006, 99.

husbands' households, and the interdependent nature of their relationship resulted in the creation of connections through patronage in both directions.

In addition to rewarding and honouring loyal servants, patronage by the king of the queen's servants reflected honour and respect for the queen herself and demonstrated her effectiveness as a patron. Early modern sources show that courtiers were keenly interested in who the queen favoured and to whom she distributed rewards. For instance, Anne Boleyn's gift of a gold chain to Lord Leonard Grey before he left for Ireland was reported in a letter to Lady Lisle, who was away from court, in Calais with her husband.[17] A year or so later, Lady Lisle also heard from her court informant that Jane Seymour, the new queen, often spoke favourably of Lady Lisle after the two had met at Dover.[18] Although we do not have similar reports on Catherine's or Margaret's activities, it is highly likely that the rewards that their servants received would have been noted by others at court, especially by those eager for reward themselves. Success in obtaining rewards for their servants would encourage others to seek out Catherine and Margaret because they had established reputations as successful patrons.

Catherine's and Margaret's ability to reward their servants was bolstered by the informal nature of patronage in the sixteenth century, which allowed them to use personal relationships and influence to gain rewards for their servants. However, this informality has made it difficult to ascertain the true extent of their involvement in the distribution of rewards, as their influence tends not to be documented.[19] The extent of queenly patronage is often disguised by the survival of grants, charters or royal warrants that only reveal the actions of the king and not the informal influence of the queen.[20] In most instances, the only evidence of a reward to a servant of the queen is a formal document signed by the king. However, the wide variety of patronage distributed to their households without specific reference to their intervention, indicates that Catherine and Margaret must have been successful in obtaining patronage for their households beyond what was within their own gift.

The rare survival of multiple royal warrants for one reward reveals how Catherine and Henry worked together to reward her servants and demonstrates the potential of hidden queenly intervention in royal patronage. On 4 February 1511 Catherine issued a warrant to Sir John Cutt, under-treasurer of England,

---

[17] *Lisle letters*, ii. 468.
[18] Ibid. iii. 753.
[19] In general, women played an important, if complicated, role in the patronage networks of the elite of Europe. The informal nature of patron-client relationships gave women significant opportunities to participate in the indirect exercise of influence, but its informality has also led to fewer records being available for historians to trace these relationships: Sharon Kettering, 'The patronage power of early modern French noblewomen', *HJ* xxxii (1989), 818.
[20] During the later reign of Henry VIII, grants were prepared by a series of officials so that the true identity of the patron was similarly obscured: Linda Levy Peck, *Court patronage and corruption in early Stuart England*, Boston 1990, 40.

stating that the king has granted a reward of £40 to servants of her Wardrobe of the Beds: Henry Roper, yeoman, George Brygus, groom, Matthew Johns, page. Cutt had already received warrants from Henry specifying what funds the reward was to come from, and Catherine now pleaded that her servants receive their reward 'rather for our sake', stating that 'ye shall minister under us full good pleasure to your thanks hereafter'.[21] A few days later, on 7 February, Henry reinforced his wife's warrant with a warrant of his own, restating his order, and referring to Roper, Brygus and Johns as 'servants to our dearest wife the Queen'.[22] The series of warrants demonstrates how Catherine and Henry worked together to distribute rewards to her household. Her servants likely told her that they were having difficulties with Cutt, and Catherine responded not only by writing a warrant of her own, but also by making Henry aware of the problem as well, hence his second warrant. This situation was obviously unusual, but it reveals the behind-the-scenes activities that Catherine could engage in to support her household and work with her husband. Without the second warrant, there would have been no official record of Catherine's involvement in the reward, demonstrating how easily her agency could be obscured by official records.[23]

Catherine's influence in obtaining rewards for her servants may have lacked documentation, but that does not mean that it went unnoticed. Even for relatively simple rewards a number of people, including secretaries, clerks and messengers, were required to distribute the funds, which in the case above originated through a forfeit to the king from unnamed persons. The number of people who knew about the reward could have increased beyond those initially involved because of the oral circulation of news and gossip at the court. Moreover, it is more than likely that Roper, Brygus and Johns would have shared news (and possibly the spoils) of their good fortune with their friends, thus spreading the knowledge of Catherine's act of patronage beyond the parties involved.

Margaret and James also worked together to reward members of her household, and occasionally the sources indicate that it was specifically through the queen's influence that the reward was granted. In May 1507 Margaret's usher Charles Maxton was granted lands in Culcreif by James IV. The lands were 'remittand hym at the instance of the qwene, to quham he standis in service'.[24] Other members of Margaret's household received lands, wards and privileges from James without reference to Margaret's specific intervention, but they are named in these grants as members of the queen's household. For example, in the grant of lands given to William Ogilvy and

---

[21] TNA, MS E404/87, no. 108. For a summary of the warrant see also *LP* i/1, 683.
[22] TNA, MS E404/87, no. 114.
[23] See also Hayward, *Dress*, 157.
[24] RSS i. 1471.

his wife Alison Roule, she is named as a servant of the queen's.²⁵ Ogilvy was a personal servant of the king's and James had sent him on diplomatic missions to France and England.²⁶ Although Margaret's specific influence was not acknowledged as it was in Charles Maxton's grant, her servants are identified with her household, perhaps indicating her behind-the-scenes influence.²⁷

Catherine had an additional independent source of patronage as queen in the form of her dower estates granted to her upon her marriage. Unlike Margaret, who did not come into possession of her estates until her husband's death, Catherine administered her lands from the beginning of her queenship. She used these estates in part to create connections to her husband's household and the English elite more generally. Catherine's lands were extensive, and thus required her to employ numerous officials to oversee their administration.²⁸ Many of these officials were members of the king's household and the English nobility. Although their duties were probably performed by deputies, their connection to the queen through these often lucrative positions could be useful for Catherine.²⁹ It is unlikely, for example, that Charles Brandon, duke of Suffolk and the king's brother-in-law, personally performed his duties as steward of Catherine's estates in the duchy of York, or that Henry Courtenay, earl of Devon and first cousin of the king, acted as her steward of Cramborne and keeper of Marshwood Park.³⁰ Granting these sinecures to the English nobility was a form of patronage for Catherine, which created bonds of obligation between the queen and her husband's subjects. This included less exalted, but very influential, courtiers, such as Sir William Kingston and Sir Nicholas Carew, members of Henry's Privy Chamber, both of whom were officials on Catherine's manors.³¹ Just as the king rewarded members of the queen's household, so Catherine had opportunities to grant positions and rewards to her husband's closest servants and companions, strengthening her own ties to the English nobility in the process.

Scottish queens did not have such resources, and Margaret was financially dependent on her husband for nearly all of her career as queen consort. She only

---

[25] *RMS* ii. 3171, 3269.

[26] *RSS* i. 2482

[27] *RSS* i. 1423, 1640, and appendix, 619.

[28] For more on the landownership of Tudor queens consort see Dakota L. Hamilton, 'The learned councils of the Tudor queens consort', in Charles Carlton (ed.), *State, sovereigns & society in early modern England: essays in honour of A. J. Slavin*, New York 1998, 87–101. See also Michelle L. Beer, 'A queenly affinity? Catherine of Aragon's estates and Henry VIII's Great Matter', *Historical Research* xci (2018).

[29] For more on the granting of stewardships to the nobility see Catherine Kelly, 'The noble steward and late-feudal lordship', *HLQ* xlix (1986), 133–48.

[30] See Figures 2, 4 above.

[31] BL, MS Royal appendix 89, fos 84r–87v. See also *LP* vii. 352. Eric Ives argues that this document is a list of fees and annuities from Catherine's lands, and thus a record of her previous administration as it transitioned to the new queen, Anne Boleyn: *Anne Boleyn*, 215.

appears to have had a separately funded and administered household for eight or nine months in 1508, when her accounts were kept by her knight comptroller, Sir Duncan Forester. During the rest of her queenship Margaret's household expenses were paid by James's officials, and the fees and liveries for her servants were covered by the king's household.[32] However, although Margaret's household was paid by the king's officials, it was still treated as a separate entity within royal accounts, indicating that her servants were seen as a distinct group. The fees for her household were paid and listed separately from the fees of the king's household, as were the liveries for her household.[33] Significantly, after 1508, Forester became the comptroller of James IV's household as well, thereby combining the offices for both the king's and queen's households.[34] Margaret's financial inexperience and dependence in part explains some of the problems that she had in running her own household during her widowhood. While she was queen, however, she had opportunities to maintain and reward her household through her own personal patronage and her relationship with the king.

In addition to grants of lands and money, Catherine, Margaret and their servants participated in gift-exchanges at the English and Scottish courts. These were an important form of reward that fostered relationships and maintained connections between the queen and the royal court.[35] Gift-giving was also a material component of the hospitality that both Catherine and Margaret presided over in at their marital courts. Felicity Heal has rightly pointed out that royal giving was a performative act, one of the 'gestures of majesty' that had an audience beyond the internal court elite, which could include the wider political elite and international observers.[36] This made gift-giving, especially the highly ritualised gift-giving at New Year, an important opportunity for Catherine and Margaret to demonstrate their honour and position within the patronage exchanges of England and Scotland.

Fostering relationships through gifts was especially important for foreign-born queens such as Catherine and Margaret, who needed to form new connections

---

[32] Murray, 'Crown revenue of Scotland', 219-20.

[33] NRS, MS E34/2, fos 6r -7r. See also *LHTA* ii. 336; iii. 118-20; NRS, MS E21/ 7, fo. 89r. See also *LHTA* iii. 324-5; iv. 67.

[34] *ERS* xiii. pp. lxxx, 258-9.

[35] Since the work on gifts and gift exchanges by key theorists and anthropologists such as Marcel Mauss, historians have begun to use gift theory as an important lens for understanding patronage and clientage, hospitality, diplomacy and honour in the pre-modern world: Marcel Mauss, *The gift: forms and functions of exchange in archaic societies*, trans. Ian Cunnison, New York 1967; Natalie Zemon Davis, *The gift in sixteenth-century France*, Madison 2000; Peck, *Court patronage*, and 'Benefits, brokers and beneficiaries: the culture of exchange in seventeenth-century England', in B. Y. Kunze and D. D. Brautigam (eds), *Court, country and culture: essays on early modern British history in honor of Perez Zagorin*, Rochester 1992, 109-27; Sharon Kettering, 'Gift-giving and patronage in early modern France', *French History* ii (1988), 131-51.

[36] Felicity Heal, *The power of gifts: gift exchange in early modern England*, New York 2015, 89, 92.

with members of their household and the native nobility. Clothing and plate, some of the most common (and best-recorded) kinds of gifts exchanged at the Renaissance court, could sustain a patronage relationship, even when those involved in the exchange were far apart.[37] In addition, while plate and silver made for durable gifts that held value over time, clothing could evoke a personal connection, especially if it went beyond traditional livery allowances.[38] Catherine and Margaret also gave and received other types of gifts, including food gifts and books, although the former was not particularly well recorded during this period.[39] Queens such as Margaret or Catherine, who did not have access to the same vast patronage resources as their husbands, could use traditional giving rituals, such as the New Year or a client's wedding, to strengthen their relationships with courtiers and the native nobility.[40]

New Year's Day was the most important occasion for gift exchange at the English and Scottish courts, and the ritual was an opportunity for the king and queen to foster bonds of loyalty and obligation with members of the royal court and the nobility.[41] Both Henry VIII and James IV gave New Year's gifts to their wives and their households, and this was an important way of demonstrating the strength of their relationship with their wives and maintaining connections to the queen's household. Indeed, during Catherine's divorce crisis, Henry used the New Year's gift exchange in January 1532 to deliberately snub Catherine, her ladies and her daughter, by forbidding his household to send gifts to them and refusing to accept the queen's gift.[42] Normally, the English king and queen would receive gifts formally on the morning of New Year's Day. During the reign of Henry VII, Elizabeth of York would receive her gifts sitting on the end of her bed, surrounded by attendants. The queen's chamberlain and ushers

---

[37] Idem, 'Food gifts, the household and the politics of exchange in early modern England', *P&P* cxcix (May 2008), 45; Steven J. Gunn, 'The structures of politics in early Tudor England', *Transactions of the Royal Historical Society* v (1995), 85; Mario Damen, 'Gift exchange at the court of Charles the Bold', in Marc Boone and Martha C. Howell (eds), *In but not of the market: movable goods in the late medieval and early modern economy*, Brussels 2007, 91-2.

[38] Damen, 'Gift exchange', 91, 94-5.

[39] See, for example, NRS, MSS E21/6, p. 280, 319; E21/9, fos 64r, 98r, 98v. See also *LHTA* ii. 411, 448; iv. 71, 132, 133; *LP* iv/2, 2475. Catherine was the recipient of at least seven book dedications during her lifetime, which were probably accompanied by presentation copies, but here the line between a gift recipient and (potential) patron is difficult to discern, as some dedications were a result of Catherine's direct patronage, while others may have been a gift in hopes of receiving patronage in return: Schutte, 'Early modern book dedications', 17-18.

[40] For the deployment of clothing and gifts in this fashion see Sarah Bercusson, 'Giovanna d'Austria and the art of appearances: textiles and dress at the Florentine court', *RS* xxix (2015), 683-700. Kings would also use clothing as part of their informal patronage: Maria Hayward, 'Fashion, finance, foreign politics and the wardrobe of Henry VIII', in Richardson, *Clothing culture*, 165-78.

[41] Heal, *Power*, 92.

[42] *CSP Spanish*, iv/2, 880.

would present her with the gifts delivered to her chamber door, whereupon the queen would decide how to reward the bearer.[43] Later accounts of Henry VIII's gift ceremonies reveal that the ritual had become more formalised and elaborate, eventually including the display of gifts in a special chamber and the creation and retention of formal gift rolls.[44] Unfortunately, we do not know precisely when these changes began or whether Catherine would have participated in this more elaborate ritual.

At the Tudor court, the queen's gift to the king was the first gift that he received on New Year's Day, indicating the primacy of the king and queen's relationship, which was also reflected in the size and worth of the queen's gift and the reward offered to the servant who brought it. According to the Household Ordinances of 1494, the queen's messenger would receive ten marks in reward from the king, while messengers from a duke would receive only five marks.[45] Catherine's gifts to Henry were suitably impressive, especially because she could draw upon a distinctive and personal source of plate. When Catherine came to England in 1501 she brought with her Spanish gold and silver plate worth 15,000 *scudi*, and many of those pieces were recorded as gifts to the king in the 1521 Jewel Book.[46] One piece in particular, a pair of gilt candlesticks meant for the king's chapel, was recorded as Catherine's New Year's gift to Henry.[47] The only recorded New Year's gift from Henry to Catherine was in 1513. Henry gave her a pair of gilt pots, which were apparently so complex and 'curious' to make that the goldsmith, William Holland, begged additional funds from the king to complete them.[48]

James and Margaret also exchanged gifts at the New Year, and although there is no record of the precise ceremony involved, it does appear that they were often together during the Yule season, as several of James's gambling debts to the queen were incurred in December and January.[49] James's gifts to Margaret were often jewellery of some sort, and each year they were different. His first New Year's gift in January 1504 was two sapphire rings, and in 1512 he gave her a knotted gold chain worth £28 Scots.[50] One unusual New Year's gift

---

[43] BL, MS Add. 38174, fos 19v–20v, 37r.

[44] Jane A. Lawson, *The Elizabethan New Year's gift exchanges, 1559–1603*, Oxford 2013, 4–5.

[45] BL, MS Add. 38174, fo. 37r; Lawson, *New Year's gift exchanges*, 4–5.

[46] English documents assume that 1 *scudo* equalled 4s. 2d. which means that Catherine brought about £1,500 worth of plate to England: *CSP Spanish*, i. 364. It is likely that many of the other Spanish pieces in the inventory were gifts from Catherine as well: 'King Henry VIII's jewel book', ed. Edward Trollope, *Associated Architectural Societies* xvii/2 (1883–4), 155–229.

[47] Philippa Glanville, *Silver in Tudor and early Stuart England: a social history and catalogue of the national collection*, London 1990, 35.

[48] *LP* i/1, 1549; Glanville, *Silver*, 35.

[49] NRS, MSS E21/6, p. 281; E21/7, fo. 125r; E21/9, fo. 74v. See also *LHTA* ii. 412; iii. 180, 181; iv. 92. See chapter 3 above for gambling in the queen's chamber.

[50] NRS, MSS E21/6, p. 282; E21/10, fo. 102r. See also *LHTA* ii. 412; iv. 323.

from James was a jewelled serpent's tongue, set with precious stones, given to Margaret in 1507.[51] Serpent's tongues were supposed to protect against poison and were popular amongst royalty; Catherine of Aragon owned one in 1534.[52] The serpent's tongue may have had some personal significance for James, as it matches the description of a similar jewel owned by his mother, Margaret of Denmark.[53] January 1507 marked the beginning of a new phase in James and Margaret's marital relationship: she was expecting their first child (Prince James was born on the twelfth) and had probably already taken to her chambers when James gave her the serpent's tongue. It seems possible that James felt that the gift of a family jewel was an appropriate way to mark Margaret's impending motherhood and the deepening of their marital ties. The only New Year's gift recorded from Margaret to James is a salt cellar decorated with a figure of the Virgin Mary, also given in 1507. The gift was recorded because James subsequently gave it away to a visiting French knight.[54]

In addition to giving gifts to each other, the king and queen also distributed gifts at New Year to prominent members of the nobility and members of their households. Accounts of Catherine's gifts, which are partially preserved for c. 1520, 1522 and 1528, show her engaging in similar gift-giving activity to her husband, though on a smaller scale.[55] Although there are no records for Margaret's New Year's gifts to Scottish courtiers, the pattern of giving at the Scottish court by James IV indicates that this was an established tradition in which Margaret most likely would have been a participant. During her widowhood, when Margaret had fled to England in 1515, she wrote to Cardinal Wolsey, requesting funds for New Year's gifts for those attending her. Even in the difficult circumstances of her return to England, Margaret understood the importance of the New Year's gift ritual to her own honour.[56]

When James IV distributed New Year's gifts in 1504, he used gift-giving to incorporate into the Scottish court Margaret's new English attendants, who were starting a new life away from home and family. Margaret's gentlewomen typically received jewellery from the king. At least one of these gifts, a chain of gold with an image of St Andrew, Scotland's patron saint, may have had symbolic significance. Given to one of Margaret's English chamberers, Margaret Dennet, the image of St Andrew may have been deliberately chosen to welcome her to Scotland.[57] James's gesture was certainly not wasted, as Margaret Dennet remained in Scotland and would marry one of his squires,

---

[51] NRS, MS E21/8, fo. 85v. See also *LHTA* iii. 359.
[52] Glanville, *Silver*, 309.
[53] *LHTA* i. 84. There is no record in the royal accounts of a payment for the serpent's tongue, which indicates that it was already part of the king's treasure.
[54] NRS, MS E21/8, fo. 87v. See also *LHTA* iii. 364.
[55] TNA, MSS SP1/73, fos 70r–85v; SP1/233, fos 233r–269v, E101/420/4. See also *LP* v. 1711, Add. i/1, 367.
[56] *Original letters*, i. 130.
[57] NRS, MS E21/6, p. 282. See also *LHTA* ii. 413.

Sir Alexander Ogilvy, sometime before January 1507.[58] Other gifts were more practical, usually consisting of chains of gold decorated with gold coins, such as one given to the English gentlewoman Eleanor Jones, worth £6 9s. 10d. Scots.[59] The king would continue to give chains and coins to Margaret's gentlewomen over the years.[60]

James also distributed gifts to other English members of Margaret's household; yeomen and ushers of her chamber were given gifts of cash worth £21 Scots total in 1504 and would continue to receive New Year's money from the king until 1508.[61] The majority of Margaret's English household left Scotland sometime around 1509, at the same time that there is a gap in the Scottish Lord Treasurer's accounts. However, when the accounts resume in 1512, James no longer gave New Year's gifts to the new Scottish yeomen and ushers of Margaret's chamber, indicating that the earlier gifts were intended to bind her English attendants more closely to the king's service. Margaret's Scottish attendants, many of whom had previously served James in his own household, required no such reward.[62] In 1512 James was still distributing New Year's gifts to the ladies of the court, only now the queen's retinue had changed, and it included many more Scottish gentlewomen and noblewomen.[63]

Just as James IV sought to honour Margaret's household and to create connections through New Year's gifts, so Catherine of Aragon used New Year's gifts to maintain alliances with particular friends within the English nobility and to reward her English and Spanish servants. Between 1524 and 1530 Catherine spent between £350 and £424 a year on gifts, a little less than 10 per cent of her total annual budget. She also spent around £100 per year on 'rewards to people bringing presents', essentially gratuities to those who delivered gifts to the queen, showing that she was at the centre of a significant exchange of gifts at Henry's court.[64] Although no formal roll of the queen's gifts survives, accounts from c.1520, 1522 and 1528 listing the delivery and distribution of gold and silver plate show recipients of the queen's gifts, and the servants and household members who delivered them.[65] These documents

---

[58] NRS, MS E21/8, fo. 85v. See also *LHTA* iii. 360.

[59] NRS, MS E21/6, p. 282. See also *LHTA* ii. 413.

[60] In 1505 five of Margaret's ladies received gifts; in 1506 eight ladies were given coins attached to string. Also in 1506 the king gave velvet, satin and damask to two English ladies worth a total of £81 12s. Scots: NRS, MSS E21/6, p. 343; E21/7, fos 79r, 121v-122r. See also *LHTA* ii. 472; iii. 177-8, 111. In 1507 Margaret's ladies received chains and saint's images: NRS, MS E21/8, fo. 85v. See also *LHTA* iii. 359-60.

[61] NRS, MS E21/6, p. 282. See also *LHTA* ii. 413.

[62] They did, however, continue to receive issues of livery from James: NRS, MS E21/10, fos 72r-74r. See also *LHTA* iv. 266.

[63] NRS, MSS E21/10, fo. 102r; E21/12, fo. 20v. See also *LHTA* iv. 324, 401.

[64] BL, MS Cotton appendix LXV, fos 11v, 10r, 7v, 5v, 8r. See also *LP* iv/3, 6121.

[65] The first account, from about 1520, is a list of plate provided to Catherine by several

can thus be used to reconstruct the web of relationships between Catherine, her household and members of the English elite.

The exchange of New Year's gifts at the court of Henry VIII and Catherine of Aragon was in most cases carried out by their servants or attendants. Catherine's household attendants, primarily the servants who waited on the queen in her chambers or her Wardrobe, delivered her gifts at the New Year. Some gift-bearers were more elite attendants, including ladies and gentle-women to the queen, such as Lady Darrell, wife of the queen's vice-chancellor.[66] Maria de Salinas, Lady Willoughby, Catherine's Spanish lady-in-waiting, delivered two gifts in about 1520, one to the queen's chancellor, Sir Robert Dymoke, and the other to the king's nurse.[67] The bearers of gifts in 1522 were also members of Catherine's household or courtiers closely connected to her.[68] Upon delivery, non-elite gift-bearers would receive a reward for their trouble, which could be quite generous and further incorporated the queen's household into the New Year's gift exchange. William Cholmeley, cofferer for the duke of Buckingham, gave 100s. to 'a servant of the Queen, bringing a New Year's gift' in 1521.[69] Lady Katherine Courtenay, dowager countess of Devon and aunt of Henry VIII, gave the queen's servant 53s. for her New Year's gift in 1524.[70]

The delivery of plate by Catherine's household on her behalf is an unusually well documented interaction between the queen and members

---

goldsmiths, and it lists the gift, its weight, the recipient of the gift and who delivered it: TNA, MS SP1/73, fos 70r-85v. The manuscript is dated by the editors of the *Letters and papers* to 1531. However, one of the gift recipients is the duke of Buckingham (fo. 76r), who was executed in spring of 1521, so this list probably dates from between January 1517 and January 1521, from when Maria de Salinas married and became Lady Willoughby (fo. 70v; see pp. 117-18 below) and when the duke was executed. See also *LP* v. 1711. Another list from 1522 is similar in format to the goldsmith's list, but it also includes items given away from the queen's personal store of plate, an even stronger indication that this list documents Catherine's gift-giving: TNA, MS SP1/233, fos 233r-269v. See also *LP*, Add. i/1, 367. Finally, there is an incomplete list of gifts given for the New Year in 1528, primarily listing women of the court, which is also a likely list of the queen's gifts: TNA, MS E101/420/4. Maria Hayward has also argued that the 1522 and possibly the 1528 list record Catherine's gifts: 'Gift giving at the court of Henry VIII: the 1539 New Year's gift roll in context', *Antiquaries Journal* lxxxv (2005), 129, 133.

[66] TNA, MS SP1/233, fos 233r-269v; *LP* Add. i/1, 367. Of the seventy-three entries in the 1520 account, sixty-five indicate the bearer of the plate: TNA, MS SP1/73, fos 70r-85v; *LP* v. 1711.

[67] TNA, MS SP1/73, fo. 70v-r; *LP* v. 1711. For Lady Willoughby's marriage see Melissa Franklin-Harkrider, *Women, reform and community in early modern England: Katherine Willoughby, duchess of Suffolk, and Lincolnshire's godly aristocracy, 1519-1580*, Woodbridge 2008, 30.

[68] The 1522 list, which has eighty-seven entries of recipients, with no repeats, also indicates who delivered the gift for sixty-five of those entries: TNA, MS SP1/233, fos 233r-269v.

[69] *LP* iii/3, 1285.

[70] *LP* iv/1, 771.

of the English nobility. The practice of gift-giving allowed the Spanish-born queen to create connections to the English elite through the distribution of material goods that were valuable monetarily and symbolically. In 1522, when George Talbot, the fourth earl of Shrewsbury, was given a gilt cup with a cover, Catherine would have reinforced her relationship with a leading nobleman at the court of Henry VIII.[71] These relationships developed over many years and included the servants bearing the gifts, as some of them delivered gifts to the same person each year. Although there are only two years' worth of lists to compare, there are some consistent links forming between the queen's household and gift recipients. When comparing the two extant lists for Catherine's gifts, there are nineteen recipients whose plate was delivered to them by the same person in both c. 1520 and 1522. Some of these relationships hint at potential connections between the recipient and the bearer. John Glynn, one of Catherine's yeomen ushers, delivered a New Year's gift to Thomas Howard, duke of Norfolk, in about 1520 and 1522. Glynn may have been well-known to Norfolk because of his involvement with the Scottish campaign in 1513; Glynn was the messenger whom Catherine sent to deliver the bloody coat of James IV to Henry VIII after Norfolk's (then earl of Surrey) great victory at Flodden.[72]

The practice of using repeated contacts between the queen's household attendants bearing gifts and the noble recipients of her gifts allowed Catherine to use the exchanges to reinforce bonds between her household and with the wider Tudor elite. Most of the repeat-bearers were simple yeomen and gentlemen ushers of Catherine's household without any clear relationship with the recipient whom they visited; however, they often delivered gifts to the same recipient every year. This would have given Catherine's attendants some personal knowledge and familiarity with specific members of the Tudor elite, which could prove useful for their mistress. However, some of the gifts were delivered by members of the queen's household who were already well-acquainted with each other and connected to Catherine through multiple ties of obligation and affinity, and their role as gift-bearers possibly reflects more personal and status-related elements to the gift exchange. For instance, when the queen's gentlewoman Mistress Cook delivered a gilt pot with a cover to Lady Anne Grey in 1522, she would have known Lady Grey from their previous service together in the queen's household at the Field of Cloth of Gold. Other pairings denote an element of deference based on years of service rather than social rank, as when Lady Willoughby delivered a gift to the king's nurse in 1520.[73] Lady Willoughby also delivered plate to the

---

[71] TNA, MS SP1/233, fo. 253v. The earl of Shrewsbury proved to be sympathetic to Catherine, and told the Spanish ambassador that he would refuse to crown Anne Boleyn: G. W. Bernard, 'Talbot, George, fourth earl of Shrewsbury and fourth earl of Waterford (1468–1538)', ODNB.

[72] TNA, MSS SP1/73, fo. 79v; SP1/233, fo. 245r; LP i/2, 2268.

[73] TNA, MS SP1/73, fo. 70v; LP iii/1, 704.

queen's chancellor Sir Robert Dymoke, and her secretary Richard Decons, both of whom had acted as guarantors of Lady Willoughby's jointure for her marriage.[74]

One of the most interesting features of the New Year's gift-exchange is the distribution of gifts 'from the queen's own store' in 1522 to women who were particularly closely connected to the queen. These would have been gifts of plate and jewels that Catherine already held in her treasury, some of which had come to her as gifts in previous years. Catherine saved gifts from her own store for her intimate friends, such as Margaret Pole, countess of Salisbury and Princess Mary's governess, and Mary Tudor Brandon, duchess of Suffolk and Catherine's sister-in-law.[75] Many of these women were Catherine's ladies-in-waiting or were married to her household officials, while others were wives and widows of peers. The range of social rank in this category – from the wife of the king's Spanish physician to the king's sister – indicates that intimacy with the queen, and not status, was important in determining who received these particular gifts.

Catherine's gifts from her own treasury tended to be more varied and distinctive than the gilt cups, salts and spoons bought from the goldsmiths for other recipients, and thus indicate a more personal connection between the queen and the recipient. For instance, Agnes Howard, duchess of Norfolk, was given a pendant shaped like an 'A' made of pearls and set with diamonds; Lady Margaret Grey and Lady Gertrude Blount Courtenay were both given similar crucifixes with five diamonds and a pearl. Mary Tudor Brandon was given a gold ring with a heart-shaped diamond and nine garnets. Lady Fitzwilliam, a former gentlewoman of Catherine's whose marriage had been in part arranged by the king, received a gold pomander enamelled with the passion of Christ, which had originally been given to Catherine by the earl of Devon.[76] 'Re-gifting' items that were originally given to the queen by someone else was not an uncommon phenomenon in the sixteenth century. There was no insult or stigma attached to repurposing these items, and it could be seen as a sign of personal favour.[77]

The turnaround for re-distributing gifts could often be quite quick. Lady Darrell was given 'a pomander given by the earl of Shrewsbury that same year', and Lady Margaret Pole received 'a pax that the elder countess of Devon gave to

---

[74] TNA, MSS SP1/73, fo. 71r; SP1/233 fo. 245v. The recipient is only named as 'the queen's chancellor'. Depending on the exact date of the document it could be referring to Sir Richard Poyntz, who was Catherine's chancellor until 1520.

[75] The other recipients were Lady Elizabeth Boleyn, Lady Mabel Fitzwilliam, Lady Alice Darrell, Gertrude Blount Courtenay countess of Devon, Lady Margaret Grey marchioness of Dorset, Anne Hastings countess of Huntingdon and daughter of the second duke of Buckingham, Agnes Howard duchess of Norfolk, and Mistress Victoria, wife of Henry's Spanish physician: TNA, MS SP1/233, fo. 264.

[76] Ibid. fo. 264v. For her marriage see Harris, *English aristocratic women*, 226.

[77] Hayward, 'Gift giving', 137.

the queen in the same year'.[78] Unfortunately, the sources do not reveal if there was a particular reason why gifts were redistributed, although there are connections between some of the previous givers and a new recipient; for instance, Lady Margaret Pole and the elder countess of Devon were first cousins, so Catherine may have felt that the pax that she had been given would have had particular meaning for its new owner.[79]

The redistribution of previous gifts provides some indication of the gifts that Catherine received from members of court, although there is no surviving list of the items that she received for any year.[80] Undoubtedly Catherine did receive gifts from her courtiers and the nobility, and they would have been a sign of honour and respect from the giver and could act as a reminder of obligations or an affirmation of friendship. There are scattered references in other accounts to gifts that the queen received. The duke of Buckingham in 1520 gave the queen a pomander and a chain of gold. That same year he gave the king a goblet of gold and Cardinal Wolsey a cup of gold with a cover.[81] Gertrude Blount Courtenay, younger countess of Devon, gave Catherine fine linen cloth, worth £63.[82] Her gift reflects her close relationship with the queen; Lady Courtenay's father was Catherine's Lord Chamberlain, and Lady Courtenay would remain one of Catherine's staunchest supporters during the divorce crisis. Instead of giving the more customary gold plate, she chose to give the queen a luxurious fabric, an equally valuable gift which probably reflected her own knowledge of the queen's tastes and preferences.[83] Catherine's gift in 1522 to Lady Courtenay, of a crucifix with diamonds, reflected a similar intimacy.[84]

Catherine and Margaret also used gifts of clothing to reward members of their husbands' households. Margaret seems to have been particularly fond of William Dunbar, James's court poet who celebrated her marriage in 1503 with the poem 'The Thrissil and the Rois'. Many of Dunbar's poems are set in the queen's chamber or in the company of the queen, and they paint a lively picture of life in the queen's household. It is therefore unsurprising that Margaret would wish to reward the poet with the gift of a doublet from her Wardrobe. Dunbar was particularly concerned with the importance of gift-giving at James's court and wrote several poems on the subject, including two

[78] TNA, MS SP1/233, fo. 264v.
[79] See Figure 2 above.
[80] Systematic accounts of gifts to the king were kept in the latter half of Henry's reign: Hayward, 'Gift giving', 127-9.
[81] LP iii/1, 1070.
[82] LP iv/1, 1792.
[83] For examples of this type of gift-giving at the court of Elizabeth I see Catherine L. Howey, 'Fashioning monarchy: women, dress and power at the court of Elizabeth I: 1553-1603', in Cruz and Suzuki, Rule of women, 149-50.
[84] TNA, MS SP1/233, fo. 264v.

about Margaret's gift.[85] Dunbar criticises Margaret's Master of the Wardrobe, James Dog, for being uncooperative and slow to release the doublet to him. Although Dunbar used this poem to tease and humiliate Dog, his familiarity with the queen's household as well as her evident desire to reward him shows that Margaret understood the benefit of rewarding the king's household.[86] Dunbar's poem provides a glimpse of the informal and occasional rewards that were probably one of the most commonplace ways in which Margaret could distribute rewards and patronage at the Scottish court.

Catherine rewarded members of her husband's household in similar ways to the gift of Dunbar's doublet. She ordered her Wardrobe to make a doublet of cloth of gold worth £8 as a gift for Sir Edward Neville, a close companion and gentlemen of Privy Chamber to the king.[87] Although the record of the gift is undated, the doublet may have been a reward for Neville after he represented the queen in a suit involving the title to some of her properties in Kent in July 1516.[88] In 1520 her Wardrobe gave two of the king's minstrels tawny broadcloth for a gown and black velvet for a doublet.[89] She also patronised Giles Duwes, another musical member of Henry's household. Duwes had a varied career at the early Tudor court, tutoring the children of Henry VII and later Catherine's daughter Mary in music and going on to oversee Henry VII's library at Richmond. Catherine employed Duwes as a clerk for her own library and gave him cloth for a gown and doublet worth 52s. 6d. in 1520. Duwes served the king through the 1520s, and his duties appear to have included service to both the king and queen.[90] Justice also delivered black satin for a doublet for Thomas More, clerk of the privy seal to the king, on the command of Sir Robert Poyntz, Catherine's Chancellor, and Richard Decons, her receiver.[91] As two of the chief administrators of Catherine's estates, Poyntz and Decons would possibly have encountered More as they transacted business, and the doublet was an acknowledgement of their relationship with him, and by extension, of More's relationship with the queen.

Catherine also gave away items of her own clothing to members of her household and others at court. Catherine's and Margaret's households received liveries that extended the queen's presence at court, but their attendants also received clothing as individual gifts. Catherine had grown up in a court where

[85] Hepburn, 'Household', 150.
[86] Dunbar, *Poems*, 101–2. For Margaret's relationship with Dunbar see chapter 3 above.
[87] TNA, MS E101/418/6, fo. 26v.
[88] The wardrobe book that records the gift is damaged and missing dates, but some pages include internal dates of 1514–17: TNA, MS E101/418/6; E298/17; *LP* Add. i/1, 165. Neville was also Catherine's steward for several manors in Surrey and Kent: *LP* vii. 352.
[89] JRL, MS Latin 239, fo. 14r.
[90] In June 1527 the king granted Duwes the privilege of importing Gascon wine, a lucrative investment opportunity: *LP* iv/2, 3213. The household accounts of Henry VIII also show (iv/1, 1673) that Duwes received robes from the king's Wardrobe.
[91] JRL, MS Latin 239, fo. 9r.

the distribution of one's own clothing was an important sign of favour. Her mother Isabella admonished her eldest son and heir, Juan, to give away his clothing when he was as young as eight.[92] As queen, Catherine distributed clothing as a method of forming connections to the Tudor elite. Catherine gave the duchess of Norfolk a gown of crimson velvet with Spanish sleeves lined with green cloth of gold damask, and she gave Lady Maltravers a gown of white satin. Lady Darrell, the queen's chamberer, and Mistress Victoria, the wife of Henry's Spanish physician, all received gifts of gowns from Catherine in 1516 and 1517.[93] These gifts of Catherine's own clothing were both more personal and made of finer materials than the usual issuances of livery that members of Catherine's household would have received. They would have been kept as treasured possessions, possibly passed down to other family members, as when in 1531 Maud Parr, one of Catherine's gentlewomen, bequeathed rosary beads given to her by Catherine to her daughter (and the future queen) Katherine Parr.[94]

Weddings were a significant occasion for the queen to extend her largesse to members of her household. When Elizabeth Collins, Catherine's chamber servant since 1511, married in 1516, Catherine gave her russet satin for a gown, a kirtle of black satin hemmed with crimson velvet, and mink fur to line the gown.[95] Catherine's tailor, John Scutt, was given 7 yards of violet cloth worth 70s. on his marriage.[96] Members of Margaret's household also received clothing upon their marriage from the king's Wardrobe. Edmund Levisay, Margaret's long-serving English usher who was also a favourite of James IV, received a wedding gown of grey and crimson satin from the king in 1512.[97] Further up on the social scale, Isabel Stewart, daughter of John Stewart, earl of Atholl, and one of Margaret's ladies, was given two new gowns, one of tawny satin and one of grey satin, for her marriage to John Stewart, earl of Lennox.[98] Both Catherine

---

[92] Ruth Matilda Anderson, *Hispanic costume, 1480–1530*, New York 1979, 12–13. On the other hand Catherine's sister Juana hoarded or destroyed clothing rather than present it to servants whom she found unworthy: Bethany Aram, *Juana the Mad: sovereignty and dynasty in Renaissance Europe*, Baltimore 2005, 28–9.

[93] TNA, MS E101/418/6, fos 11r, 9v. Mistress Phillips, John Glynn and several others also received gifts of Catherine's clothes. The recipients of the clothes probably would not have worn them, but often the clothing would be pulled apart for the material to make other items of clothing, or would be sold. Occasionally, they might be kept as mementos of the giver: Hayward, 'Fashion, finance, foreign politics', 177; Howey, 'Fashioning monarchy', 146.

[94] TNA, MS PROB 11/24/153. Elizabeth I's gifts were similarly treasured: Howey, 'Fashioning monarchy', 146.

[95] TNA, MS E101/418/6, fos 47r, 38r.

[96] Ibid. fo. 39r. In view of Scutt's profession, it is likely that the cloth would be sold on or used for a paying client, rather than worn by Scutt himself.

[97] NRS, MS E21/10, fo. 59v. See also *LHTA* iv. 249.

[98] Isabel Stewart (also called Elizabeth) was descended from Joan Beaufort, mother of James II, and her second husband, Sir John Stewart. She was thus related to both the Scottish royal family and to Margaret Tudor, through her grandmother Margaret Beaufort, which

and Margaret were involved in arranging marriages for their gentlewomen, but they also supported members of their households at their marriages through gifts of clothing, even if they did not have a hand in arranging their marriages themselves.

The material wealth of the Scottish and English courts was deployed to create and reinforce relationships of obligation and affinity between the queen, the king, her household and the nobility. Gifts were a signifier of favour and largesse that was particularly important during ritual occasions, such as New Year, when Catherine's and Margaret's households participated in the exchange of gifts which created connections between the queen's household and the elite of England and Scotland. Distributing clothing, gifts and plate to members of the household was a crucial part of good queenship that both enriched the queen's household and added to the magnificence and splendour of the court as a whole. In addition to the connections created through rewards and gift-giving, Catherine and Margaret also formed relationships through the arranged marriages of their foreign ladies, which would link them to their new homelands through ongoing, even generational, relationships with the native nobility.

Arranged marriages and royal patronage

Marriages were an important way for Catherine and Margaret to create connections between themselves, their households and the native nobility, and they were another opportunity for these queens to support and reward their closest ladies. Because the most high profile members of Catherine's and Margaret's foreign households were their ladies-in-waiting and gentlewomen, these matches helped to connect Catherine and Margaret more closely with important members of their nobility. Their native-born ladies also benefitted from marriages arranged by the queen, and a place in the queen's household was often sought by mothers wishing to arrange marriages for their daughters, as royal courts across Europe were elite marriage markets.[99] Indeed, one of the most important purposes for socialisation at court, and in the queen's chamber particularly, was the formation of marriage alliances. The spectacles and entertainments at court gave Catherine's and Margaret's ladies unsurpassed opportunities to display their accomplishments and features to the eligible and powerful men of the kingdom, in hopes of catching the interest of a future husband.

---

may explain why she received so many lavish wedding clothes from the royal wardrobe: James Balfour, *The Scots peerage: founded on Wood's edition of Sir Robert Douglas's peerage of Scotland*, 1904, i. 442; William Fraser, *The Lennox*, Edinburgh 1874, ii. 192-200.

[99] Harris, *English aristocratic women*, 217, 226; Barbara Stephenson, 'Maintaining the antiquity of the house: Marguerite de Navarre, noble marriage and dynastic culture in early sixteenth-century France', *TCH* x (2005), 15-24; Bercusson, 'Duchess' court', 132.

While many of these ladies would have had their marriages arranged by their families, it was Catherine's and Margaret's duty, as the heads of the household, to see that their foreign ladies, for whom they acted *in loco parentis*, were provided for. As these marriages were public, often festive occasions which produced (hopefully) lasting alliances, they were opportunities for queens not only to fulfil their duties as heads of households but also to celebrate publicly their own patronage and to attract or influence yet more clients. Thus the marriage of Margaret's maid-of-honour, Elizabeth Barlow, to the Scottish nobleman Alexander Elphinstone, in or around August 1507, for example, was a triumph both for Elizabeth herself and for Margaret as a demonstration of her ability to secure favour for her ladies.

These matches often resulted in higher-status husbands for the queen's women than they would have been able to secure if they had stayed at home; and procuring good matches for her ladies was also a sign of success for the consort. In sixteenth-century France, for example, placing a girl in a royal woman's household, such as the household of Marguerite de Navarre, sister of Francis I, improved her chances of making a good match.[100] During the reign of Margaret's son James V, his consort Marie de Guise would successfully marry several of her French ladies to Scotsmen.[101] The failure of Catherine's sister Juana to marry any of her ladies into the Burgundian nobility after her marriage was a sign of Juana's lack of authority and her own marginalised position at court.[102] In contrast, when Catherine became queen in 1509, the Spanish ladies who remained with her in England made important marriages that closely linked Catherine's new English household officials with her loyal and trusted Spanish attendants. Of the four Spanish ladies-in-waiting who attended Catherine at the coronation, two married into the English nobility.[103]

The marriages of Catherine's and Margaret's foreign attendants offered their husbands the opportunity to recommit to the foreign alliance formed by their own marriage by incorporating the nobility into similar marriage alliances. Even before Catherine became queen, she promoted marriages for her ladies with the English nobility. In 1504 one of Catherine's maids of honour, Maria de Rojas, was a potential marriage partner for the heir of the earl of Derby. The match itself never took place, but it indicates the desirability of Catherine's ladies as marriage partners at a moment when

---

[100] Stephenson, 'Maintaining the antiquity of the house', 44. Habsburg empresses in the seventeenth century also had a hand in arranging marriages: Clarissa Campbell Orr, 'Introduction', to Orr, *Queenship in Europe*, 11.

[101] Rosalind K. Marshall, *Mary of Guise*, London 1977, 72.

[102] Aram, *Juana the Mad*, 46.

[103] Of the others, Katherine Fortes returned to Spain to become a nun: *LP* i/1, 473. It has proved impossible to trace Dame Maria de Guevara, who was more senior and possibly already married. She presumably returned to Spain: TNA, MS LC9/50, fos 181v, 216r. See also *LP* i/1, 82.

Catherine's political value was high.¹⁰⁴ Once Henry VII decided to reject the Spanish alliance and Catherine as a bride for his son, offers for Catherine's ladies dried up, until Catherine unexpectedly became queen and the Spanish alliance was once again royal policy. As the new king Henry VIII wrote to his new father-in-law Ferdinand, it was 'very desirable' to unite English and Spanish families through marriage.¹⁰⁵ Henry was referring to the marriage of one of Catherine's ladies, Inés de Vanegas (sometimes Anglicised to Agnes), who married William Blount, Lord Mountjoy, in 1509. Inés had served Catherine since 1500, and probably knew the queen for far longer through her mother, who had been Catherine's nurse since 1495.¹⁰⁶ Although his marriage to Inés did not last long – Mountjoy had remarried by 1515 – she was likely an asset to Mountjoy in his diplomatic service to Spain. It is possible that Inés journeyed with her husband when he was sent to Spain in early 1513 as the English envoy to Ferdinand. Even if she was not with her husband, Mountjoy's marital connections to a Spanish court family could have been useful to him during diplomatic missions.¹⁰⁷

For their foreign ladies, Catherine and Margaret acted in the place of relatives during marriage negotiations, inquiring about marriage portions, providing dowries and guaranteeing jointures through their household officials. The marriage of another of Catherine's Spanish ladies to an English nobleman brought together several members of Catherine's household to support the new marriage. Maria de Salinas was a long-serving lady in Catherine's household, and she is well-known for her continuing loyalty to Catherine, even defying Henry to visit the dying Catherine in 1536.¹⁰⁸ Catherine's arrangements for Maria's marriage shows how the members of the queen's household as a whole were connected through networks of family and obligation to each other as well as to the queen. Maria married Lord William Willoughby d'Eresby after being naturalised as an English subject in May 1516. Lord Willoughby was a baron with manors in Lincolnshire, Norfolk and Suffolk worth over £900 *per annum*.¹⁰⁹ The couple was granted manors in Lincolnshire as a gift from the king, and Catherine provided Maria with a handsome dowry of 1,100 marks.¹¹⁰ Key members of Catherine's household acted as guarantors of Maria's jointure, including the queen's Lord Chamberlain, vice-chamberlain, secretary and chancellor. Lord Willoughby

---

¹⁰⁴ *CSP Spanish*, i. 413, 420.
¹⁰⁵ Ibid. ii. 20.
¹⁰⁶ Ibid. i. 246; Earenfight, 'Raising infanta Catalina', 430–2.
¹⁰⁷ Mountjoy was first connected to Catherine's household through his step-father, the earl of Ormond, Lord Chamberlain to Elizabeth of York and later to Catherine: James P. Carley, 'Blount, William, fourth Baron Mountjoy (c. 1478–1534)', *ODNB*.
¹⁰⁸ *LP* x. 28.
¹⁰⁹ Susan Wabuda, 'Bertie, Katherine, duchess of Suffolk (1519–1580)', *ODNB*.
¹¹⁰ *LP* ii/1, 1953, 2172; Harris, *English aristocratic women*, 50; Franklin-Harkrider, *Katherine Willoughby*, 30.

was connected to the queen's household through his cousin Christopher Jenny – Catherine's attorney – who was also a guarantor of Maria's jointure.[111] These connections and bonds of loyalty would be useful to both Catherine and Maria when Lord Willoughby died in 1526 and Maria entered into a protracted legal battle over his estates and the inheritance of her daughter, Katherine. By using men whom she trusted from within her own household, Catherine did her best to ensure that Maria's jointure and marriage were legally protected, much in the same way as a father would oversee his daughter's marriage portion and jointure.[112]

Catherine took an interest in the marriages of many of her ladies, not only those Spanish ladies for whom she was essentially *in loco parentis*. In a letter to Cardinal Thomas Wolsey in 1525 the queen was anxious to arrange a marriage between one of her English maids of honour (and probably her namesake and god-daughter), Lady Katherine Grey, and Henry Fitzalan, the heir to the earldom of Arundel.[113] Catherine was intimately involved in negotiating the match, and she used her influence with Wolsey to ask for a favourable decision regarding a suit of Fitzalan's that was before Wolsey's court. A favourable decision, she claimed, would allow Fitzalan to obtain his father's consent to the marriage and, more critically, provide a jointure for Katherine Grey.[114] Catherine's letter demonstrates that she was involved at a detailed level with the complex negotiations that prefaced an aristocratic match, and that she was willing to extend her personal influence to broker an agreement. In this instance Catherine was successful, and the marriage went ahead.[115]

Marriage to one of the queen's ladies could result in ongoing patronage for the new couple from the king and queen, as demonstrated by the grants given to one of Margaret's maids of honour, Elizabeth Barlow. After Elizabeth made a good match to one of James IV's favoured courtiers, the couple continued to receive rewards from the king and queen. Elizabeth was probably the daughter of John Barlow and Christian Berlay, from a minor gentry family.[116] John Barlow was attainted for his involvement in the Perkin Warbeck conspiracy, and his lands were given to the earl of Oxford. Elizabeth's marriage prospects

---

[111] Franklin-Harkrider, *Katherine Willoughby*, 30, 33.

[112] For the safeguards that fathers tried to put in place for their daughters' marriages see Harris, *English aristocratic women*, 51–3.

[113] Lady Katherine Grey was the daughter of Thomas Grey second marquess of Dorset: see Figure 3 above. She had been in Catherine's household as a maid of honour since at least 1520, when she was around eleven years old, so she probably had an especially close relationship with the queen: JRL, MS Latin 239, fos 9r, 18r; Julian Lock, 'Fitzalan, Henry, twelfth earl of Arundel (1512–1580)', *ODNB*.

[114] *LP* iv/2, 1032.

[115] Lock, 'Fitzalan, Henry'.

[116] Peter Sherlock, 'Monuments, reputation and clerical marriage in Reformation England: Bishop Barlow's daughters', *G&H* xvi (2004), 60.

were probably materially damaged by her father's attainder. Her prospects improved when she was introduced to the English court, probably through a family connection to the countess of Oxford.[117] In March 1503 Elizabeth Barlow was paid a fee for attending upon Margaret, so she was in the young queen's household before they left for Scotland.[118] Elizabeth was probably roughly the same age as the queen, and they seem to have become close friends while living in Scotland. As a young daughter of a minor, disgraced gentry family, her service to the queen in Scotland greatly improved her social prospects and possibly helped her family as well.

In 1507 Elizabeth married Alexander Elphinstone, James IV's close friend and a courtier who would eventually become, through James's patronage, the first lord Elphinstone. Elizabeth's marriage to a Scottish baron favoured by the king was likely a better match than she would have made if she had stayed in England.[119] Although there is no documentation about the role that Margaret played in negotiating her marriage, Elizabeth and Elphinstone were greatly favoured by both Margaret and James. Elphinstone was a frequent participant in James's courtly revels and, given Elizabeth's attendance on Margaret, she probably was too.[120] In August 1507 Elizabeth received a new gown, a featherbed and bedclothes from the royal wardrobe.[121] This entry in the records, which is dated two days before the first royal charter that gave lands to Elizabeth and her new spouse, was clearly part of the preparations for her marriage, ensuring that the queen's gentlewoman was provided for honourably. Elizabeth's dowry, provided by James IV, was to be the lands and the castle in Kildrummy, a valuable collection of lands and privileges.[122]

The Elphinstone-Barlow wedding gifts were merely the beginning of royal patronage of the new couple, a patronage which was clearly linked to Elizabeth Barlow's relationship with the queen and the queen's own favour. The timing of James and Margaret's patronage indicates that the patronage itself was closely tied to milestones in Margaret's own queenship. The Elphinstone-Barlow marriage itself took place by August 1507, after the birth of Margaret's first child in January 1507 and the court's spectacular progress to Whithorn

---

[117] Montague Barlow, *Barlow family records*, London 1932, 46-7. Elizabeth may have been somewhat educated, as three of her four brothers took holy orders and became prominent clerics in the reformed Henrician Church: 'Barlow, William (d. 1568)', *ODNB*; Sherlock, 'Bishop Barlow's daughters', 62.

[118] TNA, MS E404/84.

[119] Elizabeth's brothers, for example, all had to make their own way, one became a merchant-explorer while the other three rose through the Church: Sherlock, 'Bishop Barlow's daughters', 62.

[120] For Elphinstone's role in James's tournaments see pp. 83-4 above.

[121] NRS, MS E21/8, fo. 65v. See also *LHTA* iii. 322.

[122] William Fraser, *The Elphinstone family book of the Lords Elphinstone, Balmaerino, and Coupar*, Edinburgh 1897, i. 42-6.

that July.[123] Several years later Alexander Elphinstone was created a lord of parliament as part of the ceremonies surrounding the baptism of James and Margaret's second son, Arthur.[124] Over the course of the marriage James granted the couple the baronies of Inverlochty and Kildrummy, in addition to other lands and privileges. These gifts were ongoing through the reign of James IV, and despite no mention of Margaret's specific influence, the charters indicate that the lands were closely tied to Elizabeth's connection to the queen. One charter stated that the lands were a continuation of Elizabeth's dowry, and it connected her marriage and position in Scotland with her service to Margaret. Elizabeth was described in the charter as she 'whom we caused him [Alexander Elphinstone] to take to wife and made her live beyond her native land in service with our dearest consort the queen, within our kingdom'.[125] The timing of these rewards, in addition to the charter explicitly citing Elizabeth's service to Margaret, indicates that James's patronage of Alexander Elphinstone was closely bound to his marriage to Margaret's lady and therefore to Margaret. James's affirmation of the marriage at key moments in the reign through the formal granting and thus witnessing of charters for lands also re-affirmed Margaret's patronage of the couple and would have demonstrated before the court Margaret's success in gaining rewards for her ladies.

The matches made by Catherine and Margaret for their foreign ladies allowed them to extend their own connections to the nobility of their marital kingdoms. The nobility of early modern Scotland and England interacted through complex networks of kin, friends and neighbours, and Catherine and Margaret used their ladies' marriages to form bonds of kinship and loyalty to their subjects, while at the same time fulfilling their duties to their ladies.[126] In return, Scottish and English men who married one of the queen's ladies forged links to court and gained access to patronage and support through their wives' relationships with the queen.

The partnership between Catherine and Margaret and their husbands was the most important factor in enabling them successfully to reward their households and act as patrons at court. Because Catherine and Margaret had productive relationships with their husbands, which were frequently displayed at court through their roles as honoured audience and hostess, they were able to use their close connections and access to the king to influence the distribution of patronage. This patronage was often informal or took place behind the scenes, but when Catherine and Margaret were engaging in ritual gift-giving or enacting appropriate gender roles by arranging marriages for

---

[123] The first charter granting the couple lands is dated 8 August 1507: *RMS* ii. 3115.
[124] Fraser, *Elphinstone family book*, 46–7.
[125] NRS, MS GD156/9. See also Fraser, *Elphinstone family book*, 48–9.
[126] On the role of wives in the creation of networks through marriage in the English nobility see Harris, *English aristocratic women*, 175–205.

their ladies, their activities as patrons were more marked. Gifts of clothing or plate at New Year served to affirm bonds of obligation and loyalty between the foreign queens and their native nobility, while their ladies' marriages created lasting connections between their households and the nobilities of England and Scotland. These lasting connections continually demonstrated the queen's success as a patron to those who also might wish to gain favour at court. As patrons, Catherine and Margaret are often difficult to trace, but when their activities are placed alongside the patronage activities of their husbands, there is evidence of successful partnerships, each of which served to create bonds of obligation and loyalty between the queen and her court.

5

Queenship and Pre-Reformation Piety

'the said Quene [Margaret] remayned in the said Towne of York. At Ten of the Clok that Day she was conveyed to the Church, with the sayd Archbyschop, the Byschops of Durham, Morrey, aud Norrwysche, the Prelates before mentioned, and other honourable Folks of the Churche, my Lord of Surrey, the Lord hyr Chammerlayn, and other Nobles, Knyghts, Squyers and Gentylmen, and the said Mayre, Aldermen, and Scheryffes, to the Nomber of Two hundreth and more: With hyr wer Ladies and Gentylwomen of hyr Company, and Straungers, to the Nombre of xl. And so was shee conveyed to the Church. It was a fair Syght for to see the Company so richly apoynted'.[1]

According to the herald John Young's account, when Margaret Tudor attended mass in the city of York, she did so in full view of over two hundred people, including members of her household, local prelates and governors, and a throng of curious onlookers. Young's account shows that this was only one in a series of pious practices that Margaret observed as she and her entourage journeyed to Scotland in 1503. When she entered the town of Tuxford, for example, the bishop of Moray offered her a cross to kiss, and at Hexham Margaret was greeted by the abbess and the nuns and again kissed a cross.[2] Margaret's own entourage and common folk witnessed her observance of Christian rites when she entered a town, which demonstrated her piety before a wide audience. When Margaret heard mass at York, the Minster was completely full of ladies, gentlemen and townsfolk, all there to see the queen and to witness her piety.[3] As the queen of Scotland and an English princess, Margaret was expected not only to be a devout and pious Christian but also to display this piety as a moral leader of her people.

Margaret's devotions on her wedding journey were part of an array of practices that made up her public piety in the early sixteenth century and, as queen, her honour and authority rested in part on her reputation as a devout Christian. Although some insight into Catherine's and Margaret's personal faith can be gained by examining their clerical patronage, reading habits and scant records of personal devotions, their public pious practices were more widely known to their people and closely associated with the office of queen.[4] This chapter will

---

[1] Young, 'The fyancells of Margaret', 273.
[2] Ibid. 269, 275.
[3] Ibid. 274.
[4] Catherine's and Margaret's personal faith is difficult to reconstruct, but they probably held beliefs similar to Margaret Beaufort, whose piety combined personal austerity and

focus on two forms of public piety that connected Catherine's and Margaret's queenship with their pious practice: almsgiving and pilgrimages. Almsgiving not only fulfilled their duties before God and their kingdom, but also gave them claims to sacerdotal monarchy through the Royal Maundy. While their almsgiving separated Catherine and Margaret from the pious practices of most of their people, it create a closer bond to their people through the obligation of charity. Meanwhile, Catherine's and Margaret's pilgrimages to shrines in England and Scotland brought them closer to the shared pious experiences of their subjects, while displaying their status to remote regions of the kingdom along pilgrimage routes. Together these practices of queenly piety served to establish Catherine and Margaret as sacred royal partners, magnificent consorts and good Christians.

The pre-Reformation context of royal piety

Catherine and Margaret were queens in the British Isles at the dawn of the Reformation, in a world where religious ritual, pious acts, visual imagery and belief were deeply intertwined.[5] Pious lay belief and ritual practice in Europe had grown in intensity and variety since the thirteenth century.[6] In both pre-Reformation England and Scotland, the Catholic culture of lay piety combined aspects of modern devotion, including humanist education and support of newly reformed orders such as the Observant Franciscans, with older traditions such as almsgiving and pilgrimages. Many of these pious practices, both old and new, had a public and communal face. Devotion to the sacraments, especially the eucharist, manifested itself in confraternities such as the confraternity of the Holy Blood in Edinburgh, of which James IV was a member, while pilgrimages continued to be popular until reformers in England and Scotland destroyed shrines.[7] Catherine and Margaret shared in some of these pious practices through royal variations on the largely community-based

---

devotion to the eucharist with her continuing obligations as a great householder: Jones and Underwood, *King's mother*, 197-9.

[5] In England, the minority heretic group of Lollards questioned the efficacy of church ritual and images, but they were a small and persecuted segment of the population before Protestant ideas began circulating in the 1520s: Margaret Aston, *Lollards and Reformers: images and literacy in late medieval religion*, London 1984. Scotland had little or no traditions of heresy: Alec Ryrie, *The origins of the Scottish Reformation*, New York 2006, 18-19.

[6] In recent decades, many historians have investigated the changing nature of lay belief in late medieval Europe and its vibrancy and strength before the Reformation: Eamon Duffy, *The stripping of the altars: traditional religion in England, c.1400-c.1580*, New Haven, CT 2005; John Bossy, *Christianity in the West, 1400-1700*, Oxford 1985, 4; Gail McMurray Gibson, *The theater of devotion: East Anglian drama and society in the late Middle Ages*, Chicago 1989; Miri Rubin, *Corpus Christi: the eucharist in late medieval culture*, Cambridge 1991.

[7] Mairi Cowan, *Death, life, and religious change in Scottish towns, c. 1350-1560*, New York 2012, 67-70, 137, 180-2; G. W. Bernard, 'Vitality and vulnerability in the late medieval

beliefs and practices of the laity. They participated in devotions that reflected their concerns as wives and mothers, and they continued to support chaplains and orders that had a long history of serving them and their families. Moreover, their devotions were practised in a pre-Reformation society that expected devotional behaviour to be displayed before the community. As Eamon Duffy has argued, late medieval, pre-Reformation Britain expected and supported forms of piety that emphasised the community, and queens, of course, were a crucial part of the community of the realm.[8]

As queens, Catherine and Margaret were considered moral leaders and exemplars, and nearly every pious act, from gifts of alms to public pilgrimage, had a role in influencing others. Despite interest in Catherine's posthumous reputation as queen, very little scholarly attention has been given to the public faith of the last pre-Reformation queens in the British Isles. As with many aspects of their queenships, later controversies about religion and politics have obscured understanding of how Catherine and Margaret fulfilled their roles as queens. Catherine's faith has tended to be singled out (for good or ill) specifically because of the role that it played in the divorce crisis which precipitated Henry VIII's break from Rome. Where it has been discussed at all, Catherine's famed piety has been described in somewhat dour generalities, perhaps put best by Catherine's first modern biographer: '[t]he strain of piety which had made Isabella's [Catherine's mother] last years seem those of a crowned nun was beginning to show in the daughter'.[9] Margaret has merely been described as 'devout in an entirely orthodox way'.[10] Like her sister-in-law, she was resistant to her brother's break from Rome and died a Catholic.

Aside from the later political ramifications of their faiths, little has been said about how Catherine's or Margaret's piety informed their queenship. Scholars have focused instead on Catherine's posthumous reputation for piety because of its use in the propaganda wars of the Reformation. Anti-Protestant propaganda by English Catholics depicted her as a Catholic martyr, but later English Protestants attempted to reclaim and rehabilitate her history for their own use.[11] Judith Richards has argued that as the sixteenth century wore on,

---

Church: pilgrimage on the eve of the break with Rome', in John Lovett Watts (ed.), *The end of the Middle Ages? England in the fifteenth and sixteenth centuries*, Stroud 1998, 200-1.

[8] Duffy, *Stripping of the altars*, 4.

[9] Mattingly, *Catherine of Aragon*, 168; Catherine's entry in the *ODNB* also stresses the similarities between Catherine's piety and that of her mother: C. S. L. Davies and John Edwards, 'Katherine (1485-1536)', *ODNB*.

[10] Fitch, 'Mothers and their sons', 164.

[11] Amy Appleford, 'Shakespeare's Katherine of Aragon: last medieval queen, first recusant martyr', *JMEMS* xl (2010), 149-71; Hansen, 'And a queen of England, too'; Georgianna Ziegler, 'Re-imagining a Renaissance queen: Catherine of Aragon among the Victorians', and Carole Levin, 'The taming of the queen: Foxe's Catherine and Shakespeare's Kate', in Levin, Carney and Barrett-Graves, *'High and mighty queens'*, 203-22, 171-86; Richards, 'Public identity and public memory'; Carolyn P. Collette, *Performing polity: women and agency in the Anglo-French tradition, 1385-1620*, Turnhout 2006, 6.

Catherine's reputation in England began to improve. She was no longer the Catholic 'villain' of the Henrician Reformation, and partisan historians such as John Foxe and Edward Hall had to acknowledge that Catherine was personally popular. Richards suggests that this resurgence 'may reflect understandable popular distaste for Henry's marital history' and that 'support for Katherine may have been much wider than [is] usually understood'.[12] Richards is careful to point out that the true nature of Catherine's public image and reputation for piety is difficult for historians to assess, because it seems to be based on oral traditions and rumour.[13] By focusing on Catherine's public pious acts as queen, this chapter will argue that Catherine presented her piety in a queenly, but very public, way that connected her own faith with that of her people while maintaining her status as an anointed queen.

Matthew Hansen also argues that Catherine's reputation began to change in the late sixteenth century, but he notes that later discussions of Catherine tend to de-emphasise the religious controversy of Henry's divorce by transforming Catherine into a sympathetic exemplar of suffering womanhood.[14] This transformation made it possible for even staunch Protestant propagandists like John Foxe to valorise Catherine without confronting her Catholicism.[15] By the seventeenth century even Catherine's foreignness has been 'Englished', thus removing the two most controversial elements of Catherine's history – her Catholicism and her Spanishness – to allow her fully to inhabit the roles of suffering queen and wronged woman.[16]

Catherine's later reputation as a pious queen was undoubtedly grounded in the public practice of her faith before a variety of audiences, which helped her become a moral leader of her people. Both Catherine and Margaret demonstrated their piety publicly, before audiences that were perhaps the most widespread of any that they encountered. Their piety was witnessed by the Church, their courtiers, servants and the elite of England and Scotland, but it also reached the poor and indigent through almsgiving and ordinary country folk along their pilgrimage routes. Indeed, because their public display of piety took place in a variety of circumstances, from elaborate courtly ceremonies and rituals to the distribution of alms and largesse at their gates, it served as an exemplar before the entire kingdom. Historians of both late medieval and early modern Britain have argued that queens could substantially influence society and the king's court through their piety.[17] Because many queens, such as

---

[12] Richards, 'Public identity and public memory', 208, 207.

[13] Ibid. 208.

[14] Hansen, 'And a queen of England, too', 81, 86; Collette, *Performing polity*, 6.

[15] Hansen, 'And a queen of England, too', 91.

[16] Ibid. Other authors have noted that Catherine is no longer the subject of political or religious controversy by the seventeenth century: Scherb, '"I'de have a shooting"', 136–7.

[17] Anne Crawford, 'The piety of late medieval English queens', in Caroline M. Barron and Christopher Harper-Bill (eds), *The Church in pre-Reformation society: essays in honour of F. R. H. Du Boulay*, Dover 1985, 48–9. Seventeenth-century consorts could also become public

Elizabeth of York, were popular with the larger public, their images were useful in establishing models and ideals of social behaviour. Catherine and Margaret also acted as exemplars for their kingdoms, and as Britain's last queens before the beginnings of the English and Scottish Reformations, they were also some of the last consorts to share their pious practices with the vast majority of their subjects.[18]

Queens were incorporated into the sacred aspects of the British monarchies from the moment of their coronation, which also contributed to their ability to become both exemplars and moral leaders for their people. Both Catherine and Margaret had coronations (not all sixteenth-century queens did), and both were anointed with holy oil, giving them quasi-sacerdotal status.[19] The English queen's coronation service further emphasised the queen's special relationship with God by enjoining her to cultivate virtue and spread the Christian faith.[20] Although sacral monarchy has been primarily seen as a masculine, Christ-centred development, the partnership of the king and queen gave her some claims to sacred status as well. The association of the queen with the king through ritual, beginning with her marriage and coronation but lasting throughout her queenship, and her association with the Virgin Mary, empowered queens as partners in sacred monarchy.[21] In pre-Reformation England, the Virgin's coronation was often depicted in parish churches, where she is shown being crowned by the Holy Trinity.[22] Worshippers would have been familiar with the visual iconography of the crowned Queen of Heaven and the sacred nature of queens as well as kings. Catherine certainly understood the important connection between her authority as queen and the rite of coronation. During the divorce crisis, Catherine emphasised that her

---

images of virtue: Sybil Jack, 'In praise of queens: the public presentation of the virtuous consort in seventeenth-century Britain', in Broomhall and Tarbin, *Women, identities and communities*, 211–24.

[18] This is in contrast to their queenly successors. See, for example, Adam Morton, 'Sanctity and suspicion: Catholicism, conspiracy and the representation of Henrietta Maria of France and Catherine of Braganza, queens of Britain', in Helen Watanabe-O'Kelly and Adam Morton (eds), *Queens consort, cultural transfer and European politics, c. 1500–1800*, New York 2017, 172–201.

[19] In 1509 Catherine of Aragon was anointed with holy oil during her joint coronation with her husband Henry VIII, whereupon she drank from a chalice, a practice usually reserved for priests. Margaret was anointed during her coronation, which immediately followed her marriage ceremony: Alice Hunt, *The drama of coronation: medieval ceremony in early modern England*, Cambridge 2008, 32; Young, 'The fyancells of Margaret', 294; Laynesmith, *Last medieval queens*, 99–100; Jennifer Loach, 'The function of ceremonial in the reign of Henry VIII', *P&P* (Feb. 1994), 53.

[20] Laynesmith, *Last medieval queens*, 103.

[21] Ernst H. Kantorowicz, *The king's two bodies: a study in medieval political theology*, Princeton 1957, 88–9; Theresa Earenfight, 'Partners in politics', in Theresa Earenfight (ed.), *Queenship and political power in medieval and early modern Spain*, Burlington, VT 2005, 11.

[22] Christine Peters, *Patterns of piety: women, gender, and religion in late medieval and Reformation England*, New York 2003, 64–5.

legitimacy as Henry's wife and queen was confirmed not only by their legal marriage, but by her public anointing and coronation.[23]

Catherine's and Margaret's devotions frequently took place before an audience of some kind. The nature of the royal court meant that as soon as Catherine or Margaret left her inner chamber, courtiers and servants could observe their actions. At the English court, the king or queen heard mass in the royal chapel on major church feast days, which involved a ritual procession from their chambers to the chapel. According to Fiona Kisby, for Henry VII and Henry VIII this was a 'moment of emergence from the private to the public arena, a crucial instant set in a devotional context that drew attention to the king's conventional and conspicuous piety'.[24] Processions to the royal chapel were also significant moments of interaction between the monarch and courtiers.[25] The organisational structure of Catherine's household closely mirrored the king's, and thus her procession to the royal chapel took place in a very similar manner and context.[26] In the fifteenth century, Margaret of Anjou regularly took part in the procession to the royal chapel, more often than her famously pious husband.[27] At the least, Catherine probably attended the royal chapel on the same days as her husband: Sundays, Christmas, Easter and forty-five other feast days.[28] Margaret's devotions were well enough known at the Scottish court for the English ambassador, Dr Nicholas West, to report on them when he visited in March 1513. Despite not actually being at court on Easter Saturday, he wrote that the queen received communion that day.[29] West had a number of meetings with James and Margaret in their chapel after attending a service, so the Scottish royal chapel, like the English Chapel Royal, was a space for the monarch to conduct business as well to attend to their devotions.[30]

Not every pious act that Catherine or Margaret performed was part of such a public ceremony as mass in the royal chapel. Catherine and Margaret both

---

[23] *State papers of Henry VIII*, i. 398.

[24] Fiona Kisby, '"When the king goeth a procession": chapel ceremonies and services, the ritual year, and religious reforms at the early Tudor court, 1485-1547', *JBS* xl (2001), 56.

[25] Ibid. 45, 56-7.

[26] For example, regulations for the king's household in 1526 show that the queen's household had a similar organisational structure, 'Ordinances for Eltham', 170, 173.

[27] Laynesmith, *Last medieval queens*, 252.

[28] Fiona Kisby, 'The royal household chapel in early Tudor London', unpubl. PhD diss. Royal Holloway 1996, 133.

[29] *LP* i/1, 1735, p. 791.

[30] In 1498 the Spanish envoy also remarked that James IV conducted urgent business immediately after hearing mass: *CSP Spanish* i. 210, p. 169; Kisby, 'Procession', 55-6. James IV founded the Scottish royal chapel at Stirling, making it a centre not only of household worship, but also a nationally important centre of cultural and religious patronage: Theo van Heijnsbergen, 'The Scottish chapel royal as cultural intermediary between town and court', in A. A. MacDonald and Jan Willem Drijvers (eds), *Centres of learning: learning and location in pre-modern Europe and the Near East*, Leiden 1995, 299-301.

had privy closets for their private devotions, led by their private chaplains.³¹ According the Venetian ambassador, Henry VIII habitually heard Vespers and Compline in the queen's chamber, possibly before or after they had dined together.³² These evening offices and domestic habits suggest a closeness in their marital lives and devotions that mirrored the public partnership that they presented through royal ceremony and pageantry. The fact that the Venetian ambassador knew of the king and queen's private devotional habits indicates that, even in private, the piety of the monarchy was discussed and commented upon.

Alms, the Royal Maundy and the sacralisation of queenship

Almsgiving was one of the most consistently public ways in which queens could model Christian behaviour before large numbers of their subjects, and it was also a pious practice that many sixteenth-century Christians engaged in: thus the queen's piety was closely connected to that of her people. Charity, especially household alms, was often associated with women because of their responsibility for hospitality, something that queens shared with married women.³³ Juan Luis Vives argued that wives, as managers of the household, should give generously to the poor and see that their servants were well taken care of.³⁴ At the same time, almsgiving was recognised by contemporaries as an important mark of elite, queenly status. Conduct books like Christine de Pizan's *The treasure of the city of ladies* encouraged princesses to distribute largesse in many different circumstances 'with great discretion and prudence'.³⁵ Queens in particular were expected to bestow charity in a prominent and public way, so that their own generosity would inspire generosity in others. Christine de Pizan urged princesses to distribute alms to foreigners so that the princess's reputation for generosity would spread beyond the borders of her own kingdom.³⁶ Catherine, unsurprisingly, gave alms to Spanish friars, although it seems likely that it was their connection to Spain, as well as their potential for

---

[31] Kisby, 'Royal household chapel', 132; Dunbar, *Scottish royal palaces*, 135. Margaret's private closet was furnished with an altar cloth: NRS, MS E21/8, fo. 39v. See also *LHTA* iii. 285.

[32] Giustiniani, *Four years*, ii. 312; *LP* iv/1, 2215.

[33] Peters, *Patterns of piety*, 52.

[34] Vives, *Education of a Christian woman*, 261.

[35] Pizan, *Treasure*, 54. Almsgiving was also particularly praised by Pizan in her more well-known work, *The book of the city of ladies*, which was translated into English by a member of Catherine's household and was probably read by Catherine herself: Christine de Pizan, *The book of the city of ladies*, trans. Rosalind Brown-Grant, London 1999, 192–5; Johnston, 'How the *Livre*'.

[36] Pizan, *Treasure*, 55.

spreading her reputation, that made them objects of her interest.³⁷ Later, after the divorce, Catherine's public almsgiving became a point of political significance. According to the Spanish ambassador, Anne Boleyn forbade any contact between Catherine and the poor, because 'the alms she has been accustomed to give have attracted the love of the people'.³⁸ Understanding Catherine's and Margaret's almsgiving practices, both as part of their household routines and as significant royal rituals, demonstrates the importance of pre-Reformation piety to the construction of their queenship.

As the heads of great households, Catherine's and Margaret's charity was part of their daily lives, and this giving took different forms. Institutional charity in the form of regular almsgiving at the queen's residence, during her devotions and on her travels, was under the purview of her almoner. Her almoner was also responsible for overseeing ceremonies such as the Royal Maundy, which involved specific acts of poor relief in a ritual setting. Catherine and Margaret also distributed spontaneous gifts to the poor when they were travelling around their kingdoms. Although evidence for Catherine's and Margaret's almsgiving is fragmentary, the picture that emerges reveals that they consistently and regularly gave alms as part of their obligation as moral leaders of the Christian community.

The evidence for Catherine's and Margaret's almsgiving contrasts with the surviving sources for the almsgiving of their predecessor, Elizabeth of York. Anne Crawford identifies Elizabeth's distribution of alms, 'small-scale but universal', as being a key component in the successful practice of queenly piety, which in turn fostered her positive reputation and widespread affection amongst the populace.³⁹ Elizabeth of York's pious practices are more well-known because of the survival of the Privy Purse account book from the last year of her life. This source reveals that Elizabeth of York made offerings at mass, being especially generous on major feast days, and that she had her almoner distribute food, money and clothing as part of her household alms. She also gave alms informally to those whom she encountered who were in need: to a friar of St John's, or to a man who had lodged her uncle, Earl Rivers, before he was executed.⁴⁰ Elizabeth of York thus emerges as a truly generous and pious queen, seemingly more so than her predecessors or successors. Because the evidence of Catherine's and Margaret's charity is scattered throughout royal accounts, a different picture emerges of their charity that owes more to the survival of sources than to changes in queenly piety. Privy Purse accounts for Catherine or Margaret have not survived, although there is evidence that both women had access to similar types of funds.⁴¹ It is therefore necessary to piece

---

37 TNA, MS E101/418/6, fo. 29v.
38 *LP* vii. 469.
39 Crawford, 'Piety', 52–3.
40 Ibid; *Privy Purse expenses*, 78.
41 Catherine of Aragon's receiver's accounts lists the queen's Privy Purse expenses as being

together Catherine's and Margaret's almsgiving from different sources, but bearing in mind that a true comparison across their queenships is, as always, fraught with difficulty.

Catherine's receiver's accounts give a general idea of how much, if not to whom, Catherine gave in alms. Catherine's almsgiving was between £160 and £190 a year from 1525 to 1530, though this sum does not include alms given using other sources of funds, for instance, Catherine's Privy Purse, or in her name by the king.[42] The queen's almoner was not the only official who distributed charity on her behalf. Catherine's receivers gave alms to specific foundations or individuals associated with her estates and often these gifts were a continuation of what her predecessors had given. For instance, the convent of Sheen received £7 6s. 8d. from Catherine's receiver as part of a grant originally made by Henry's ancestors out of the lordship of Wareham. Catherine herself also directed that alms be granted by her receivers, giving 13s. 4d. to John Benton, an anchorite of Marlborough in April 1518.

Margaret's alms are more difficult to trace because of the lack of household accounts. The Scottish Lord High Treasurer recorded offerings made by the king in the royal accounts, but apart from a few isolated entries, there is no systematic accountings for Margaret's offerings. In addition, because most of her household accounting was not independent of the king's, any household-based alms, such as the broken meats from her table, are indistinguishable from the king's. Margaret did have a small pension of £1,000 Scots per year, and it is likely that at least some of her offerings and alms came out of this purse. These alms, if they existed, were most likely of the occasional variety and were probably similar to the few references to Margaret's charity in the Lord High Treasurer's accounts, such as when Margaret's chaplain was given £3 12s. Scots to give away after presenting a token from Margaret to the Lord High Treasurer. This exchange indicates that Margaret had access to some sort of system which allowed her to distribute charity from the king's treasury.[43]

We can gain a slightly clearer picture of Catherine of Aragon's occasional charity because of the survival of some of her wardrobe accounts. Catherine distributed charity both in money and in kind, and her wardrobe accounts show that she gave clothing to the poor or pious whom she encountered. Catherine supported poor friars from her Spanish homeland by giving two of them grey habits worth 21s. 4d., and she gave russet broadcloth to the friars at

---

between £160 and £260 per year, which was probably accounted for in a now lost Privy Purse account book: BL, MS Cotton appendix LXV, fos 11v, 10r, 7v, 5v, 8r. See also *LP* iv/3, 6121. Margaret was given a pension of £1,000 Scots per year, at least part of which was probably considered her 'Privy Purse': NRS, MSS E21/6, p. 74; E21/7, fos 19v, 25v; E21/8, fos 28r, 31r. See also *LHTA* ii. 243; iii. 37, 46, 268, 27.

[42] BL, MS Cotton appendix LXV, fos 11v, 10r, 7v, 5v, 8r. See also *LP* iv/3, 6121. Anne Boleyn's alms were probably more, and her biographer argues that £1,500 a year, though an exaggeration, is 'just about credible': Ives, *Anne Boleyn*, 284.

[43] NRS, MS E21/6, p. 312. See also *LHTA* ii. 441.

Newark. The grey habits of the Spanish friars indicates they were Observant Franciscans, as were the friars of Newark.[44] The Observant Franciscans were one of Catherine's favourite orders, an order favoured by her parents as well as the Tudors.[45] The same account book reveals that Catherine also ordered clothing of linen and russet, as well as shoes, for nine poor women, a similar provision to her Maundy charity.[46] Elizabeth of York had also given occasional alms to poor friars or nuns, and it is reasonable to assume that Catherine's Privy Purse accounts would have reflected similar donations in coin as well as the gifts of clothing recorded in her wardrobe accounts.[47]

Catherine's and Margaret's choice of almoners reflected the importance of their almsgiving. They selected highly educated clerics for whom they also obtained additional positions in the English and Scottish Churches. The queen's almoner was responsible for overseeing their institutional and household alms, as well as administrative and ceremonial duties in their chapels.[48] All of Catherine's and Margaret's known English almoners were educated at Cambridge, and three held doctorates of divinity.[49] The Cambridge connection, although slight, is probably significant, because Margaret Tudor's grandmother Margaret Beaufort, who oversaw the creation of both Margaret Tudor and Catherine's first households, was closely connected to Cambridge though her patronage of two colleges there. It is possible that her Cambridge connections brought these clerics to the royal households. In the case of Catherine's first almoner, Dr Robert Bekinsall, it was undoubtedly Margaret Beaufort's influence that furthered his career, as he was previously her almoner before serving the queen.[50]

In general, both queens preferred and promoted almoners from their natal lands at the beginning of their lives abroad. In Scotland, Margaret's two known chaplains, Dr Henry Babington and James Carvenall, were both English and

---

[44] TNA, MS E101/418/6, fos 30r, 38v. Newark was founded by Henry VII sometime around 1499: William Page (ed.), 'Friaries: observant friars of Newark', in *A history of the county of Nottingham*, ii, London 1910, 147–8.

[45] Richard Rex, 'The religion of Henry VIII', *HJ* lvii (2014), 20–1; Jones and Underwood, *King's mother*, 180; Manuel de Castro, 'Confesores Franciscanos en la corte de los reyes Catolicos', *Archivo Ibero-Americano* xxxiv (1974), 55–126.

[46] TNA, MS E101/418/6, fo. 34v.

[47] *Privy Purse expenses*, 56, 57; Crawford, 'Piety', 52–3.

[48] R. A. Houston, 'What did the royal almoner do in Britain and Ireland, c. 1450–1700?', *EHR* cxxv (2010), 288. In sixteenth-century France the queen's almoner was the head of her chapel establishment, but the English king's chapel was headed by a dean, so it is unclear whether Catherine's almoners were also the head of her private chapel, or if that role was filled by another chaplain: Kolk, 'Household of the queen of France', 18; Kisby, 'Royal household chapel', 75–6.

[49] *Alumni cantabrigienses: a biographical list of all known students, graduates and holders of office at the University of Cambridge, from the earliest times to 1900*, ed. J. A. Venn, Cambridge 1922, i. 62, 157, 303; iv. 69.

[50] Jones and Underwood, *King's mother*, 269.

had travelled to Scotland as part of Margaret's first household. Babington was Margaret's almoner until his death in 1507, while James Carvenall returned to England sometime after 1512 to become chaplain to Henry VIII.[51] After Babington's death in 1507, it is unclear who may have taken his place in Margaret's household, although Carvenall would have been a strong candidate until his departure in 1512. Both were given positions in the Scottish Church by the king; James made Babington archdeacon of Aberdeen, and Carvenall was nominated to the archdeaconry of Dunkeld.[52] Carvenall had a hard time obtaining his appointment, however, as it was contested in Rome by George Ferne, a clerk at Dunkeld, who claimed that the appointment was his. James even enlisted his brother-in-law Henry VIII in support of 'zowre[our] familiare clerk and chaplane', possibly the only time that the two kings ever worked harmoniously together.[53]

Catherine's almoner was initially John de Rebelos, an Englishman who had served her mother in Spain; however, like many of her household staff, he seems to have left her service before she became queen.[54] When she became queen in 1509, Catherine's almoner was an Englishman, Dr Robert Bekinsall, who had served Margaret Beaufort and probably Elizabeth of York as well.[55] Bekinsall probably served Catherine until his death in 1526; his successor, Dr Robert Shorton, is mentioned as Catherine's almoner beginning in 1528.[56] Shorton had risen to prominence through his administration of St John's College, Cambridge, and later he became the dean of Cardinal Thomas Wolsey's chapel.[57] Given his numerous connections, it is therefore difficult to determine precisely how Shorton came into Catherine's orbit, although it is likely that his appointment in 1529 as dean of the college of Stoke by Clare was Catherine's doing, as this post had been held by Bekinsall from 1517 to 1525.[58]

Because they were responsible for the public face of the queen's charity and had access to the royal court, serving as Catherine's or Margaret's almoner was an important and potentially advantageous position. As high-ranking

---

[51] NRS, MS E21/8, fo. 35v. See also *LHTA* iii. 278; *LP* ii/2, 2837; A. D. M. Barrell, 'Royal presentations to ecclesiastical benefices in late medieval Scotland', *IR* lv (2004), 197-9.

[52] NRS, MS E21/8, fo. 35v. See also *LHTA* iii. 278; *LP* i/1, 1300. James IV held the right of appointment to certain ecclesiastical benefices in the Scottish Church from a papal Indult of 1487, but this did not stop rival claimants from frequently appealing to Rome. The archdeaconry of Aberdeen had been a contested appointment in 1499 as well: Peter Iver Kaufman, 'Piety and proprietary rights: James IV of Scotland, 1488-1513', *SCJ* xiii (1982), 85-8.

[53] *LP* i/1, 1296, 1300.

[54] *CSP Spanish*, i. 288, *La casa de Isabel la Católica*, ed. Antonio de la Torre, Madrid 1954, 130.

[55] *LP* i/1, 82; Neal, 'The queen's grace', 161.

[56] *Fasti ecclesiae anglicanae, 1300-1541*, ed. John Le Neve, London 1964, i. 29.

[57] Malcolm G. Underwood, 'Shorton, Robert (d.1535)', *ODNB*.

[58] William Page (ed.), 'Colleges: Stoke by Clare', in *A history of the county of Suffolk*, ii, London 1975, 145-50.

members of the queen's household, almoners received diets at the queen's table and liveries, in addition to their yearly fee. Margaret's English almoner Dr Babington received £10 sterling for his half-year fee in 1503, which made him the third highest paid male member of her English household, after her chamberlain and treasurer.[59] Catherine's almoner was the fourth highest-ranked male member of her chamber at her coronation, behind her chamberlain, vice-chamberlain and confessor. At New Year, her almoners received valuable gifts of plate. In 1522 Catherine's almoner was given a large gilt cup with a cover, roughly the same size as the cup given to Catherine's chancellor, the official who headed her council and oversaw the administration of her estates.[60] Since New Year's gifts were distributed based on rank and personal connection to the queen, the almoner's gift reflects his important role in the queen's household.

Almoners fulfilled several roles for the queen, not only overseeing almsgiving, but also acting as administrators for their chapels. Margaret's almoner performed administrative tasks for the queen's religious establishment, overseeing the running of her chapel. In December 1511 Margaret's almoner was given cloth for vestments and towels for the queen's altar, which indicates that he was responsible for furnishing the queen's chapel as well as distributing alms.[61] Catherine's almoner, moreover, served on her council and was involved in administering her estates. At least one petition to the queen's council was initially addressed to her almoner, as 'one of her most distinguished council'.[62] This petition may have been directed towards the queen's almoner because of his role as an intermediary between the queen's household and the wider world.[63] Bekinsall, who was Catherine's longest-serving almoner, was an arbitrator in several suits and settlements not involving the queen's household, so he had the kind of legal and judicial experience that would have made him a useful councillor to the queen.[64] On a practical level, because the almoner was responsible for large amounts of money and goods assigned for distribution to the poor, it would make sense for him to be involved in the financial administration of the queen's revenues or the organisation of her chapel.[65]

---

[59] *LHTA* ii. 336.

[60] TNA, MS SP1/233, fo. 202r. See also *LP* Add. i/1, 367. The cup weighed 34 oz, roughly the same as cups given to Catherine's chancellor and larger than the cups given to most of the other members of her household. Catherine's almoner also received New Year's gifts in 1528: *LP* iv/2, 3748.

[61] NRS, MS E21/10, fo. 36r. See also *LHTA* iv. 209.

[62] TNA, MS E298/6. The petition is undated, although the catalogue at the National Archives assigns it to Catherine's council.

[63] Houston, 'Royal almoner', 286.

[64] Ibid. 286–7.

[65] Dakota Hamilton does not include the queen's almoner as a typical member of her council, and it is possible that his involvement was based on personal ability rather than institutional organisation: 'Learned councils', 87.

The status and rewards given to the queen's almoner demonstrate how important almsgiving was to Catherine's and Margaret's public piety. Nearly all of the almoner's duties involved mediating between the queen and the wider world, acting as the queen's representative and organiser of public spiritual occasions. When, for instance, Catherine's almoner fined the Church of St Lawrence in Reading for failing to ring the bells when the queen entered the town, he combined both public and pious aspects of his responsibilities.[66] Additionally, as the public face of the queen's household piety, Bekinsall, Babington and others helped to organise public religious ceremonies that involved almsgiving, including the Royal Maundy.

The Royal Maundy was the most important almsgiving event for Catherine and Margaret during the ritual year and the ceremony was a powerful statement about the sacerdotal power of the king and his queen. Maundy Thursday (also called Skire Thursday in Scotland) occurred the day before Good Friday, and since at least the fourteenth century had been celebrated by the kings of England by giving alms to poor men and women. By the sixteenth century, the ceremony had evolved into a solemn court spectacle which took place in the royal chapel.[67] At the English court on Maundy Thursday, the king would process from his chamber to the royal chapel, where he would hear mass. After mass he returned to his chamber for a meal. He then processed back to the chapel in the afternoon, where he would kneel on a cushion while the dean stripped and washed the altars. Only then would the king perform the *pedilavium*, the ritual washing of the feet of selected poor men, using a towel, basin and perfumes given to him by his almoner. After the *pedilavium* the king distributed clothes and alms to the poor men and then returned to his chambers.[68] Washing the feet was meant to emulate the Last Supper, when Jesus washed the feet of his disciples.[69] The ceremony was thus a part of the sacralisation of the monarch by associating him with Christ, and monarchs used ceremonies such as the Royal Maundy to enhance their sacred status.[70] Catherine and Margaret, who almost certainly participated in the same ceremony alongside their husbands, shared their claims to the sacred status of royalty.

---

[66] C. Kerry, *A history of the municipal church of St. Lawrence, Reading*, Reading 1883, 92.

[67] There seems to be no eyewitness description of the Scottish Maundy. The English ambassador, Nicholas West, was at the Scottish court during Holy Week 1513, but he does not record a Maundy ceremony, though he spoke to Margaret on Holy Saturday within her traverse of the Royal Chapel: LP i/1, 1735. James IV had a tradition of retreating to the convent of the Observant Franciscans at Stirling during Holy Week, so it is possible that he did not take full advantage of the performance opportunities of the Royal Maundy, although he certainly distributed clothing and alms both at Stirling and at the gates of his other castles, Linlithgow and Edinburgh: MacDonald, 'Princely culture in Scotland', i. 150; *LHTA* ii. 71.

[68] Kisby, 'Royal household chapel', 159–60.

[69] Brian Robinson, *The Royal Maundy*, London 1977, 25–6.

[70] Kisby, 'Procession', 62; Carole Levin, '"Would I could give you help and succour": Elizabeth I and the politics of touch', *Albion* xxi (1989), 195.

During Henry VIII's reign the Royal Maundy became a religious ritual that was useful in supporting the power of the Tudor monarchy, and this continued after the Royal Supremacy made this power paramount over the English Church. The Royal Maundy has been of particular interest to scholars of Mary I and Elizabeth I, the first English queens regnant, both of whom had to adapt new strategies for legitimating their rule.[71] Carole Levin in particular has argued that the Royal Maundy ceremony was part of Elizabeth's deliberate strategy to use liturgical ceremonies to claim sacred status for the monarchy.[72] In the Tudor period, the ceremony focused on the monarch personally, as the number of poor recipients of royal alms was made equal to the age of the monarch.[73] For the Tudors, Levin argues that this focus 'marks a major difference from other Maundies, and places more emphasis on the specific monarch as Christ figure, rather than simply as an anonymous representative of the church'. Furthermore, Levin argues that the gender of Elizabeth and Mary was emphasised through the performance of the *pedilavium* on women, not men, as had been the case with male monarchs.[74]

While Elizabeths and Mary's Royal Maundy, especially their performance of the *pedilavium* on women, may have emphasised their gender as queens, it was not an unprecedented ritual act. Instead, their Maundies drew upon the tradition of queenly Maundies practised by their mothers and grandmothers before them.[75] When Henry VII and Henry VIII developed the Royal Maundy as an important royal ritual, they did so with their wives at their sides. The Royal Maundy for queens consort was a symbol of their status as the sacred public partners of their husbands. Both Catherine and Margaret participated in Royal Maundy ceremonies that were gendered in the same way as Mary's and Elizabeth's Maundies, by washing the feet of poor women. Performed in the same ritual space and in a similar manner as their husbands' Maundies, the ceremony made implicit claims for the sacredness of their queenship. This ritual, which spoke to both courtly and non-courtly audiences, was a religious performance of the queen's status as an anointed consort, her relationship with her husband, and her fulfilment of pious Christian ideals of charity. Moreover, Margaret's Maundy ceremony incorporated unique elements that tied its performance closely to her identity as both the wife of James IV and also an English princess and physical embodiment of a political alliance.

---

[71] See, for example, Carole Levin, *The heart and stomach of a king: Elizabeth I and the politics of sex and power*, Philadelphia 1994, and Caroline McManus, 'Queen Elizabeth, dol common, and the performance of the Royal Maundy', *English Literary Renaissance* xxxii (2002), 189-213.

[72] Levin, '"Would I could give you help and succour"', 198.

[73] Robinson, *Royal Maundy*, 25. Sometimes the number of recipients equalled the monarch's age plus one, for 'a year of grace'.

[74] Levin, '"Would I could give you help and succour"', 202.

[75] Ives, *Anne Boleyn*, 284.

The Royal Maundy ritual for queens encompassed (and thus did not ignore) their gender through the use of female recipients of the *pedilavium*, and their gender did not prevent Catherine and Margaret from fully participating in the sacralising rite of the Maundy. Because the Maundy was above all a ritual of charity, it was entirely within the appropriate gender expectations for queens to participate in its rites, but because it was a ritual closely associated with the actions of Christ and a Christo-centric monarch, it elevated their charity. By placing the queen's ritual on a near-equal footing to her husband's, the Royal Maundy reaffirmed their partnership and asserted the queen's high estate next to the king. When performed alongside their husbands, the Maundy was a quasi-sacerdotal act that reaffirmed their own sacred authority as anointed queens. The rite is therefore an excellent example of how Catherine and Margaret both conformed to widely-held social expectations for women while also superseding those gendered roles through their unique status as the king's public partner.

Henry VIII understood the distinctive power and quasi-sacred authority that Royal Maundies could give to the queen. During Henry's divorce crisis the celebration of the Royal Maundy by Catherine as queen became a point of contention. In 1534 Catherine was prevented from holding her Maundy while she was under house arrest. In 1535 Catherine insisted on holding her Maundy, and her jailor wrote to the king for instructions on how to handle the situation.[76] Henry decided that Catherine could hold her Maundy only if she did so as a royal widow, in conformity with how other elite women, including Henry's grandmother Margaret Beaufort, held their Maundies, and not as a queen, which indicates that queenly Maundies had significant symbolic power.

Royal Maundies were especially elaborate and sacred, but Maundy Thursday was observed by other Christians as well. Many pre-Reformation religious, including abbesses, and lay men and women distributed alms on Maundy Thursday. For instance, instructions for the household of the earl of Northumberland show that both the earl and his countess gave alms to poor men and women equal to each of their ages.[77] Although it is unclear what the specific differences were between Margaret Beaufort's Maundy and a queenly Maundy, the restrictions placed upon Catherine perhaps hint that non-queenly Maundies were less public affairs, taking place in private chapels and chambers rather than churches or the Chapel Royal. Catherine was 'to keep her Maundy in her chamber' thus lessening the potential audience for the ceremony, had it been held in her chapel or the parish church. Moreover, if Catherine attempted to keep the Maundy as queen, 'she is to be told that she and all her officers and such as receive it will be guilty of high treason'.[78] Henry's instructions,

---

[76] 'Original documents relating to Queen Katharine of Arragon', *Gentlemen's Magazine and Historical Review* cxxxv/2 (1854), 573-4.

[77] Robinson, *Royal Maundy*, 26. Cardinal Wolsey, along with other high-ranking clerics, also held Maundies.

[78] *LP* viii. 435.

which punish not only the queen and her officers, but also the paupers who received her alms, reveal that the public performance of the queen's Maundy was a distinct privilege of queens consort that set them apart from others' Maundies. Henry, and his contemporaries, understood that queenly Maundies were powerful rituals that gave the queen a spiritual authority and moral capital that contributed to the support that she received from the populace during the divorce.[79]

Maundy Thursday was closely bound to the material culture of the royal court through the distribution of clothing as alms and the use of material culture to proclaim the magnificence of the monarchy, and records of the material preparations for the ceremony provide the best evidence for how Catherine and Margaret performed the ritual. Because Maundy Thursday was a solemn church feast day and day of mourning, it was an occasion for crown-wearing and dressing in either blue (the colour of royal mourning) or purple.[80] In March 1504 Margaret's Wardrobe made the queen a gown of purple velvet and cloth of gold, possibly in preparation for the Royal Maundy.[81] In 1514 Catherine's Maundy gown was of violet cloth.[82] The Maundy gown was of particular significance because traditionally it was given to one of the poor almswomen after the ritual was complete.

Catherine's and Margaret's performance of the Maundy was specifically tied to them as individuals *via* their age and the gender of the recipients. Although no eyewitness descriptions of their Maundies survive, account books show that Catherine and Margaret both followed the tradition of distributing suits of clothes to female recipients, the number of whom was related to their own ages. For Margaret's first Maundy in Scotland in April 1504, clothing was ordered for fifteen poor women which equalled Margaret's current age plus one, often referred to as a year of grace.[83] Like her husband, Catherine also distributed alms in line with her age. In March 1520 her wardrobe bought ninety-six yards of cloth for the gowns of thirty-five poor women, in addition to smocks for a total cost of £16 9s. 5d.. Like their royal predecessors, both queens gave alms to poor women, gendering the ceremony to their queenship.[84]

---

[79] Kisby, 'Procession', 62. For a discussion of public opinion of Catherine during the divorce see Elston, 'Widow princess', 19-23, 26-7. Elston has noted that during this incident Catherine is attempting to continue her charitable ritual while calling Henry's bluff that she is now 'merely' a royal widow.

[80] Hayward, *Dress*, 132-3.

[81] NRS, MS E21/6, p. 54. See also *LHTA* ii. 225.

[82] TNA, MS E101/416/8, fo. 21v.

[83] NRS, MS E21/6, p. 95. See also *LHTA* ii. 259. This order sharply illuminates the difference in ages between the royal couple, as James IV's gift was to thirty-two poor men: Robinson, *Royal Maundy*, 46.

[84] Elizabeth of York also gave alms to thirty-seven poor women (her age) in 1502: Robinson, *Royal Maundy*, 26. Margaret of Denmark also participated in the Royal Maundy: Thomas

The foot-washing portion of the Royal Maundy was perhaps the most significant element of the ritual, because it most directly imitated the actions of Christ and placed the king in a priestly, almost divine role. Scholars have argued that queens consort did not perform the foot-washing because of its sacerdotal character.[85] While this aspect of the ceremony is the most difficult to discern in the sources for Catherine and Margaret, there is evidence that both women performed the *pedilavium*, as did their predecessor Elizabeth of York. As with other aspects of the Royal Maundy ceremony, the queen consort participated in the *pedilavium* alongside the king, as his partner in sacred monarchy.

The purchase of items needed for the foot-washing ceremony by the queen's almoner is a good indication that the queen participated in this aspect of the Maundy. Tudor protocol books describe Henry VIII being provided with a towel, basin and perfumes before performing the *pedilavium*.[86] When Elizabeth I performed the Royal Maundy in the late sixteenth century, she and her ladies were provided with aprons before washing the feet of poor women (whose feet had already been washed by three other household officials).[87] In 1502 Elizabeth of York reimbursed her yeoman almoner for new bowls and for heating water in the kitchen in preparation for her Maundy, a strong indication that she would be performing the *pedilavium* that year.[88] For Margaret's Maundy in 1504, one indication that she may have participated in the *pedilavium* was the purchase of four ells of Holland cloth for the queen and her almoner.[89] The account entry shows that the remainder of the fabric was made into towels for the king. This fabric, clearly suitable for towels, was not the type of fabric used for the other elements of the Maundy – clothing for the poor women or the queen – and thus it is highly likely that it went to make the queen's own towels for the footwashing ceremony. Similarly, the purchase of aprons and towels for Catherine and her almoner in both 1514 and 1520 suggest that she participated in the *pedilavium* as well.[90]

Margaret's Royal Maundy featured a unique aspect that identified the ritual with the queen personally as both a Scottish queen consort and an English princess. In addition to the distribution of clothing and the *pedilavium* at the Royal Maundy, poor men and women were also given purses with alms, usually containing a symbolic amount tied to the monarch's age. For instance, in 1505 James IV gave thirty-three men 33s Scots as alms on Maundy

Riis, *Should auld acquaintance be forgot ... Scottish-Danish relations c.1450–1707*, Odense 1988, 247, 249.

[85] Carole Levin states, following Robinson, that queens consort did not perform the footwashing portion of the Maundy: "'Would I could give you help and succour'", 194, 202; Robinson, *Royal Maundy*, 26.
[86] Kisby, 'Royal household chapel', 160.
[87] McManus, 'Performance of the Royal Maundy', 195–6.
[88] *Privy Purse expenses*, 4.
[89] NRS, MS E21/6, p. 297. See also *LHTA* ii. 426.
[90] TNA, MS E101/418/6, fo. 22r; JRL, MS Latin 239, fo. 1v.

Thursday. Margaret also distributed alms in purses, and in 1505 she gave sixteen women 16d. in English coin.[91] While there is no indication in the accounts as to why Margaret's alms were in English coin, it was a practice that continued throughout her marriage.[92] This custom would have served to reassert Margaret's identity as both Scottish queen and English princess, while also making her part of the Royal Maundy distinctive from the king's.[93]

The Royal Maundy was a ceremony that even before the Reformation in England and Scotland was an important ritual, which enhanced the status of the monarchy and had political as well as religious significance. Evidence of the purchase of towels for the footwashing for both Margaret and Catherine indicates that both performed the *pedilavium* and almsgiving as queens consort. Their Maundies were specifically tailored to their personal status as queens, reflecting their age, gender and, in the case of Margaret Tudor, her national origin. By performing this important religious and royal ceremony, Margaret and Catherine incorporated the sacrality of monarchy into their own queenship and claimed a significant place alongside their husbands as part of divinely sanctioned royal partnership. In the profoundly religious society and culture of the early sixteenth century, the participation by the monarchy in religious rituals reaffirmed the status of the monarch as one chosen by God.[94] By sharing in these same rituals, Catherine and Margaret claimed the importance of queenly piety by placing their pious acts alongside their husbands' Maundies.

Pilgrimage and the display of piety

While Catherine's and Margaret's Royal Maundies served to exalt their authority and link their queenly piety to their husbands, their participation in royal pilgrimages brought them significantly closer to the religious practices of pre-Reformation Britons. Despite their rapid destruction during the Reformation, shrines in both England and Scotland were popular pilgrimage

---

[91] NRS, MS E21/7, fo. 35r. See also *LHTA* iii. 57.

[92] For the 1512 Royal Maundy alms see NRS, MS E21/10, fo. 22v. See also *LHTA* iv. 185.

[93] It may appear that this practice was part of an attempt to inflate the value of Margaret's alms: as Margaret was significantly younger than the king, her alms would have been significantly less than his. By using English pennies instead of Scottish shillings, the value of Margaret's alms may seem to come closer to the value of the king's, and thus may have preserved some notion of 'fairness.' However, the decision to use pennies instead of shillings negates any increase in value gained by using different currency. As James gave out his alms in Scottish shillings, which were worth 12 Scottish pence or roughly 36 English pence, his alms were worth far more than Margaret's even when currency conversions are taken into account. It seems unlikely that there was a deliberate economic motivation behind using English currency.

[94] Richardson, *Renaissance monarchy*, 22.

sites in the early sixteenth century.[95] Many of the shrines that Catherine and Margaret visited were holy sites of national, or even international, stature. Moreover, in pre-Reformation England, the gendered division of roles within the household, associating women with the care and nurturing of the family, meant that it was expected that women, including queens, would go on pilgrimages to 'procure the well-being of members of the family' and the kingdom.[96] Pilgrimage was also a social and public expression of piety for common folk and queens alike, sanctioned by religious authorities and witnessed by the public.[97] At the same time, Catherine's and Margaret's pilgrimages were necessarily different in form and scale from most early sixteenth-century pilgrimages. These official pilgrimages by the royal court, either with the king and queen or with the queen alone, were highly performative expressions of royal piety and devotion.

Any royal progress or lengthy journey, whether its destination was a holy site or royal palace, could be considered a type of pilgrimage if it featured a prominent display of kingly or queenly piety.[98] While travelling across the countryside beyond the usual routes of the royal court, Catherine and Margaret frequently stopped in towns, monasteries or colleges to venerate local relics and pay their respects to local churchmen. Thus both queens performed their piety to a wide public audience, and their presence would have been broadcast to the surrounding areas through the ringing of bells, the traditional form of welcome for the king and queen in the sixteenth century.[99] When they entered towns, they were welcomed by the leaders of the community and then immediately performed an act of devotion. For instance, the first place at which Margaret stopped during her wedding journey to Scotland in 1503 was Grantham, where she was given a cross to kiss by the bishop of Norwich. According to John Young, this began a series of public displays of piety by the young queen: '[a]nd thus was doon continually, lastyng the said Veyage throrough the Reyme of Inglaund in all the Places wher she cam'.[100] Catherine too visited local shrines or chapels in the areas where she stayed.

---

[95] Cowan, *Religious change*, 70; Ryrie, *Scottish Reformation*, 19. Bernard explains how pilgrimage could be simultaneously popular and vulnerable to critique on the eve of the Reformation: 'Vitality and vulnerability'.

[96] Peters, *Patterns of piety*, 15.

[97] Susan Signe Morrison, *Women pilgrims in late medieval England: private piety as public performance*, London 2000, 4.

[98] Robert N. Swanson, 'Political pilgrims and political saints in medieval England', in Antón M. Pazos (ed.), *Pilgrims and politics: rediscovering the power of the pilgrimage*, Burlington, VT 2012, 30; Neil Samman, 'The progresses of Henry VIII, 1509–1529', in Diarmaid MacCulloch (ed.), *The reign of Henry VIII: politics, policy and piety*, New York 1995, 71.

[99] Gunn, 'Public opinion', 135. It was the royal almoner's duty to ensure that the bells were rung. He could levy fines if a town did not do so: Kerry, *St Lawrence*, 92.

[100] Young, 'The fyancells of Margaret', 268.

In addition to pilgrimages that took place in the course of royal progresses, Catherine and Margaret took part in large-scale pilgrimages that were tied to their desire for children and the trouble that they faced in childbirth, and which also reaffirmed their roles as the continuators of the royal dynasties and communicated both their anxieties and their hopes to the kingdom at large. Catherine's and Margaret's motivations for going on pilgrimage were similar to those of many other women pilgrims of the period whose primary concerns centred around fertility, childbirth and the health of their family.[101] In July 1507 Margaret, accompanied by her husband, household and the royal court, made a grand pilgrimage to St Ninian's shrine at Whithorn as a thanksgiving for her recovery from a difficult birth. Catherine made several pilgrimages to the shrine of the Virgin at Walsingham in Norfolk, which had a special affinity with women and fertility. Both pilgrimages took the queens beyond the areas of the kingdom usually frequented by the royal court and thus displayed their piety to a wider audience.

Catherine and Margaret shared their pilgrimage tastes, and sometimes their journeys, with their husbands. Walsingham and Whithorn saw visits from Henry VIII and James IV respectively, which is unsurprising for two of the most renowned shrines in their kingdoms. James IV was a regular pilgrim to Whithorn, travelling there nearly every spring, usually around Easter.[102] Henry VIII's pilgrimage habits have been debated by historians in an attempt to determine the king's attitude towards traditional religion before the Reformation.[103] Although he may not have been quite as enthusiastic about Walsingham as his first wife nor as regular in his journeys as James IV, Henry visited the shrine at least twice and paid handsomely to glaze the chapel.[104] The reason for Henry's first visit to Walsingham, in January 1511, was to give thanks for the birth of his first child and heir, the short-lived Prince Henry. It is tempting to speculate as to why none of the births of Henry and Catherine's other children provoked such a display of piety from the king, but there is no evidence that Henry withdrew his support from the shrine until the break with Rome.[105]

Margaret's most significant pilgrimage to Whithorn was also associated with childbirth, when she travelled there five months after the birth of her first child Prince James. The birth had been difficult for the seventeen-year-old queen. While Margaret suffered some sort of childbed fever, her husband rode to Whithorn to pray for her recovery.[106] When Margaret had recovered enough to

---

[101] Morrison, *Women pilgrims*, 16.

[102] Margaret did not usually accompany him on these trips, but James would make an offering there for the queen as well: NRS, MS E21/9, fo. 33r. See also *LHTA* iv. 39.

[103] Rex, 'Religion', 7–9; Bernard, 'Vitality and vulnerability', 231–2.

[104] Rex, 'Religion', 7.

[105] Ibid.

[106] Leslie, *History of Scotland*, ii. 122.

travel, her pilgrimage in the summer became one of thanksgiving for her own recovery and for the successful fulfilment of her primary duty, that of providing an heir to the throne.[107] Margaret's journey echoed a similar pilgrimage made by James IV's parents in 1473, when they went to Whithorn together to give thanks for the birth of their heir.[108] The timing of Margaret's pilgrimage, and its nature, also echoed the atmosphere and motivation behind many women's churchings, and Margaret's journey could be seen in one sense as a kingdom-wide churching.[109]

Margaret's pilgrimage would have connected her to a popular practice of Scottish lay piety while also exposing a new area of the kingdom to her presence. The cult of St Ninian at Whithorn was not only favoured by the elite, it was also a genuinely popular pilgrimage site for Scots, as well as travellers from the British Isles and beyond.[110] As it was in the south-western portion of Scotland, in Galloway, the shrine itself was quite a distance from the court's usual territory around Edinburgh. For Margaret and most Lowland Scots, the pilgrimage to St Ninian's involved the additional complication of a language and culture barrier. Galloway was still primarily Gaelic-speaking in the sixteenth century, and so the young queen would have encountered a new and quite different linguistic and cultural region of Scotland.[111] Despite these challenges, St Ninian was probably Scotland's most popular native saint, and Margaret's journey there would have connected her pious practice with that of many of her subjects.

Margaret's journey was a public occasion that allowed the royal couple to see and be seen across their kingdom. Great care was taken to ensure that the queen's retinue would make the correct impression of royal splendour and magnificence. Three new gowns of satin and a new cloak were made for Margaret in June in preparation for her journey.[112] Additionally, the queen's stables were busy preparing her stable gear and harnesses in anticipation of the journey, providing her with practical necessities such as bits and stirrups, as well as more elaborate and ornate items such as a cloth of gold harness and two velvet saddles.[113] Margaret was accompanied by her ladies and gentlewomen, who rode horses and brought their own servants. The most visible of Margaret's servants, her footmen and littermen, were outfitted to match the

---

[107] Prince James lived for a year before dying in February 1508, so he was not the future James V, but in July 1507 the succession looked assured.

[108] *LHTA* i. 29, 44.

[109] For churching see chapter 2 above.

[110] Cowan, *Religious change*, 64, 70.

[111] David Ditchburn, '"Saints at the door don't make miracles?" The contrasting fortunes of Scottish pilgrimage c. 1450-1550', in Julian Goodare and A. A. MacDonald (eds), *Sixteenth-century Scotland: essays in honour of Michael Lynch*, Leiden 2008, 91.

[112] NRS, MS E21/8, fos 29v-30r. See also *LHTA* iii. 269-70.

[113] NRS, MS E21/8, fo. 102. See also *LHTA* iii. 399.

royal splendour with new suits of clothes in the Scottish royal livery colours of red and yellow.[114]

Margaret's journey was also an occasion that allowed James and his queen to visit important members of the noble and clerical elite, thus serving a political as well as a spiritual purpose. It took the royal court about a month for the whole journey, which was conducted at a leisurely pace and eschewed a direct route, instead stopping at major Scottish towns including Glasgow, Paisley and Peebles.[115] Local elites greeted James with gifts ranging from cherries to horses. A generous gratuity given by the king to the bishop of Glasgow's master cook indicates that the king and queen were feasted by local elites.[116] Numerous gifts and gratuities to musicians in the employ of Scottish noblemen demonstrates the lively reception that greeted James and Margaret along the way.[117] In turn, the royal accounts give a festive picture of a large court on the move. In addition to their servants and personal attendants, James and Margaret brought Italian minstrels to entertain them along the route.[118] Local musicians entertained the royal couple as well, such as the 'clarschaar' (an Irish harpist) of Ayr to whom the king gave 5s. Scots.

The journey provided opportunities for Margaret to see more of her kingdom and interact with her subjects. Along the route to Whithorn, Margaret and her ladies stopped for refreshments, pausing to drink 'by the gate' with a local woman, who was given 14d. Scots for her trouble.[119] In another instance Margaret stopped to drink and gave 14s. Scots for 'belcher' or good entertainment, at the village of Monaebrugh, on the road from Glasgow to Stirling.[120] These small instances probably indicate a larger pattern of Margaret's interactions along her pilgrimage route with the villages and towns where the royal entourage stopped, either to spend the night or to take refreshment on a summer's day. When taken together with James's similar gifts and interactions, it becomes clear that Margaret's pilgrimage to Whithorn in July 1507 was an important royal progress, possibly the most important progress since her wedding in 1503.[121] Because the journey was a festive occasion, giving thanks

---

[114] NRS, MS E21/8, fo. 65r. See also *LHTA* iii. 321.

[115] Ditchburn, 'Scottish pilgrimage', 95; The most direct route from Edinburgh to Whithorn was 120 miles, but the journey could be much longer if James went out of his way to stop by Glasgow and other major towns, as he did in 1507: Mairi Cowan, 'Lay piety in Scotland before the Protestant Reformation: individuals, communities, and nation', unpubl. PhD diss. Toronto 2003, 137.

[116] NRS, MS E21/8, fo. 104v. See also *LHTA* iii. 405.

[117] *LHTA* iii. 403.

[118] *LHTA* iii. 399, 404.

[119] NRS, MS E21/8, fo. 103r. See also *LHTA* iii. 401.

[120] NRS, MS E21/8, fo. 104v. See also *LHTA* iii. 405.

[121] Mairi Cowan makes a similar point in her discussion of James's pilgrimages, but 1507 was the first time that Margaret and her household were included in this important royal display: 'Lay piety in Scotland', 140-1.

for the birth of an heir and the queen's recovery, Margaret and James had an opportunity to proclaim the strength and success of the monarchy through their splendid display in a relatively remote corner of the kingdom. However, the triumphal nature of their pilgrimage should not obscure the spiritual impulse at the root of it: personal thanksgiving after Margaret's recovery from illness.[122]

Margaret's journey of thanksgiving to Whithorn stands in contrast to a great many pilgrimages made by English and Scottish queens in the fifteenth and sixteenth centuries, which were journeys of supplication. A far more common reason for queenly pilgrimages was to pray for the birth of an heir to the throne, not to celebrate the birth itself.[123] Catherine's pilgrimages to the shrine of the Virgin at Walsingham appear to conform to this type of practice, though it should be emphasised that she was not unique amongst English and Scottish queens in seeking divine help with fertility issues. Moreover, although no contemporary sources explicitly state the motivations for Catherine's pilgrimages, because of its association with fertility and childbirth, Walsingham was a natural focus for queens worried about fulfilling their dynastic duties.

Like Whithorn in Scotland, Walsingham was a popular shrine in late medieval and early modern England with elites as well as more humble folk, but it enjoyed a higher international profile. English queens visited the shrine with their husbands, but queens facing fertility problems made journeys on their own. In the fifteenth century both Margaret of Anjou and Elizabeth Woodville had gone on separate pilgrimages to Walsingham. Margaret went to give thanks for her long-awaited pregnancy and to pray for a son.[124] Elizabeth Woodville had planned to go to Walsingham in 1469, though it is unclear if the visit was cancelled because of the rebellion of the earl of Warwick. If she made the journey, she was probably praying for the birth of a prince after a succession of four daughters.[125] Elizabeth of York, too, had visited the shrine in 1495, possibly because of the recent loss of her four-year old daughter and the birth of a premature son.[126]

---

[122] Margaret made other pilgrimage journeys to Scottish shrines, including the shrine of St Duthac at Tain, in the far north-east of the kingdom, though none of these were explicitly associated with her childbearing or fertility. In the spring of 1510 Margaret and James travelled to Tain by way of Elgin: ERS xiii. 292.

[123] For instance, Mary of Guise, Margaret's daughter-in-law, went on pilgrimage to St Adrian's shrine on the Isle of May in 1539 to pray for a child: Marshall, *Mary*, 78. James IV visited the Isle of May nearly every year, though there is no record of Margaret joining him.

[124] Pre-modern popular and learned authorities held a variety of beliefs on when the sex of the foetus was determined in the uterus, so Margaret's prayers for a son after conception would have seemed appropriate to many of her subjects anxious for a male heir: Ian Maclean, *The Renaissance notion of woman: a study in the fortunes of scholasticism and medical science in European intellectual life*, Cambridge 1980, 37-9.

[125] Laynesmith, *Last medieval queens*, 111, 134.

[126] Ibid. 111.

QUEENSHIP AND PRE-REFORMATION PIETY

From her first successful pregnancy, Catherine connected Walsingham with childbearing and fertility. The birth of Prince Henry on New Year's Day 1511 caused enormous celebration at court, and the new father immediately ordered a pageant performed that celebrated the royal couple, using Catherine's badge of pomegranates and the Tudor rose. Before Catherine was churched and returned to court life, Henry also rode to Walsingham to give thanks for his heir.[127] Catherine appears to have been planning to visit the shrine as well. In a letter to her husband in 1513, she mentions wishing to go to the shrine to fulfil a vow she made long ago.[128] Events seemed to have prevented Catherine from going to Walsingham until 1515, by which time she had had two additional unsuccessful pregnancies that had resulted in miscarriages or stillbirths.[129] Although Catherine did not visit the shrine until six years into her queenship, from the earliest moments of her marriage, Catherine and the English court associated the shrine at Walsingham with prayers for childbirth and pregnancy.

Catherine of Aragon's childbearing problems and tragedies have been much discussed by historians, and the period during which Catherine went on pilgrimage to Walsingham coincides with her most difficult childbearing years. Catherine was pregnant between five and six times from the beginning of her marriage in 1509 until 1518.[130] Three of those pregnancies resulted in a miscarriage or a stillbirth, and two resulted in children who lived for only a matter of weeks. Prince Henry was born in January 1511 and died six weeks later. In 1516 Catherine gave birth to Princess Mary, the future queen regnant of England. Catherine's pilgrimages to Walsingham took place from 1515, after her third failed pregnancy, to 1521, three years after her last pregnancy. Catherine probably entered the menopause shortly after this last pilgrimage, which may be why she appears to have stopped visiting the shrine.[131] Nevertheless, Catherine continued her devotion to the shrine until the end of her life, requesting in her will that 'some personage' make a pilgrimage to Walsingham on her behalf and distribute 20 gold nobles along the way.[132]

On a practical level, Catherine had a strong association with Walsingham and the pilgrimage route there. As queen she had been assigned the manors of Great and Little Walsingham as part of her dower, and while on pilgrimage

[127] Dillon, *Hall's Chronicle*, 37.
[128] *LP* i/2, 2268. It is possible that this vow was initially made after (or during) her successful delivery in 1511, which would have been the most appropriate moment for the vow before 1513.
[129] Dewhurst, 'Alleged miscarriages', 51–2.
[130] The number and dates of Catherine's pregnancies and their tragic outcomes are surprisingly difficult to pin down, but they are outlined in great detail ibid. 49–54. See also Whitley and Kramer, 'New explanation', 829–30.
[131] Starkey, *Six wives*, 163; Neil Samman, 'The Henrician court during Cardinal Wolsey's ascendancy, c.1514–1529', unpubl. PhD diss. Bangor 1988, 63.
[132] BL, MS Cotton Titus C VII, fo. 44v.

she may have stayed at those manors.¹³³ Catherine held many other manors in Suffolk and Norfolk as well, which she may have visited along the way. She was also hosted by the local nobility and friends during these trips, including her Spanish lady-in-waiting, Maria de Salinas, Lady Willoughby, and her sister-in-law Mary Tudor Brandon, duchess of Suffolk.¹³⁴

Those friends and local elites who joined Catherine on pilgrimage served to expand her own entourage and project royal magnificence. For the 1517 pilgrimage, for example, Catherine was accompanied by her sister-in-law Mary and her husband. The couple brought along their own substantial households, which, in addition to Catherine's train, would have created an impressive and memorable spectacle. Suffolk, who had been informed of the queen's route by the king's chief minister Cardinal Wolsey, met her at Pykenham Wade and the following day his wife and her servants joined them.¹³⁵ Suffolk wrote to Wolsey that he and his wife attended to Catherine 'with as good herte and mynd as hir own servantes, according to our duties'.¹³⁶ Other groups also sought to accommodate the queen as she made her pilgrimages; for example in 1521 the city of Norwich presented her with 100 marks upon her entry into the city.¹³⁷ Catherine's pilgrimages were highly public affairs that were seen by many different groups of people across the countryside and served to project not only Catherine's piety but also her queenly splendour. Catherine also followed a slightly different route each time, and thus she was seen by different groups of people and hosted by different towns and noblemen.

Local audiences and other current and former pilgrims to Walsingham would have associated Catherine's pilgrimages to Walsingham with her concerns about childbearing and fertility. The Chapel of Our Lady at Walsingham had always been closely associated with devout women and the Virgin: in the legend of the shrine's founding, a wealthy widow, Richeldis de Faveraches, had founded the shrine based on a vision of Mary's house in Nazareth.¹³⁸ Throughout East Anglia, church art was dominated by the imagery of childbirth, which complemented and magnified the shrine at Walsingham. The route to Walsingham was lined with churches and smaller shrines that featured

---

¹³³ *LP* i/1, 94. For discussion of Catherine's dower lands see also Beer, 'A queenly affinity?'.

¹³⁴ Brandon was married to Henry VIII's sister Mary: *LP* i/1, 94; Samman, 'Henrician court', 62.

¹³⁵ TNA, MS SP1/15, fo. 33v. See also *LP* ii/2, 3018.

¹³⁶ TNA, MS SP1/15, fo. 33v.

¹³⁷ Samman, 'Henrician court', 62.

¹³⁸ Richard Pynson printed the legend in ballad form in 1496, making it widely available. Pynson's decision to print the ballad suggests not only the shrine's popularity, but also the widespread knowledge and appeal of its founding legend, which placed devout women and the Virgin at the centre of events: J. C. Dickinson, *The shrine of Our Lady of Walsingham*, Cambridge 1956, 124–30.

images of female saints or saintly mothers and their children.[139] Catherine and her entourage stopped at these churches along the way, performing devotions to local shrines, which would have reinforced the reasons for her pilgrimage through their own emphasis on women and childbirth. On at least three of her pilgrimages, for example, Catherine stayed in the town of Litcham, which was known for its rood screen depicting female saints.[140] The overall experience of her pilgrimages would have emphasised for Catherine, her household and any observers, not only the queen's own public piety but also her anxiety about having children.

News of the queen's pilgrimages would have been widely reported throughout the countryside as important and interesting events.[141] Ambassadors at the court mentioned Catherine's absences on these trips in their dispatches, and those who saw Catherine's or Margaret along the road would have passed the news along to others whom they met.[142] Given the well-documented interest of the sixteenth-century populace in royal gossip, it is likely that most folk knew something of Catherine's or Margaret's fertility troubles and thus a possible reason for their pilgrimages.[143] Their journeys would have served as an exemplar to others and possibly as a source of comfort or at least identification for women experiencing similar problems. Although grand in scope and fraught with political ramifications, Catherine's and Margaret's pilgrimages at their core connected their queenly piety with the pious practices and personal problems of their people, especially their female subjects.

Catherine's and Margaret's piety was closely connected to a tradition of queenly piety that encompassed almsgiving, pilgrimages and late medieval religious ritual as expressions of faith and good works, which could also serve as Christian exemplars to their English and Scottish subjects. Participation in ceremonies like the Royal Maundy closely allied Catherine's and Margaret's queenships with the sacerdotal character of the English and Scottish monarchies as a whole and drew upon personal and gendered signs of piety to associate both queens with powerful conceptions of royal holiness. On another level, the Royal Maundy was part of a larger programme of almsgiving that was both a duty for queens as social and moral leaders of their people and also a potentially political performance of their own elite nobility and largesse. In contrast, pilgrimages made by Catherine and Margaret exhibited their piety to a wider audience, while also acknowledging the personal triumphs and tragedies that both women experienced as queens, wives and mothers. Pilgrimages linked the queens' own piety with the beliefs and experiences of

[139] I have relied on Susan Signe Morrison's excellent work on women pilgrims and Walsingham, *Women pilgrims*, 27–8.
[140] Samman, 'Henrician court', 338, 354, 359; Morrison, *Women pilgrims*, 27.
[141] Morrison, *Women pilgrims*, 17.
[142] *CSP Venetian*, iii. 167.
[143] Adam Fox, *Oral and literate culture in England, 1500–1700*, Oxford 2000, 340, 361.

their subjects, emphasising their roles as leaders of the Christian community. Their people largely shared Catherine's and Margaret's entirely orthodox beliefs, and a range of audiences witnessed their public piety. These audiences could connect the queens' public piety with their own lives, thus creating a powerful bond between Catherine and Margaret and their people. As queens consort, almsgiving and pilgrimages were powerful public expressions of piety that connected Catherine and Margaret to the sacred mystique of monarchy and the personal religious practices of their people.

Conclusion

'My husband, for hastynesse, w[ith]Rogecrosse I coude not sende your Grace the pece of the King of Scotts cote which John Glyn now bringeth. In this your grace shal see how I can kepe my premys, sending you for your banners a King's cote. I thought to send hymself unto you, but our Englishmens herts wold not suffre it. It shulde have been better for hym to have been in peax than have this rewarde. Al that God sendeth is for the best.'[1]

When Catherine of Aragon wrote to Henry VIII on 16 September 1513 he was campaigning in northern France, and had made his wife queen regent and governor of England in his absence. While the bulk of Henry's armies were fighting in France, James IV invaded the north of England and sacked several towns before meeting the English army that Catherine had sent north, commanded by Thomas Howard, earl of Surrey. In a stunning victory, Surrey destroyed the Scottish army at the battle of Flodden Field on 9 September, killing the Scottish king and nearly a hundred of his nobility. It was the greatest military victory of Henry's reign and made the Scottish border secure for the English for a generation. Flodden also caused havoc in Scotland, wiping out a generation of Scottish noblemen and putting Margaret Tudor at the head of a minority government for her infant son, now James V. Although occurring under very different circumstances, the regencies of Catherine and Margaret were the ultimate official acknowledgement of the public partnership between queens and their kings during this period.

Not all queens were granted the responsibility of regency, although it was a historically acceptable role for them to fulfil in Western Europe. Usually they were appointed regents for their under-age sons. Catherine, of course, was regent for an adult king who was temporarily absent from his realms, but her situation echoed familiar Spanish practices. The Iberian kingdoms had a strong tradition of female regency and lieutenancy, and queens had frequently acted as regents for under-age heirs and while their husbands were on campaign. The kingdom of Aragon had developed the role of queen-lieutenant, who acted as a co-ruler while the king was visiting his other kingdoms or on campaign. Catherine's paternal grandmother, Juana Enriquez, was an able queen-lieutenant who had taught her son much about Aragonese politics.[2] In Castile, Catherine's celebrated English great-grandmother, Catalina of

---

[1] *Original letters*, i. 88.
[2] Theresa Earenfight, *The king's other body: María of Castile and the Crown of Aragon*, Philadelphia 2010, 138-40.

Lancaster, had served as regent twice.³ Given her family traditions, Catherine of Aragon probably expected to be named regent while Henry was in France, although in England this tradition was less developed. Female regency may even have been seen as a negative institution after the attempts of Margaret of Anjou to rule for her insane husband.⁴ Despite this precedent, Catherine's regency seems to have been considered a success, as Henry would go on to appoint one of her successors, Katherine Parr, regent when he invaded France again in 1544.⁵

Scotland also had a tradition of queen mothers involving themselves unofficially in the government for minority heirs, although Margaret Tudor was Scotland's first official queen regent. In the fifteenth century Margaret Tudor's great-great aunt, Joan Beaufort, widow of James I, was guardian of her son James II, and a generation later Mary of Guelders had a leading role in the minority government of her son James III.⁶ In naming Margaret regent in his will, James IV made official what was already a common practice for the Stuart kings. Catherine's and Margaret's regencies were both unusual moments of public political power and responsibility and traditional extensions of their careers as queens consort and partners in the Scottish and English monarchies.

Catherine's letter after Flodden also reveals more about her personal relationship with her husband and her personality than most of the documents cited in this study. Her tone implies an intimacy and partnership between the married couple that belies the formal wording of sixteenth-century correspondence. In this letter Catherine is witty, jesting with Henry that she has sent him a king's coat for his banner in France. Her quip refers to her activities of a few months ago, when she and her ladies were busy sewing standards, banners and badges for the English army. In her letter Catherine jokes that she has now sent Henry a new banner, one created in a more martial manner.⁷ This jest may also have been a reference to Henry's earlier 'gift' of a prisoner, the duc de Longueville, whom he had captured while on campaign and had sent to England in late August.⁸ As ambassadors around Europe passed along the news of Catherine's victory, some observed that while Henry had sent Catherine a captive duke, she could send him the body of a king.⁹

---

3   Ibid. 23.

4   Laynesmith, *Last medieval queens*, 159-60.

5   Marie de Guise, Margaret's successor and wife of James V, became queen regent for her daughter Mary queen of Scots, when Mary was an adult monarch living in France as the dauphine: Blakeway, *Regency*, 23. French kings such as Henry II appointed their wives or close female relatives to head regency councils while the king was on campaign. For French regency see Crawford, *Perilous performances*, 21-2.

6   Downie, *She is but a woman*, 141-2, 157-74.

7   *Original letters*, i. 83.

8   *Letters of royal and illustrious ladies*, i. 163-5.

9   *CSP Venetian*, ii. 328.

CONCLUSION

Catherine was just as martial-minded as her male contemporaries, if not more so, a trait she shared with her mother Isabella, who had successfully fought for her throne and accompanied her armies during the conquest of Granada.[10] Catherine had marched north with the English vanguard, making it as far as Buckingham before news of the victory reached her. She may even, according to one report, have made a speech to the troops 'in imitation of her mother Isabella'.[11] In her letter she claimed to have considered sending James's body to Henry as proof of her victory, but it seems that the more squeamish English thought that was a bad idea.[12] And, as Catherine's letter shows, just as her mother had believed that God supported her military campaigns against the Muslim kingdom of Granada, so her daughter believed that God had given the English their victory at Flodden.

Catherine's brief tenure as regent of England shows her queenship in a new mode. Henry had named her, in a grant made June 1513, regent and governess of England. Catherine had the power to issue commissions of array to muster troops, to distribute church patronage, appoint sheriffs and issue warrants under her own signature to the king's treasurer, John Heron.[13] For a few months in 1513 she became the centre of government in England, and she took these duties seriously. By 18 July she was authorising Heron to send money to the king in support of the war effort in France at the same time as she was issuing orders in preparation for England's defence against the Scots.[14] Catherine also had to deal with potential challenges to her authority, and she handled them efficiently. The town of Gloucester was evidently slow to respond to her call to arms, and in August she warned them in no uncertain terms that the Scots were invading and that they must respond without delay.[15] When the archbishop of Canterbury, William Warham, decided to rekindle his jurisdictional dispute with the bishop of Winchester while the king was in France, Catherine called Warham before her council to reprimand him and ordered him to stop 'vexing' Winchester's commissioners.[16]

Supporting Henry's war effort and England's defence kept both the queen and her household busy. Catherine's household was so important to her ability to function as regent that the king granted her officials and councillors (many of whom were noblemen with military retinues of their own) a special licence exempting them from military service in France, so that they could stay in

---

[10] Elizabeth A. Lehfeldt, 'Ruling sexuality: the political legitimacy of Isabel of Castile', *Renaissance Quarterly* liii (2000), 44–5; Jansen, *Monstrous regiment*, 12–18.
[11] *LP* i/2, 2299.
[12] *Original letters*, i. 88.
[13] *LP* i/2, 2055, no. 46.
[14] TNA, MSS E101/417/2, no. 5; E101/417/12; E36/215; E36/264.
[15] *LP* i/2, 2143, p. 968.
[16] *LP* i/2, 2098, 2163.

England and support the queen.[17] With the king and a large part of the English court away in France, the men and women of Catherine's household stepped into new roles. Catherine's Groom of the Robes, Richard Justice, who for over a decade had provided finery for royal women, now found himself responsible for a much more martial set of cloth when he was issued royal standards with the arms of England and Spain in preparation for Catherine's army.[18] Elis Hilton, who in peacetime served as the head of Catherine's Wardrobe establishment, was temporarily put in charge of ordnance left behind in Plymouth and Southampton.[19] Catherine's ladies, too, did their part for Henry's war effort, busily sewing badges and standards for the king to use in France.[20]

Catherine's time as regent probably deepened her understanding of the machinery of the English government, because in addition to war preparations she also oversaw the mundane business of the Crown. As regent, she had the power to distribute the Crown's church patronage worth less than 40 marks, and her warrants show her presenting churchmen with positions in the royal gift.[21] Catherine also distributed secular royal patronage during her regency, including grants of wardships, licences to acquire lands and bailiffships, all small but necessary acts that kept royal affairs running smoothly.[22] These activities, coupled with her extensive involvement in the defence of the realm, would have given Catherine a thorough understanding of how royal government operated on a daily basis as well as the experience of working with some of the king's most experienced administrators and bureaucrats, including Sir Thomas Lovell, treasurer of the household; Thomas Englefield, royal councillor and speaker of the House of Commons; and Sir John Cutte, treasurer of the chamber.[23]

During her time as regent Catherine continued to perform the usual duties of queenship. Her letters during this period are full of her concerns for the king's health and spiritual well-being. Because Catherine did not wish to distract the king, she sent some of her letters to Thomas Wolsey, then the king's almoner, who reported back news of the king's health and his movements. Catherine also ensured that she would have a steady stream of information from the campaign in France, using a system of two messengers, where one 'shal tarye there til another commeth and thi[s] [w]ay I shal here every weke fromthens'.[24] In her letter to Henry of 16 September 1513 she thanks God for the English

---

[17] TNA, MS SP 1/229, fo. 211. See also *LP* i/2, 1985.
[18] TNA, MS E101/417/3. See also *LP* i/2, 2243.
[19] *LP* i/2, 2059.
[20] *Original letters*, i. 83.
[21] *LP* i/2, 2137, no. 22; i/2, 2222, no. 2.
[22] *LP* i/2, 2137, nos 26, 30; i/2, 2222, no. 1.
[23] For the various activities of these councillors see Steven J. Gunn, *Henry VII's new men and the making of Tudor England*, New York 2016, ch. xvi.
[24] *Original letters*, i. 80.

victories and gently reminds the king to do the same: 'I am suer your Grace forgetteth not to doo this.'[25] Her piety goes further, as she then informs Henry that she will make a pilgrimage to Walsingham to pray for his safe return.

Catherine's regency was a once in a lifetime event, an extraordinary opportunity for her to wield power and govern England at the head of a regency council appointed by the king. Her success in that role probably cemented her reputation in England and across Europe as an admirable queen and formidable opponent.[26] As is clear from Catherine's letters, her position as regent was inseparable from her position as queen consort. Her concern with her husband's well-being, her close relationship with him and his household (shown in her letters to Wolsey), her deployment of magnificence to outfit her army correctly with royal banners (flying not only the king's arms but her own as well), and her thanks to God after Flodden were all natural extensions of her queenship. The circumstances of her regency brought her actions into greater relief by requiring the use of letters to convey thoughts that might have otherwise been expressed verbally, and by highlighting Catherine's actions because she was also the centre of government for a time. But when looked at closely, underneath the exciting stories of battlefield speeches was a truly competent queen carrying out her duties to king and kingdom as she always had done.

Margaret Tudor also became queen regent in 1513, though in drastically different and far more fraught circumstances than her sister-in-law. Catherine's triumph at Flodden was, for Margaret, a personal and political tragedy, as her husband and a large swathe of the Scottish nobility were killed fighting the English that day. Sometime before his death James had named Margaret both regent and guardian for their infant son James V in his now-lost testament. James's decision indicates the confidence that he had in his wife's ability to safeguard their son's inheritance. Regardless of what was to follow, the beginning of Margaret's regency is a powerful statement of the trust that James placed in his queen and the success of their royal partnership as it had developed over the past decade. Moreover, Margaret's regency, based on James IV's testament, was 'the only [Scottish] example of a sixteenth-century regent provided with an unambiguous, legally watertight and widely accepted statement of monarchical delegation to underpin her rule'.[27] According to Amy Blakeway, Margaret initially had support for her regency from the Scottish elite, and there is evidence that she was a politically active regent, who attended council sessions and had a degree of success in influencing their proceedings.[28]

---

[25] Ibid. i. 88.

[26] The popular prose pamphlet *Jack of Newbury* (1597) retains the memory of Catherine's regency during the Scottish invasion. See Roze Hentschell, *The culture of cloth in early modern England: textual construction of a national identity*, Aldershot 2008, 64–6.

[27] Blakeway, *Regency*, 24.

[28] Ibid. 71–3.

Like Catherine's, Margaret's regency reflected the roles and, in her case, the limitations of her career as James IV's queen consort, in both the success that she initially experienced as regent and the problems that she later faced, which ultimately cost her the regency and forced her to flee for England. Margaret's regency began to break down due to a combination of factors, some of which were outside her control: the old hatred of the Scots for the English; the strong preference of some Scots for turning the regency over to John, duke of Albany, and the heir presumptive, who had the backing of the king of France.[29] However, it was her critical error in hastily marrying Archibald Douglas, earl of Angus, in August 1514 that legally voided the terms of her regency and lost her the support of the council. Margaret's marriage to Angus not only legally terminated her rights to the regency, but it also subjected the queen to the control of a new, politically inept, husband. It is not clear why Margaret chose to marry Angus: her decision may be related to the challenges that she faced upon suddenly becoming a young widow. Margaret had generally been dependent on her relationship with James IV during her queenship. Her financial resources, household organisation, and relative youth meant that much of her patronage, influence and financial support were closely bound up with her dependence on the king. When reading Margaret's letters to her brother and his advisors after Flodden, it is clear that one of her constant concerns was her inability to access her dower funds, and thus properly reward her household and equip herself as queen mother.[30] Facing issues like these in late 1514, Margaret may have felt that she needed the support that only a marriage to Scottish magnate like Angus could provide. Although this turned out to be serious error of judgement on her part, nevertheless, like her sister-in-law, Margaret's regency was closely tied to her experience as queen consort, and her successes and failures should be considered within this context.

This study has sought to understand how Catherine and Margaret created and maintained their roles as queens at the Renaissance courts of Britain. These women could easily be defined solely in terms of their relationships to their families: as daughters, wives or mothers. And these were important relationships to them, as is clear from their activities as patrons, courtly audiences, devout Christians and diplomats. But there were ultimately other rights and responsibilities that were part of Catherine's and Margaret's queenships. Following the example set by their predecessor Elizabeth of York, they were heads of households, patrons, hostesses, audiences, pilgrims and gift-givers. Taken together, these roles gave Catherine and Margaret access to loyal service, honourable status, cultural influence and political power. The pre-modern monarchies of England and Scotland greatly benefited from these queens, and not solely because they provided for the continuation of their dynasties.

---

[29] Ibid. 24–7.
[30] *Letters of royal and illustrious ladies*, i. 224–5, 229–30, 233.

CONCLUSION

Catherine's and Margaret's queenships meant opportunities for the expansion of monarchical power, as Henry and James worked with their wives to distribute rewards at court, amplify the monarchy through spectacle and magnificence and foster alliances amongst their nobility and abroad. Moreover, sixteenth-century moralists would have argued that their people benefitted from their social and moral examples as virtuous, pious and Christian queens.

Queenship was not something that was simply given to Catherine and Margaret. Throughout their lives, both women continually reasserted their positions in order to claim and maintain their honour and status as queens. Catherine and Margaret repeatedly used magnificence to maintain their queenly estate, harnessing the material culture and spectacle of the royal court to enhance their own roles. The use of fine fabrics for clothing and furniture was an expected and necessary part of being a queen, and the colours, furs, clothes and gems served to embody their queenly dignity to any who might see and know them as queens. Fine apparel supported Catherine and Margaret at moments of triumph, such as tournaments, court entertainments and public almsgivings as well as moments of crisis, such as their first confinements. This magnificence encompassed more than the queen's own body, as it included the granting of liveries and gowns to their servants, officers and ladies, who in turn amplified their performance of queenship whenever they accompanied the queen or acted in her name.

At court, Catherine and Margaret were the chief hostesses of the kingdom, and they presided over lavish spectacles and informal pastimes, which strengthened their public image and their relationship with their husbands. Hosting entertainments and acting as the audience to the king's exploits connected these queens and their ladies with the wider world of the court and their husband's households. This provided the opportunities for patronage and reward which made Catherine and Margaret sought-after patrons and cemented their reputation as good and generous ladies. Their patronage also worked to create ties between these foreign consorts and the native nobility through gift-giving and arranged marriages with their ladies. While nearly every foreign consort was expected to promote the marriages of her ladies, the willingness of both Henry and James also to promote these marriages signalled the strength of the royal partnerships.

This study has also shown that Catherine and Margaret connected and interacted with their subjects in a number of ways not easily understood from narrative accounts of their reigns. At court, both women provided important opportunities for sociability and royal display, which benefited their households as well as their own status as the king's public partners. On a wider scale, Catherine's and Margaret's performance of piety linked their personal religious beliefs and practices with their people through the distribution of alms and their pilgrimages. As devout Catholic queens, Catherine's and Margaret's religious practices were intended to be a Christian example to their people, and their piety was in many cases similar to the beliefs of most pre-Reformation Britons, creating a Christian community of the realm.

In her conclusion to *The last medieval queens,* Joanna Laynesmith notes that her study of fifteenth-century queenship can provide context for Henry VIII's attitude towards his marriages, and explain why his later behaviour was both an aberration and yet the continuation of a family tradition.[31] Catherine of Aragon's queenship provides a different kind of context for Henry's later marital adventures. Catherine was indeed the first foreign queen consort of an English king in nearly fifty years, and she was able to combine the ideals of medieval queenship with the cultural and political world of the Renaissance court with great success. Henry's later wives, especially Anne Boleyn and Katherine Parr, would similarly engage in this world, but they also had to survive at a court that now saw queens as disposable. Catherine's queenship developed over decades, and her status, dignity and honour would be unmatched by her successors.

Catherine's discursive performance of queenship over several decades sheds some light on how she was able to resist Henry's attempts to divorce her for many years without facing criticism or popular derision for assuming such an uncharacteristically antagonistic position *vis à vis* her king. Considering the wealth of scholarship on Catherine's divorce is beyond the scope of this study, but I hope that my work points towards new questions and considerations of Catherine during the divorce crisis. She was not merely a 'Catholic martyr' or a dependant of her nephew, the emperor Charles V. Although many extant accounts concerning the divorce show Catherine in these roles, they do not explain her personal popularity or the unblemished reputation that protected her from the types of misogynistic insults levelled at her successor, Anne Boleyn.[32] Was Catherine's support amongst the common people connected to memories of her pilgrimages and almsgiving? Was the respect that she received a reflection of her success in deploying the magnificent trappings of Renaissance monarchy and fulfilling her social roles? Highlighting Catherine's uncontroversial decades as queen consort, expands Catherine's history beyond the religious, diplomatic and personal themes that typically feature in analyses of the divorce.

These questions reiterate the importance of successful queenship to the functioning of pre-modern monarchy. The partnership between the king and queen not only enhanced the queen's power and authority, but also gave the king new opportunities to assert his own magnificence, largesse and dynastic prestige. By establishing the queen as his true public partner, Henry VIII certainly could not have intended to provide the foundation for Catherine's future opposition to the divorce. What he surely could have anticipated,

---

[31] Laynesmith, *Last medieval queens,* 262-3. Henry VIII's grandfather Edward IV fell in love with and married an English widow, Elizabeth Woodville, instead of making a traditional foreign alliance to a virgin princess. Perhaps Henry VIII's marriage to Catherine fits this pattern of love matches, as the young Henry had known Catherine for years at his father's court and likely saw himself as her 'white knight' when her married her in 1509.

[32] For a consideration of the nature of Catherine's public support after 1533 see Elston, 'Widow princess', 20-4.

however, was that his queen could become the most valuable ally that he could hope for in ensuring the success of their dynasty. As it turns out, this partnership worked rather too well, as demonstrated by Catherine's defiance during the divorce crisis: her commitment to their daughter Mary's legitimacy and inheritance was unshakeable.[33] Margaret was certainly on her way to establishing a similar type of partnership with her husband, and James's decision to appoint her guardian and regent for their son indicates his confidence in her. The differences between Margaret's and Catherine's queenships show that this process was incomplete for Margaret in 1513. The political chaos after James's death indicates that a fuller partnership between the king and queen might have given her the experience necessary to rule alone as regent without feeling the need for remarriage. Catherine's and Margaret's reigns show that for pre-modern dynasties to survive and the power of the monarchy to continue, monarchs needed their queens to be more than royal baby-makers. Queens were necessary public partners without whom few kings could succeed.

---

[33] For a discussion of the potential consequences for Catherine and her daughter if she had acquiesced in Henry's request for an annulment see J. F. Hadwin, 'Katherine of Aragon and the veil', *JEH* lxvi (2015), 509–23.

Bibliography

Unpublished primary sources

Cambridge, St John's College archives
MS D102.11   List of officers attending on Queen Elizabeth and Princess Catherine, 1501

Edinburgh, National Records of Scotland
E21/6-12   Accounts of the Lord High Treasurer of Scotland, 16 Sept. 1502-8 Aug. 1513
E32/1   Exchequer records: household expenditure, Sept. 1511-Aug. 1512
E34/2   Miscellaneous papers and accounts relating to the royal household of James IV, 1510
GD156/9   Elphinstone muniments: miscellaneous documents, 1513
SP 13/23   State papers: indenture on receipt by William Husband, *et al.*, citizens of Carlisle, on behalf of Queen Margaret, of specified jewels and material belonging to her, 16 Sept. 1516

Kew, The National Archives
E36/123   Book of receipts and payments of Robert Fowler, clerk of John Heron, Treasurer of the Chamber, 1502-3
E36/215   King's book of payments, 1509-17
E36/216   King's book of payments, 1517-20
E36/246   Book of sales of wards, 1526-9
E101/417/2   Warrants subsidiary to accounts of Sir John Heron, Treasurer of the Chamber, 1509-20
E101/417/4   Accounts of the Great Wardrobe, Andrew Wyndsore, 1510-12
E101/417/12   Documents subsidiary to accounts of John Heron, Treasurer of the Chamber, 1512-20
E101/418/6   Account book of Richard Justice, Groom of the Robes to Catherine of Aragon, Apr. 1515-Apr. 1517
E101/420/4   New Year's gifts given at Greenwich, 1528
E298/5-31   Petitions and proceedings in equity before the queen's council, c.1509-32
E315/242/3   Account book of Elis Hilton, Yeoman of the Robes, April-May, 1520
E404/84   Warrants for issues, 1501-3
E404/87   Warrants for issues, 1509-11
E404/90   Warrants for issues, 1515-17
LC2/1   Lord Chamberlain's department: records of special events, accounts of funerals and mournings, 1500-96
LC9/50   Lord Chamberlain's accounts concerning special events, 1483-1509
PROB/11   Will registers, Probate Court of Canterbury, 1384-1858
SP 1   State papers series Henry VIII, 1509-47, accessed *via State Papers Online*

London, British Library

MS Add. 21481	Household book of Henry VIII, 1509-18
MS Add. 38174	Book of English court ceremonies, c.1485
MS Cotton appendix LXV	Accounts of Griffith Richards, Receiver-General to Catherine of Aragon, 1525-30
MS Cotton Titus C VII	Miscellaneous papers, c.1558-1625
MS Cotton Vespasian C XIV	Miscellaneous papers (originals and transcripts) concerning England, 1400-1650
MS Egerton 985	Ceremonials and heraldic proceedings, c.1485-c.1537
MS Royal 7 F XIV	State papers, Henry VIII, 1534-5
MS Royal 11 E XI	Magister Sampson, Benedictus de Opitiis and others, motets, c. 1516
MS Royal app. 89	State papers, Henry VIII, 1509-c.1600

Manchester, John Rylands Library

MS Latin 239	Account books of Elis Hilton and Richard Justice, 1520

Published primary sources

Accounts of the Lord High Treasurer of Scotland, ed. Thomas Dickson and James Balfour Paul, Edinburgh 1877-1916

Alumni cantabrigienses: a biographical list of all known students, graduates and holders of office at the University of Cambridge, from the earliest times to 1900, ed. J. A. Venn, Cambridge 1922

Anne of France: lessons for my daughter, ed. Sharon L. Jansen, Woodbridge 2004

Barlow, Montague, *Barlow family records*, London 1932

Calendar of documents relating to Scotland, ed. Joseph Bain, Edinburgh 1881-8

Calendar of letters, despatches, and state papers, relating to the negotiations between England and Spain, preserved in the archives at Simancas, Vienna, Brussels and elsewhere, ed. G. A. Bergenroth and others, London 1862

Calendar of state papers and manuscripts relating to English affairs: existing in the archives and collections of Venice, and in other libraries of Northern Italy, ed. Rawdon Brown, London 1864

La casa de Isabel la Católica, ed. Antonio de la Torre, Madrid 1954

Castiglione, Baldesar, *The book of the courtier*, trans. George Bull, New York 1978

A collection of inventories and other records of the Royal Wardrobe and Jewelhouse: and of the artillery and munitioun in some of the royal castles, ed. Thomas Thomson Edinburgh 1815

Dillon, Janette, *Performance and spectacle in Hall's Chronicle*, London 2002

Du Wés, Giles, *An introductorie for to lerne to rede, to pronounce, and to speake Frenche trewly compyled for the right high, excellent, and most vertuous lady, the lady Mary of Englande, doughter to our most gracious souerayn lorde kyng Henry the eight.*, London 1533

Dunbar, William, *The poems of William Dunbar*, ed. James Kinsley, Oxford 1979

The Exchequer rolls of Scotland, ed. John Stuart and others, 1878-1908

Extracts from the council register of the burgh of Aberdeen, 1398–1570, ed. John Stuart, Aberdeen 1844

Fasti ecclesiae anglicanae, 1300–1541, ed. John le Neve, London 1964

Fraser, William, *The Lennox*, Edinburgh 1874, ii

— *The Elphinstone family book of the Lords Elphinstone, Balmaerino, and Coupar*, Edinburgh 1897

Giustiniani, Sebastiano, *Four years at the court of Henry VIII*, ed. Rawdon Brown, London 1854

Hall, Edward, *Hall's chronicle: containing the history of England, during the reign of Henry the Fourth, and the succeeding monarchs, to the end of the reign of Henry the Eighth, in which are particularly described the manners and customs of those periods*, London 1809

'Inventories of the wardrobes, plate, chapel stuff, &c. of Henry Fitzroy, duke of Richmond and Katherine, princess dowager', ed. John Gough Nichols (Camden o.s. lxi, 1854), 23–41

'King Henry VIII's jewel book', ed. Edward Trollope, *Associated Architectural Societies* xvii/2 (1883–4), 155–229

Leslie, John, *The history of Scotland, from the death of King James I, in the year M.CCCC.XXXVI, to the year M.D.LXI*, trans. James Dalrymple, Edinburgh 1895, ii

Letters and papers, foreign and domestic, of the reign of Henry VIII, 1509–1547, ed. J. S. Brewer and others, London 1862–1932

Letters and papers of the Verney family down to the year 1639, ed. John Bruce (Camden o.s. lvi 1853)

Letters of royal and illustrious ladies of Great Britain, from the commencement of the twelfth century to the close of the reign of Queen Mary, ed. M. A. E. Green, London 1846

The Lisle letters, ed. Muriel St Clare Byrne, Chicago 1981

Madox, Thomas, *Formulare anglicanum: or, A collection of ancient charters and instruments*, London 1702

Mémoires de Martin et Guillaume Du Bellay, ed. V. L. Bourilly and F. Vindry, Paris 1908, i

'Ordinances for the household made at Eltham in the XVIIth Year of King Henry VIII AD 1526', in *A collection of ordinances and regulations for the government of the royal household, made in divers reigns*, London 1790

'Original documents relating to Queen Katharine of Arragon', *Gentlemen's Magazine and Historical Review* cxxxv/2 (1854), 572–5

Original letters, illustrative of English history; including numerous royal letters: from autographs in the British Museum, and one or two other collections, ed. Henry Ellis, London 1824.

Pinkerton, John, *The history of Scotland from the accession of the house of Stuart to that of Mary*, London 1797

Pizan, Christine de, *The book of the city of ladies*, trans. Rosalind Brown-Grant, London 1999

— *The treasure of the city of ladies*, trans. Sarah Lawson, New York 2003

Privy Purse expenses of Elizabeth of York: Wardrobe accounts of Edward the Fourth, ed. Nicholas Harris Nicholas, New York 1972

The receyt of the ladie Kateryne, ed. Gordon Kipling, Oxford 1990

The register of the great seal of Scotland, ed. John Balfour Paul, Edinburgh 1882–1914

The register of the privy seal of Scotland, ed. M. Livingstone, Edinburgh 1908

Rymer, Thomas, *Foedera, conventiones, litterae, et cujuscunque generis acta publica inter reges angliae*, London 1704-35
State papers published under the authority of His Majesty's Commission: King Henry the Eighth (Record Commission, 1830-52)
Vergil, Polydore, *Three books of Polydore Vergil's English history, comprising the reigns of Henry VI, Edward IV, and Richard III*, ed. Henry Ellis, London 1844
Vives, Juan Luis, *The education of a Christian woman: a sixteenth-century manual*, ed. Charles Fantazzi, Chicago 2000
Young, John, 'The fyancells of Margaret, eldest daughter of King Henry VIIth to James king of Scotland', in John Leland (ed.), *Joannis Lelandi antiquarii de rebus britannicis collectanea*, London 1770, iv. 258-300

Secondary sources

Ago, Renate, 'Maria Spada Veralli, la buona moglie', in Giulia Calvi (ed.), *Barocco al femminile*, Rome 1992, 53-70
Akkerman, Nadine and Birgit Houben, (eds), *The politics of female households: ladies-in-waiting across early modern Europe*, Boston 2014
Anderson, Ruth Matilda, *Hispanic costume, 1480-1530*, New York 1979
Anglo, Sydney, 'The London pageants for the reception of Katharine of Aragon: November 1501', *Journal of the Warburg and Courtauld Institutes* xxvi (1963), 53-89
— 'The evolution of the early Tudor disguising, pageant, and mask', *Renaissance Drama* i (1968), 3-44
— *Spectacle, pageantry, and early Tudor policy*, Oxford 1997
Appleford, Amy, 'Shakespeare's Katherine of Aragon: last medieval queen, first recusant martyr', *JMEMS* xl (2010), 149-71
Aram, Bethany, *Juana the Mad: sovereignty and dynasty in Renaissance Europe*, Baltimore 2005
Arthurson, Ian, '"The king of Spain's daughter came to visit me": marriage, princes and politics', in Monckton and Gunn, *Arthur Tudor*, 20-30
Ashbee, Andrew, 'Groomed for service: musicians in the Privy Chamber at the English court, c. 1495-1558', *EM* xxv (1997), 185-97
Aston, Margaret, *Lollards and Reformers: images and literacy in late medieval religion*, London 1984
Attreed, Lorraine, 'Gender, patronage, and diplomacy in the early career of Margaret of Austria (1480-1530)', *Mediterranean Studies* xx (2012), 3-27
Backhouse, Janet, 'Illuminated manuscripts, associated with Henry VII and members of his immediate family', in Thompson, *Reign of Henry VII*, 175-87
Balfour, James, *The Scots peerage: founded on Wood's edition of Sir Robert Douglas's Peerage of Scotland*, Edinburgh 1904
Barrell, A. D. M., 'Royal presentations to ecclesiastical benefices in late medieval Scotland', *IR* lv (2004), 181-204
Barrow, Lorna G., '"The kynge sent to the qwene, by a gentylman, a grett tame hart": marriage, gift exchange, and politics: Margaret Tudor and James IV, 1502-13', *Parergon* xxi (2004), 65-84
Bawcutt, Priscilla, *Dunbar the makar*, Oxford 1992

- 'Crossing the border: Scottish poetry and English readers in the sixteenth century', in Mapstone and Wood, *Rose and the thistle*, 59-76
- '"My bright buke": women and their books in medieval and Renaissance Scotland', in Jocelyn Wogan-Browne and Felicity Riddy (eds), *Medieval women: texts and contexts in late medieval Britain: essays for Felicity Riddy*, Turnhout 2000

Beer, Michelle L., 'A queenly affinity? Catherine of Aragon's estates and Henry VIII's Great Matter,' *Historical Research*

Bercusson, Sarah, 'The duchess' court in sixteenth-century Italy: a comparison of female experience', in Calvi and Chabot, *Moving elites*, 127-40
- 'Giovanna d'Austria and the art of appearances: textiles and dress at the Florentine court', *RS* xxix (2015), 683-700

Bernard, G. W., 'Vitality and vulnerability in the late medieval Church: pilgrimage on the eve of the break with Rome', in John Lovett Watts (ed.), *The end of the Middle Ages? England in the fifteenth and sixteenth centuries*, Stroud 1998, 199-233
- and Steven J. Gunn (eds), *Authority and consent in Tudor England: essays presented to C. S. L. Davies*, Aldershot 2002

Blakeway, Amy, *Regency in sixteenth-century Scotland*, Woodbridge 2015

Boardman, Steve and Julian Goodare (eds), *Kings, lords and men in Scotland and Britain, 1300-1625: essays in honour of Jenny Wormald*, Edinburgh 2014

Bossy, John, *Christianity in the West, 1400-1700*, Oxford 1985

Broomhall, Susan, 'Gendering the culture of honour at the fifteenth-century Burgundian court', in Broomhall and Tarbin, *Women, identities and communities*, 181-93
- and Stephanie Tarbin (eds), *Women, identities and communities in early modern Europe*, Aldershot 2008

Brown, Elizabeth A., '"Companion me with my mistress": Cleopatra, Elizabeth I, and their waiting women', in Susan Frye and Karen Robertson (eds), *Maids and mistresses, cousins and queens: women's alliances in early modern England*, New York 1998, 131-48

Buchanan, Patricia Hill, *Margaret Tudor, queen of Scots*, Edinburgh 1985

Bumke, Joachim, *Courtly culture: literature and society in the high Middle Ages*, trans. Thomas Dunlap, Berkeley 1991

Cahill Marron, Emma, 'Una Lucrecia del siglo XVI: los libros de Catalina de Aragón', in Sandro De Maria and Manuel Parada López de Corselas (eds), *El imperio y las Hispanias de Trajano a Carlos V: clasicismo y poder en el arte español*, Bologna 2014, 419-28

Calvi, Giulia and Isabelle Chabot (eds), *Moving elites: women and cultural transfers in the European court system*, San Domenico di Fiesole 2010

Carpenter, Sarah, 'The sixteenth-century court audience: performers and spectators', *MET* xix (1997), 3-14
- '"To thexaltacyon of noblesse": a herald's account of the marriage of Margaret Tudor and James IV', *MET* xxix (2007), 104-20

Cashman III, Anthony B., 'Performance anxiety: Federico Gonzaga at the court of Francis I and the uncertainty of ritual action', *SCJ* xxxiii (2002), 333-52

Castro, Manuel de, 'Confesores Franciscanos en la corte de los reyes Catolicos', *Archivo Ibero-Americano* xxxiv (1974), 55-126

Chapman, Hester W., *The sisters of Henry VIII*, London 1969

Collette, Carolyn P., *Performing polity: women and agency in the Anglo-French tradition, 1385-1620*, Turnhout 2006

Cowan, Mairi, *Death, life, and religious change in Scottish towns, c. 1350-1560*, New York 2012

Cox-Rearick, Janet, 'Power-dressing at the courts of Cosimo de' Medici and François I: the "moda alla spagnola" of Spanish consorts Eléonore d'Autriche and Eleonora di Toledo', *Artibus et Historiae* xxx (2009), 39-69

Crawford, Anne, 'The piety of late medieval English queens', in Caroline M. Barron and Christopher Harper-Bill (eds), *The Church in pre-Reformation society: essays in honour of F. R. H. Du Boulay*, Dover 1985, 48-57

Crawford, Katherine, *Perilous performances: gender and regency in early modern France*, Cambridge, MA 2004

— *European sexualities, 1400-1800*, Cambridge 2007

Crawford, Patricia, 'Attitudes to menstruation in seventeenth-century England', *P&P* (May 1981), 47-73

Crum, Roger J., 'Controlling women or women controlled? Suggestions for gender roles and visual culture in the Italian Renaissance', in Sheryl E. Reiss and David G. Wilkins (eds), *Beyond Isabella: secular women patrons of art in Renaissance Italy*, Kirksville, MO 2001, 37-50

Cruz, Anne J. and Mihoko Suzuki (eds), *The rule of women in early modern Europe*, Urbana 2009.

Cunningham, Sean, *Henry VII*, London 2007

Currin, John M., '"Pro expensis ambassatorum": diplomacy and financial administration in the reign of Henry VII', *EHR* cviii (1993), 589-609

Damen, Mario, 'Gift exchange at the court of Charles the Bold', in Marc Boone and Martha C. Howell (eds), *In but not of the market: movable goods in the late medieval and early modern economy*, Brussels 2007

Davies, C. S. L., 'Tudor: what's in a name?', *History* xcvii (2012), 24-42

Davis, Natalie Zemon, *The gift in sixteenth-century France*, Madison, WI 2000

Daybell, James, 'Gender, politics and diplomacy: women, news and intelligence networks in Elizabethan England', in Robyn Adams and Rosanna Cox (eds), *Diplomacy and early modern culture*, Basingstoke 2011, 101-19

Dewhurst, John, 'The alleged miscarriages of Catherine of Aragon and Anne Boleyn', *Medical History* xxviii (1984), 49-56

Dickinson, J. C., *The shrine of Our Lady of Walsingham*, Cambridge 1956

Ditchburn, David, '"Saints at the door don't make miracles?" The contrasting fortunes of Scottish pilgrimage c. 1450-1550', in Julian Goodare and A. A. MacDonald (eds), *Sixteenth-century Scotland: essays in honour of Michael Lynch*, Leiden 2008, 69-98

Dowling, Maria, *Humanism in the age of Henry VIII*, London 1986

Downie, Fiona, *She is but a woman: queenship in Scotland, 1424-1463*, Edinburgh 2006

Duffy, Eamon, *The stripping of the altars: traditional religion in England, c. 1400-c. 1580*, New Haven, CT 2005

Duindam, Jeroen, 'The politics of female households: afterthoughts', in Akkerman and Houben, *Politics of female households*, 365-70

— *Dynasties: a global history of power, 1300-1800*, Cambridge 2016

Dumitrescu, Theodor, *The early Tudor court and international musical relations*, Aldershot 2007

Dunbar, John G., *Scottish royal palaces: the architecture of the royal residences during the late medieval and early Renaissance periods*, East Linton 1999

Dunlop, David, 'The "masked comedian": Perkin Warbeck's adventures in Scotland and England from 1495 to 1497', *Scottish Historical Review* lxx (1991), 97-128

— 'The politics of peace-keeping: Anglo-Scottish relations from 1503-1511', *RS* viii (1994), 138-61

Earenfight, Theresa, 'Partners in politics', in Theresa Earenfight (ed.), *Queenship and political power in medieval and early modern Spain*, Burlington, VT 2005, pp. xiii-xxix

— 'Without the *persona* of the prince: kings, queens and the idea of monarchy in late medieval Europe', *G&H* xix (2007), 1-21

— *The king's other body: María of Castile and the Crown of Aragon*, Philadelphia 2010

— 'Regarding Catherine of Aragon', in Carole Levin and Christine Stewart-Nuñez (eds), *Scholars and poets talk about queens*, New York 2015, 137-57

— 'Raising infanta Catalina de Aragón to be Catherine queen of England', *Anuario de Estudios Medievales* xlvi (2016), 417-43

Elliott, Dyan, 'Dress as mediator between inner and outer self: the pious matron of the high and later Middle Ages', *Mediaeval Studies* liii (1991), 279-308

Elston, Timothy G., 'Transformation or continuity? Sixteenth-century education and the legacy of Catherine of Aragon, Mary I and Juan Luis Vives', in Levin, Carney and Barrett-Graves, *'High and mighty queens'*, 11-26

— 'Widow princess or neglected queen? Catherine of Aragon, Henry VIII and English public opinion, 1533-1536', in Carole Levin and Robert O. Bucholz (eds), *Queens & power in medieval and early modern England*, Lincoln 2009, 16-30

Fissell, Mary Elizabeth, *Vernacular bodies: the politics of reproduction in early modern England*, Oxford 2006

Fitch, Audrey-Beth, 'Mothers and their sons: Mary and Jesus in Scotland, 1450-1560', in Steve Boardman and Eila Williamson (eds), *The cult of saints and the Virgin Mary in medieval Scotland*, Woodbridge 2010, 159-76

Fletcher, Catherine, '"Furnished with gentlemen": the ambassador's house in sixteenth-century Italy', *RS* xxiv (2010), 518-35

Fox, Adam, *Oral and literate culture in England, 1500-1700*, Oxford 2000

Fradenburg, Louise Olga, *City, marriage, tournament: arts of rule in late medieval Scotland*, Madison 1991

— 'Sovereign love: the wedding of Margaret Tudor and James IV of Scotland', in Louise Olga Fradenburg (ed.), *Women and sovereignty*, Edinburgh 1992, 78-100

— 'Troubled times: Margaret Tudor and the historians', in Mapstone and Wood, *Rose and the thistle*, 38-58

Franklin-Harkrider, Melissa, *Women, reform and community in early modern England: Katherine Willoughby, duchess of Suffolk, and Lincolnshire's godly aristocracy, 1519-1580*, Woodbridge 2008

Fraser, Antonia, *The six wives of Henry VIII*, London 1993

Fulton, Helen, 'A woman's place: Guinevere in the Welsh and French romances', *Quondam et Futurus* ii (1993), 1-25

Gibbons, Rachel C., 'The queen as "social mannequin": consumerism and expenditure at the court of Isabeau of Bavaria, 1393-1422', *Journal of Medieval History* xxvi (2000), 371-95

Gibson, Gail McMurray, *The theater of devotion: East Anglian drama and society in the late Middle Ages*, Chicago 1989

Glanville, Philippa, *Silver in Tudor and early Stuart England: a social history and catalogue of the national collection*, London 1990

Grant, Alexander, *Independence and nationhood: Scotland, 1306–1469*, London 1984

Gray, Douglas, 'The royal entry in sixteenth-century Scotland', in Mapstone and Wood, *Rose and the thistle*, 10–37

Gunn, Steven J., 'Chivalry and the politics of the early Tudor court', in Sydney Anglo (ed.), *Chivalry in the Renaissance*, Woodbridge 1990, 107–28

— 'The early Tudor tournament', in Starkey, *Henry VIII: a European court*, 47–9

— *Early Tudor government, 1485–1558*, New York 1995

— 'The structures of politics in early Tudor England', *Transactions of the Royal Historical Society* v (1995), 59–90

— 'War, dynasty and public opinion in early Tudor England', in Bernard and Gunn, *Authority and consent*, 131–49

— 'Prince Arthur's preparation for kingship', in Monckton and Gunn, *Arthur Tudor*, 7–19

— *Henry VII's new men and the making of Tudor England*, New York 2016

Gwyn, Peter, 'Wolsey's foreign policy: the conferences at Calais and Bruges reconsidered', *HJ* xxiii (1980), 755–72

Hadwin, J. F., 'Katherine of Aragon and the veil', *JEH* lxvi (2015), 509–23

Hamilton, Dakota L., 'The learned councils of the Tudor queens consort', in Charles Carlton (ed.), *State, sovereigns & society in early modern England: essays in honour of A. J. Slavin*, New York 1998, 87–101

Hammond, P. W., 'The coronation of Elizabeth of York', *The Ricardian* vi (1983), 270–2

Hanham, Alison, 'Edmund de la Pole, defector', *RS* ii (1988), 240–50

Hansen, Matthew C., '"And a queen of England, too": the "Englishing" of Catherine of Aragon in sixteenth-century English literary and chronicle history', in Levin, Carney and Barrett-Graves, *'High and mighty queens'*, 79–100

Harris, Barbara J., 'The view from my lady's chamber: new perspectives on the early Tudor monarchy', *HLQ* lx (1997), 215–47

— *English aristocratic women, 1450–1550: marriage and family, property and careers*, New York 2002

Harris, Kate, 'Richard Pynson's "Remembraunce for the traduction of the princesse Kateryne": the printer's contribution to the reception of Catherine of Aragon', *Library* xii (1990), 89–109

Harvey, Nancy Lenz, *The rose and the thorn: the lives of Mary and Margaret Tudor*, New York 1975

Hayward, Maria, 'Fashion, finance, foreign politics and the wardrobe of Henry VIII', in Richardson, *Clothing culture*, 165–78

— 'Gift giving at the court of Henry VIII: the 1539 New Year's gift roll in context', *Antiquaries Journal* lxxxv (2005), 124–75

— 'Crimson, scarlet, murrey and carnation: red at the court of Henry VIII', *Textile History* xxxviii (2007), 135–50

— *Dress at the court of King Henry VIII: the wardrobe book of the Wardrobe of the Robes prepared by James Worsley in December 1516; edited from MS Harley 2284, and his inventory prepared on 17 January 1521, edited from Harley MS 4217, both in the British Library*, Leeds 2007

- *Rich apparel: clothing and the law in Henry VIII's England*, Burlington, VT 2009
- 'Spanish princess or queen of England? The image, identity, and influence of Catherine of Aragon at the courts of Henry VII and Henry VIII', in José Luis Colomer and Amalia Descalzo (eds), *Spanish fashion at the courts of early modern Europe*, Madrid 2014, 11-36

Heal, Felicity, *Hospitality in early modern England*, Oxford 1990
- 'Food gifts, the household and the politics of exchange in early modern England', *P&P* cxcix (May 2008), 41-70
- 'Royal gifts and gift-exchange in sixteenth-century Anglo-Scottish politics', in Boardman and Goodare, *Kings, lords and men*, 283-300
- *The power of gifts: gift exchange in early modern England*, New York 2015

Heijnsbergen, Theo van, 'The Scottish chapel royal as cultural intermediary between town and court', in A. A. MacDonald and Jan Willem Drijvers (eds), *Centres of learning: learning and location in pre-modern Europe and the Near East*, Leiden 1995, 299-313

Hentschell, Roze, 'A question of nation: foreign clothes on the English subjects', in Richardson, *Clothing culture*, 49-62
- *The culture of cloth in early modern England: textual construction of a national identity*, Aldershot 2008

Hepburn, William, 'William Dunbar and the courtmen: poetry as a source for the court of James IV', *IR* lxv (2014), 95-112

Hibbard, Caroline, 'The role of a queen consort: the household and court of Henrietta Maria, 1625-1642', in Ronald G. Asch and Adolf M. Birke (eds), *Princes, patronage, and the nobility: the court at the beginning of the modern age, c.1450-1650*, New York 1991, 393-414
- 'Henrietta Maria in the 1630s: perspectives on the role of consort queens in *ancien régime* courts', in Ian Atherton and Julie Sanders (eds), *The 1630s: interdisciplinary essays on culture and politics in the Caroline era*, Manchester 2006, 92-110

Higgins, Paula, 'The "other Minervas": creative women at the court of Margaret of Scotland', in Kimberly Marshall (ed.), *Rediscovering the muses: women's musical traditions*, Boston 1993

Hochner, Nicole, 'Revisiting Anne de Bretagne's queenship: on love and bridles', in Cynthia J. Brown (ed.), *The cultural and political legacy of Anne de Bretagne: negotiating convention in books and documents*, Cambridge 2010, 147-62

Houston, R. A., 'What did the royal almoner do in Britain and Ireland, c. 1450-1700?', *EHR* cxxv (2010), 279-313

Howe, Elizabeth, *Education and women in the early modern Hispanic world*, Aldershot 2008

Howey, Catherine L., 'Fashioning monarchy: women, dress and power at the court of Elizabeth I: 1553-1603', in Cruz and Suzuki, *Rule of women*, 142-56

Hufton, Olwen, 'Reflections on the role of women in the early modern court', *TCH* v (2000), 1-14

Huneycutt, Lois L., *Matilda of Scotland: a study in medieval queenship*, Woodbridge 2003

Hunt, Alice, *The drama of coronation: medieval ceremony in early modern England*, Cambridge 2008

Ives, Eric W., *The life and death of Anne Boleyn*, Oxford 2004

Jack, Sybil, 'In praise of queens: the public presentation of the virtuous consort in seventeenth-century Britain', in Broomhall and Tarbin, *Women, identities and communities*, 211-24

Jansen, Sharon, *The monstrous regiment of women: female rulers in early modern Europe*, New York 2002

Johnston, Hope, 'How the *Livre de la cité des dames* first came to be printed in England', in Liliane Dulac, Anne Paupert, Christine Reno and Bernard Ribémont (eds), *Desireuse de plus avant enquerre*, Paris 2008, 385-96

Johnstone, Hilda, 'The queen's exchequer under the three Edwards', in J. G. Edwards, V. H. Galbraith and E. F. Jacob (eds), *Historical essays in honour of James Tait*, Manchester 1933, 143-53

Jones, Ann Rosalind and Peter Stallybrass, *Renaissance clothing and the materials of memory*, Cambridge 2000

Jones, Michael K. and Malcolm G. Underwood, *The king's mother: Lady Margaret Beaufort, countess of Richmond and Derby*, New York 1992

Kantorowicz, Ernst H., *The king's two bodies: a study in medieval political theology*, Princeton 1957

Kaufman, Peter Iver, 'Piety and proprietary rights: James IV of Scotland, 1488-1513', *SCJ* xiii (1982), 83-99

Keen, Maurice, *Chivalry*, New Haven 1984

Kelly, Catherine, 'The noble steward and late-feudal lordship', *HLQ* xlix (1986), 133-48

Kerry, C., *A history of the municipal church of St Lawrence, Reading*, Reading 1883

Kettering, Sharon, 'Gift-giving and patronage in early modern France', *French History* ii (1988), 131-51

— 'The patronage power of early modern French noblewomen', *HJ* xxxii (1989), 817-41

Kipling, Gordon, *The triumph of honour: Burgundian origins of the Elizabethan Renaissance*, The Hague 1977

Kisby, Fiona, '"When the king goeth a procession": chapel ceremonies and services, the ritual year, and religious reforms at the early Tudor court, 1485-1547', *JBS* xl (2001), 44-75

Kolk, Caroline zum, 'The household of the queen of France in the sixteenth century', *TCH* xiv (2009), 3-22

— 'Catherine de Médicis et l'espace: résidences, voyages et séjours', in Calvi and Chabot, *Moving elites*, 51-61

Lawson, Jane A., *The Elizabethan New Year's gift exchanges, 1559-1603*, Oxford 2013

Laynesmith, Joanna L., *The last medieval queens: English queenship, 1445-1503*, New York 2004

— 'Telling tales of adulterous queens in medieval England: from Olympias of Macedonia to Elizabeth Woodville', in C. P. Melville and Lynette G. Mitchell (eds), *Every inch a king: comparative studies on kings and kingship in the ancient and medieval worlds*, Leiden 2013, 195-214

Lehfeldt, Elizabeth A., 'Ruling sexuality: the political legitimacy of Isabel of Castile', *Renaissance Quarterly* liii (2000), 31-56

Lerer, Seth, '"Representyd now in yower syght": the culture of spectatorship in late-fifteenth century England', in Barbara A. Hanawalt and Gail McMurray Gibson (eds), *Bodies and disciplines: intersections of literature and history in fifteenth-century England*, Minneapolis 1996, 139-54

L'Estrange, Elizabeth, *Holy motherhood: gender, dynasty and visual culture in the later Middle Ages*, Manchester 2008

Levin, Carole, '"Would I could give you help and succour": Elizabeth I and the politics of touch', *Albion* xxi (1989), 191–205

— *The heart and stomach of a king: Elizabeth I and the politics of sex and power*, Philadelphia 1994

— 'The taming of the queen: Foxe's Catherine and Shakespeare's Kate', in Levin, Carney and Barrett-Graves, *'High and mighty queens'*, 171–86

— Jo Eldridge Carney and Debra Barrett-Graves (eds), *'High and mighty queens' of early modern England: realities and representations*, New York 2003

Lewis, Katherine, *Kingship and masculinity in late medieval England*, New York 2013

Licence, Amy and Philippa Gregory, *Catherine of Aragon: an intimate life of Henry VIII's true wife*, Stroud 2017

Liss, Peggy K., *Isabel the queen: life and times*, Philadelphia 2004

Loach, Jennifer, 'The function of ceremonial in the reign of Henry VIII', *P&P* (Feb. 1994), 43–68

Loades, D. M., *Henry VIII and his queens*, Stroud 1996

McCleery, Iona, 'Isabel of Aragon (d. 1336): model queen or model saint?', *JEH* lvii (2006), 668–92

MacDonald, A. A., 'Princely culture in Scotland under James III and James IV', in Martin Gosman, A. A. MacDonald and Arie Johan Vanderjagt (eds), *Princes and princely culture, 1450–1650*, Leiden 2003, i. 147–72

Macdougall, Norman, *James IV*, East Linton 1998

Macfarlane, Leslie, *William Elphinstone and the kingdom of Scotland, 1431–1514: the struggle for order*, Aberdeen 1985

McIntosh, Jeri L., *From heads of household to heads of state: the preaccession households of Mary and Elizabeth Tudor, 1516–1558*, New York 2009

Maclean, Ian, *The Renaissance notion of woman: a study in the fortunes of scholasticism and medical science in European intellectual life*, Cambridge 1980

McManus, Caroline, 'Queen Elizabeth, dol common, and the performance of the Royal Maundy', *English Literary Renaissance* xxxii (2002), 189–213

Malcolmson, Cristina, 'Christine de Pizan's *City of ladies* in early modern England', in Cristina Malcolmson and Mihoko Suzuki (eds), *Debating gender in early modern England, 1500–1700*, New York 2002, 15–35

Mann, Catherine, 'Clothing bodies, dressing rooms: fashioning fecundity in the Lisle letters', *Parergon* xxii (2005), 137–57

Mapstone, Sally and Juliette Wood (eds), *The rose and the thistle: essays on the culture of late medieval and Renaissance Scotland*, East Linton 1998

Marshall, Rosalind K., *Mary of Guise*, London 1977

Martin, A. Lynn, 'National reputations for drinking in traditional Europe', *Parergon* xvii (1999), 163–86

— 'The baptism of wine', *Gastronomica* iii (2003), 21–30

Mason, Roger A., 'Beyond the Declaration of Arbroath: kingship, counsel and consent in late medieval and early modern Scotland', in Boardman and Goodare, *Kings, lords and men*, 265–82

Mattingly, Garrett, 'The reputation of doctor de Puebla', *EHR* lv (1940), 27–46

— *Catherine of Aragon*, New York 1960

Mauss, Marcel, *The gift: forms and functions of exchange in archaic societies*, trans. Ian Cunnison, New York 1967

Mears, Natalie, 'Love-making and diplomacy: Elizabeth I and the Anjou marriage negotiations, c. 1578-1582', *History* lxxxvi (2001), 442
– *Queenship and political discourse in the Elizabethan realms*, Cambridge 2005
Meikle, Maureen M., '"Holde her at the oeconomicke rule of the house": Anna of Denmark and Scottish court finances, 1589-1603', in Maureen M. Meikle and Elizabeth Ewan (eds), *Women in Scotland, c. 1100-c. 1750*, East Linton 1999, 105-11
Michalove, Sharon D., 'The education of aristocratic women in fifteenth-century England', in Sharon D. Michalove and A. Compton Reeves (eds), *Estrangement, enterprise and education in fifteenth-century England*, Stroud 1998, 117-39
– 'Equal in opportunity? The education of aristocratic women, 1450-1550', in Barbara J. Whitehead (ed.), *Women's education in early modern Europe: a history, 1500-1800*, New York 1999, 46-74
Monckton, Linda and Steven J. Gunn (eds), *Arthur Tudor, prince of Wales: life, death and commemoration*, Woodbridge 2009.
Monnas, Lisa, 'Cloth of gold', in Gale R. Owen-Crocker, Elizabeth Coatsworth and Maria Hayward (eds), *Encyclopedia of dress and textiles in the British Isles c. 450-1450*, Leiden 2012, 132-3
Morrison, Susan Signe, *Women pilgrims in late medieval England: private piety as public performance*, London 2000
Morton, Adam, 'Sanctity and suspicion: Catholicism, conspiracy and the representation of Henrietta Maria of France and Catherine of Braganza, queens of Britain', in Helen Watanabe-O'Kelly and Adam Morton (eds), *Queens consort, cultural transfer and European politics, c. 1500-1800*, New York 2017, 172-201
Muzzarelli, Maria Giuseppina, 'Reconciling the privilege of a few with the common good: sumptuary laws in medieval and early modern Europe', *JMEMS* xxxix (2009), 597-617
Nassiet, Michel, 'Anne de Bretagne, a woman of state', in Cynthia J. Brown (ed.), *The cultural and political legacy of Anne de Bretagne: negotiating convention in books and documents*, Cambridge 2010, 163-76
Nelson, Janet L., 'Medieval queenship', in Linda Elizabeth Mitchell (ed.), *Women in medieval western European culture*, New York 1999, 179-207
Nevile, Jennifer, 'Dance in Europe, 1250-1750', in Jennifer Nevile (ed.), *Dance, spectacle, and the body politick, 1250-1750*, Bloomington 2008, 7-66
Newsome, Helen, 'Reconsidering the provenance of the Henry VII and Margaret Tudor Book of Hours', *Notes and Queries* lxiv (2017), 231-4
Okerlund, Arlene, *Elizabeth of York*, New York 2009
Orr, Clarissa Campbell, 'Introduction', to Orr, *Queenship in Europe*, 1-15
– (ed.), *Queenship in Europe, 1660-1815: the role of the consort*, New York 2004
Page, William (ed.), 'Colleges: Stoke by Clare', in *A history of the county of Suffolk*, ii, London 1975, 145-50
– 'Friaries: Observant friars of Newark', in *A history of the county of Nottingham*, ii, London 1910, 147-8
Parsons, John Carmi, 'The pregnant queen as councilor and the medieval construction of motherhood', in John Carmi Parsons and Bonnie Wheeler (eds), *Medieval mothering*, New York 1996, 9-40
– 'Mothers, daughters, marriage, power: some Plantagenet evidence, 1150-1500', in John Carmi Parsons (ed.), *Medieval queenship*, Stroud 1998, 63-78
– 'Violence, the queen's body, and the medieval body politic', in Mark D. Meyerson,

Daniel Thiery and Oren Falk (eds), *A great effusion of blood? Interpreting medieval violence*, Toronto 2004, 241-67

Peck, Linda Levy, '"For a king not to be bountiful were a fault": perspectives on court patronage in early Stuart England', *JBS* xv (1986), 31-61

— *Court patronage and corruption in early Stuart England*, Boston 1990

— 'Benefits, brokers and beneficiaries: the culture of exchange in seventeenth-century England', in B. Y. Kunze and D. D. Brautigam (eds), *Court, country and culture: essays on early modern British history in honor of Perez Zagorin*, Rochester 1992, 109-27

Perry, Maria, *Sisters to the king: the tumultuous lives of Henry VIII's sisters, Margaret of Scotland and Mary of France*, London 1998

Peters, Christine, *Patterns of piety: women, gender, and religion in late medieval and Reformation England*, New York 2003

Pierce, Hazel, 'The king's cousin: the life, career and Welsh connection of Sir Richard Pole, 1458-1504', *Welsh History Review* xix (1998), 187-225

— *Margaret Pole, countess of Salisbury, 1473-1541: loyalty, lineage and leadership*, Cardiff 2003

Pollnitz, Aysha, 'Christian women or sovereign queens? The schooling of Mary and Elizabeth', in Anna Whitelock and Alice Hunt (eds), *Tudor queenship: the reigns of Mary and Elizabeth*, Basingstoke 2010, 127-44

Redworth, Glyn, *The prince and the infanta: the cultural politics of the Spanish match*, New Haven 2003

Rex, Richard, 'The religion of Henry VIII', *HJ* lvii (2014), 1-32

Richards, Judith M., 'Mary Tudor: Renaissance queen of England', in Levin, Carney and Barrett-Graves, *'High and mighty queens'*, 27-44

— *Mary Tudor*, New York 2008

— 'Public identity and public memory: case studies of two Tudor women', in Broomhall and Tarbin, *Women, identities and communities*, 195-210

— '"Unblushing falsehood": the Strickland sisters and the domestic history of Henry VIII', in Thomas Betteridge and Thomas S. Freeman (eds), *Henry VIII and history*, Burlington, VT 2012, 165-78

Richardson, Catherine, 'Introduction', to Richardson, *Clothing culture*, 1-28

— (ed.), *Clothing culture, 1350-1650*, Aldershot 2004

Richardson, Glenn, '"Most highly to be regarded": the Privy Chamber of Henry VIII and Anglo-French relations, 1515-1520', *TCH* iv (1999), 119-40

— *Renaissance monarchy: the reigns of Henry VIII, Francis I and Charles V*, London 2002

— *The Field of Cloth of Gold*, New Haven 2014

Rieder, Paula, *On the purification of women: churching in northern France, 1100-1500*, New York 2006

Riis, Thomas, *Should auld acquaintance be forgot ... Scottish-Danish relations, c.1450-1707*, Odense 1988

Robins, M. E., 'Black Africans at the court of James IV', *Review of Scottish Culture* xii (2000), 34-45

Robinson, Brian, *The Royal Maundy*, London 1977

Rogister, John, 'Queen Marie Leszczynska and faction at the French court', in Orr, *Queenship in Europe*, 186-220

Rooley, Anthony, 'Dance and dance music of the 16th century', *EM* ii (1974), 79-83

Ross, Charles, *Edward IV*, Berkeley 1974

Rubin, Miri, *Corpus Christi: the eucharist in late medieval culture*, Cambridge 1991
Rublack, Ulinka, *Dressing up: cultural identity in Renaissance Europe*, New York 2010
Ryrie, Alec, *The origins of the Scottish Reformation*, New York 2006
Sadlack, Erin A., *The French queen's letters: Mary Tudor Brandon and the politics of marriage in sixteenth-century Europe*, New York 2011
St John, Lisa Benz, *Three medieval queens: queenship and the crown in fourteenth-century England*, Basingstoke 2012
Samman, Neil, 'The progresses of Henry VIII, 1509-1529', in Diarmaid MacCulloch (ed.), *The reign of Henry VIII: politics, policy and piety*, New York 1995, 59-74
Samson, Alexander, 'A fine romance: Anglo-Spanish relations in the sixteenth century', *JMEMS* xxxix (2009), 65-94
Scarisbrick, J. J., *Henry VIII*, Berkeley 1968
Scherb, Victor I., '"I'de have a shooting": Catherine of Aragon's receptions of Robin Hood', *Research Opportunities in Renaissance Drama* xlii (2003), 124-46
Schutte, Valerie, '"To the illustrious queen": Katherine of Aragon and early modern book dedications', in Julie A. Chappell and Kaley A. Kramer (eds), *Women during the English Reformations: renegotiating gender and religious identity*, New York 2014, 15-28
Scott, Margaret, 'A Burgundian visit to Scotland in 1449', *Costume* xxi (1987), 16-25
Scottish Record Office, *Guide to the National Archives of Scotland*, Edinburgh 1996
Shenton, Caroline, 'Philippa of Hainault's churchings: the politics of motherhood at the court of Edward III', in R. G. Eales (ed.), *Family and dynasty in late medieval England: proceedings of the 1997 Harlaxton symposium*, Donington 2003, 105-21
Sherlock, Peter, 'Monuments, reputation and clerical marriage in Reformation England: Bishop Barlow's daughters', *G&H* xvi (2004), 57-82
Skinner, Quentin, *The foundations of modern political thought*, I: *Renaissance*, Cambridge 1978
Smuts, Malcolm R. and Melissa Gough, 'Queens and the international transmission of political culture', *TCH* x (2005), 1-13
Snook, Edith, *Women, beauty and power in early modern England: a feminist literary history*, Basingstoke 2011
Sowerby, Tracey A., '"A memorial and a pledge of faith": portraiture and early modern diplomatic culture', *EHR* cxxix (2014), 296-331
Staniland, Kay, 'Royal entry into the world', in Daniel Williams (ed.), *England in the fifteenth century: proceedings of the 1986 Harlaxton symposium*, Woodbridge 1987, 297-313
Starkey, David, 'Ightham Mote: politics and architecture in early Tudor England', *Archaeologia* cvii (1982), 153-63
— 'Intimacy and innovation: the rise of the Privy Chamber, 1485-1547', in David Starkey (ed.), *The English court: from the Wars of the Roses to the Civil War*, London 1987, 71-118
— 'Henry VI's old blue gown: the English court under the Lancastrians and Yorkists', *TCH* iv (1999), 1-28
— *Six wives: the queens of Henry VIII*, New York 2003
— (ed.). *Henry VIII: a European court in England*, London 1991
Stephenson, Barbara, 'Maintaining the antiquity of the house: Marguerite de Navarre, noble marriage and dynastic culture in early sixteenth-century France', *TCH* x (2005), 15-24

Stevens, John E., *Music and poetry in the early Tudor court*, London 1961

Stevenson, Jane, 'Texts and textiles: self-presentation among the elite in Renaissance England', *Journal of the Northern Renaissance* iii (2011), 39-57

Stevenson, Katie, *Chivalry and knighthood in Scotland, 1424-1513*, Woodbridge 2006

— 'Chivalry, British sovereignty and dynastic politics: undercurrents of antagonism in Tudor-Stewart relations, c. 1490-1513', *Historical Research* lxxxvi (2013), 1-18

Streitberger, W. R., 'Henry VIII's entertainment for the queen of Scots, 1516: a new revels account and Cornish's play', *Medieval and Renaissance Drama in England* i (1984), 29-35

— 'The development of Henry VIII's revel's establishment', *MET* vii (1985), 83-100

— *Court revels, 1485-1559*, Toronto 1994

Strickland, Agnes and Elisabeth Strickland, *Lives of the queens of England: from the Norman Conquest*, Philadelphia 1847

Strong, Roy C., *Splendor at court: Renaissance spectacle and the theater of power*, Boston 1973

— *Art and power: Renaissance festivals, 1450-1650*, Woodbridge 1984

Swanson, Robert N., 'Political pilgrims and political saints in medieval England', in Antón M. Pazos (ed), *Pilgrims and politics: rediscovering the power of the pilgrimage*, Burlington, VT 2012, 29-45

Thompson, Benjamin (ed.), *The reign of Henry VII: proceedings of the 1993 Harlaxton symposium*, Stamford 1995.

Thurley, Simon, *The royal palaces of Tudor England: architecture and court life, 1460-1547*, New Haven, CN 1993

Tomas, Natalie R., *The Medici women: gender and power in Renaissance Florence*, Burlington, VT 2003

Travitsky, Betty S., 'Reprinting Tudor history: the case of Catherine of Aragon', *Renaissance Quarterly* l (1997), 164-74

Tremlett, Giles, *Catherine of Aragon: the Spanish queen of Henry VIII*, New York 2010

Tudor-Craig, Pamela, 'Margaret, queen of Scotland, in Grantham, 8-9 July 1503', in Thompson, *Reign of Henry VII*, 261-79

Underwood, Malcolm G., 'The pope, the queen, and the king's mother; or, the rise and fall of Adriano Castellesi', in Thompson, *Reign of Henry VII*, 65-81

Veevers, Erica, *Images of love and religion: Queen Henrietta Maria and court entertainments*, Cambridge 1989

Vincent, Susan J., *Dressing the elite: clothes in early modern England*, New York 2003

Walker, Rose, 'Leonor of England and Eleanor of Castile: Anglo-Iberian marriage and cultural exchange in the twelfth and thirteenth centuries', in Maria Bullon-Fernandez (ed.), *England and Iberia in the Middle Ages, 12th-15th century: cultural, literary and political exchanges*, New York 2007, 67-88

Warnicke, Retha M., 'Henry VIII's greeting of Anne of Cleves and early modern court protocol', *Albion* xxviii (1996), 565-85

Watts, Karen, 'Henry VIII and the founding of the Greenwich armouries', in Starkey, *Henry VIII: a European court*, 42-6

Weir, Alison, *The six wives of Henry VIII*, London 1997

Weissberger, Barbara S., 'Tanto monta: the Catholic monarchs' nuptial fiction and the power of Isabel I of Castile', in Cruz and Suzuki, *Rule of women*, 43-63

Whitley, Catrina Banks and Kyra Kramer, 'A new explanation for the reproductive woes and midlife decline of Henry VIII', *HJ* liii (2010), 827-48
Williams, Patrick, *Catherine of Aragon*, Stroud 2012
Wormald, Jenny, 'Thorns in the flesh: English kings and uncooperative Scottish rulers, 1460-1549', in Bernard and Gunn, *Authority and consent*, 61-78
Ziegler, Georgianna, 'Re-imagining a Renaissance queen: Catherine of Aragon among the Victorians', in Levin, Carney and Barrett-Graves, *'High and mighty queens'*, 203-22

Unpublished theses

Cowan, Mairi, 'Lay piety in Scotland before the Protestant Reformation: individuals, communities, and nation', PhD, Toronto 2003
Dunlop, David, 'Aspects of Anglo-Scottish relations from 1471 to 1513', PhD, Liverpool 1988
Emond, William Kevin, 'The minority of King James V, 1513-1528', PhD, St Andrews 1988
Hepburn, William, 'The household of James IV, 1488-1513', PhD, Glasgow 2013
Kisby, Fiona, 'The royal household chapel in early Tudor London', PhD, Royal Holloway 1996
Murray, Athol L., 'The Exchequer and crown revenue of Scotland, 1437-1542', PhD, Edinburgh 1961
Neal, Derek, 'The queen's grace: English queenship, 1464-1503', MA, McMaster 1996
Samman, Neil, 'The Henrician court during Cardinal Wolsey's ascendancy, c.1514-1529', PhD. Bangor 1988

Web-based sources

Oxford dictionary of national biography, ed. H. C. G. Matthew and Brian Harrison, Oxford 2004, <http://www.oxforddnb.com>
State Papers Online 1509-1714, I: *The Tudors: Henry VIII to Elizabeth I, 1509-1603: State Papers Domestic*, < http://gale.cengage.co.uk/state-papers-online-15091714.aspx>

Index

Albany, John Stuart, 1st duke of, *see* Stuart, John
Alexander Stuart, duke of Ross (son of Margaret Tudor and James IV), 60, 91
almoners, 131-4, 138, 140 n. 99
almsgiving, 123, 128-34, 137, 138, 139
Anglo-Spanish alliance: Catherine's efforts to ensure, 25, 60, 61-3, 67-8; household marriages resulting from, 116-17. *See also* marriages.
Angus, Archibald Douglas, 6th earl of, *see* Douglas, Archibald
Anne of Brittany (duchess regnant of Brittany and queen consort of France), 4-5, 100
Anne of Cleves (queen of Henry VIII of England), 82
Anne of Denmark (queen of James VI of Scotland), 56 n. 51
Anne of York (daughter of Edward IV), 31, 32
Arthur (son of Margaret Tudor and James IV of Scotland), 120
Arthur Tudor (prince of Wales): birth, 30; christening, 32; death, 15, 28; education and upbringing, 12; marriage to Catherine of Aragon, 12, 14, 15; wedding ceremonies, 1, 13, 15, 17n. 52, 34, 35-6
Arundel, Henry Fitzalan, 12th earl of, *see* Fitzalan, Henry
Atholl, John Stewart, 1st earl of, *see* Stewart, John

Babington, Henry, 13 n. 47, 131-2, 133, 134
Barlow, Elizabeth, Lady Elphinstone, 83, 116, 118-20
Barlow, John, 118-19
Baynard's Castle, London, 35, 70, 85
Beaufort, Joan (queen of James I of Scotland), 40, 114 n. 98

Beaufort, Margaret, countess of Richmond (mother of Henry VII); almoners of Margaret Tudor and Catherine of Aragon and, 131, 132; household of, 39, 41, 132; Isabel Stewart and, 114n. 98; Margaret Tudor and, 7, 38, 42; political activities of, 27, 29-30, 32, 37, 38; relationship with Elizabeth of York, 30, 32, 38; Royal Maundy of, 136
Bedford, Jacquetta de St Pol, Countess Rivers and duchess of, *see* St Pol, Jacquetta de
Bekinsall, Robert, 131, 132, 133, 134
bells rung at royal arrivals, 134, 140
Benestede, Edward, 85 n. 77
Benton, John, 130
Berlay, Christian, 118
Black Lady and Wild Knight, Scottish tournament of (1507/1508), *see* tournaments
Black Prince (Edward of Woodstock), 15, 53
Blount, Gertrude (Courtenay), countess of Devon and marquess of Exeter, 33, 91, 111 n. 75, 112
Blount, Lord William, 4th Baron Mountjoy, 41, 44, 117
body of the queen, *see* material culture
Boleyn, Anne (queen of Henry VIII of England): almsgiving and, 129, 130 n. 42; audience and identity, 10; dower lands transitioning to, 103 n. 31; and George Talbot, 4th earl of Shrewsbury, 110 n. 71; historical afterlife of, 21; lack of household continuity with Catherine of Aragon, 40-1 n. 79; patronage of, 101; sources, 22; unpopularity of, 156. *See also* divorce of Catherine of Aragon and Henry VIII.
Boleyn, Elizabeth, 111 n. 75
Boleyn, Thomas, 1st earl of Wiltshire, 67

INDEX

books, *see* Catherine of Aragon; Christine de Pizan
Bosworth, Battle of (1485), 14, 29, 31 n. 25
Bountas (trumpeter to James IV), 95
Bourchier, Mary, *see* Say, Mary
Boyd, Marion, 91 n. 115
Brandon, Charles, 1st duke of Suffolk, 21, 80, 103, 146
Brandon, Mary Tudor, *see* Mary Tudor
Bricht, John, 43 n. 94
Brygus, George, 102
Buckingham, Edward Stafford, 3rd duke of, *see* Stafford, Edward
Buckingham, Katherine Woodville, duchess of, *see* Woodville, Katherine
Burgundian influences, *see* courtly hospitality and royal spectacle
Butler, Thomas, 7th earl of Ormond, 41, 44, 117 n. 107

Camner, James, 95
Carew, Sir Nicholas, 103
Carvenall, James, 13 n. 47, 131-2
Catalina of Lancaster, 149-50
Catherine of Aragon (queen of Henry VIII of England): as accredited ambassador, 17; Anglo-Spanish *versus* Anglo-French alliance, 25, 60, 61-3, 67-8, 89-90; apartments, as queen of England, 86; Arthur, death of, 15, 28; Arthur, marriage to, 12, 14, 15; Arthur, wedding ceremonies with, 1, 13, 15, 17 n. 52, 34, 35-6; audience and identity, 9-10; biographical information, 11-22; books dedicated to, 105 n. 39; carol written in voice of, 76; changing role over course of marriage, 19-20; childbearing struggles, 18, 48-52, 54-5, 145; disguise and correct identification of king, 81-2; dower estates, 103, 113, 145-6; dynastic connections, 14, 60, 63 n. 85, 65; education and upbringing, 11-12, 13, 27; Elizabeth of York's influence, 24-5, 27-9, 34, 36-7, 44, 71, 154; Elizabeth of York's maternal interest, 27, 38; Evil May Day apprentice boys, interceding for, 74; family tree, p. xii; at Field of Cloth of Gold (1520), 25, 46, 60-9, 79, 94; Flemish Book of Hours possibly given by Margaret Tudor to, 95-6; French acquired at behest of Elizabeth of York, 38; gift-giving, 105-6, 108-12, 113-15; on gifts given to Henry VIII by Ferdinand of Aragon, 59-60; historical afterlife of, 11, 20-1, 124-5; joint coronation with Henry VIII, 16-17, 126-7; livery, 60, 61, 64-5, 81, 94, 114; and Margaret Tudor's return to England, 1, 70, 80, 85-6; marital expectations, 13; marriage to Henry VIII, 1-3, 13, 19-20, 150; marriages arranged by, 115-18, 120; musicians and minstrels of, 93-5; palfrey given to Margaret Tudor, 85, 96; physical attractiveness, 45, 66; political activities, 1-2, 17, 19-20, 90; public and private marital relationship with Henry VIII, 1-3, 13, 19-20, 150, 156-7; as regent and governess of England, 20, 26, 149-53; sources, 22-4; victory at Battle of Flodden Field, 110, 149-53; Walsingham pilgrimages, 141, 144-7, 153; wedding with Henry VIII, 15, 16-17; wine, learning to drink, 38. *See also* courtly hospitality and royal spectacle; divorce of Catherine of Aragon and Henry VIII; household of Catherine of Aragon; households; material culture; patronage; piety.

Cecil, John de, 94
Cecily of York (daughter of Edward IV), 31, 32
charity: almoners, 131-4, 138, 140 n. 99; almsgiving, 123, 128-34, 137, 138, 139; Royal Maundy as ritual of, 136, 137, 138-9
Charles I (king of England), 100
Charles V (Holy Roman Emperor), 1 n. 2, 5, 14, 60, 62-3, 67, 68, 90
Charles VI (king of France), 56
Charles the Bold of Burgundy, 34
childbearing, *see* pregnancy and childbirth
chivalry, ideals of, 72, 75, 76, 84, 88
Cholmeley, William, 109
Christine de Pizan, 5-7, 100; *The book of the city of ladies*, 6 n. 19, 128 n. 35; *The treasure of the city of ladies*, 6, 88, 128
churching, *see* pregnancy and childbirth

175

Claude (queen of Francis I of France), 64
Clegg, Hamnet, 43 n. 94
clothing: Maundy gowns, 137; as patronage gifts, 105, 112-14; for pilgrimages, 142; significance of, 45-8. *See also* livery; material culture.
Collins, Elizabeth, 114
Compton, Sir William, 99
confinement or lying in of pregnant women, *see* pregnancy and childbirth
confraternity of the Holy Blood (Scotland), 123
conspicuous consumption, *see* courtly hospitality and royal spectacle; material culture
Cook, Mistress Margaret, 110
Cornish, William, 37, 73 n. 15, 76
coronations: creation of knights at English queens' coronations, 79 n. 46; piety, as expressions of, 126-7. *See also* Catherine of Aragon; Elizabeth of York.
Courtenay, Gertrude, *see* Blount, Gertrude
Courtenay, Henry, 2nd earl of Devon, and 1st marquess of Exeter, 33, 91, 103
Courtenay, Katherine, *see* Katherine of York
Courtenay, William, 1st earl of Devon, 31, 33-4, 36
courtly hospitality and royal spectacle, 25, 70-96, 155; ambassadors, private entertainment of, 88-90; audience, queens as, 71, 72-84; Burgundian influence on, 29, 34-5, 75-6; damage caused by queens' lack of participation, 82; disguise and correct identification of king by queen, 81-2; Elizabeth of York's legacy regarding, 29, 34-9, 71; games and gambling, 91-2; gendered social roles, 71-2, 73-5, 88, 96; hospitality, as virtue, 88-9; kings' active participation, 71, 73, 81-2, 84; ladies of the queen's household and, 72, 78, 80-1, 82-4, 90-1, 92-3; mixed-sex socialising, 72, 87, 90-3; news and gossip, exchanging, 92; passive-seeming nature of queenly involvement in, 74-5, 78, 84; queens as hostesses, 71, 72, 73, 85-95; return of Margaret Tudor to England and, 70, 80, 85-6, 95-6;

Robin Hood pageants and ballads, 74 n.18. *See also* Field of Cloth of Gold; livery; music and dancing; patronage; pregnancy and childbirth; royal entries; tournaments.
Cromwell, Oliver, 23 n. 89
Cromwell, Thomas, 1st earl of Essex, 23 n. 90, 95 n. 133
Cutt, Sir John, 101-2, 152

Dacre, Thomas, 2nd Baron Dacre of Gilsland, 57
dancing and music, *see* music and dancing
Darcy, Sir Arthur, 92 n. 122
Darrell, Alice, 109, 111 n. 75, 114
Davy, Alice, 42
de la Pole, Edmund, 3rd duke of Suffolk, 33
Decons, Richard, 111, 113
Dennet, Margaret, 107
Denton, Elizabeth, 42
d'Este, Isabella, marchesa de Mantua, 5
Devon, Gertrude Courtenay, countess of, *see* Blount, Gertrude
Devon, Henry Courtenay, 2nd earl of, *see* Courtenay, Henry
Devon, Katherine Courtenay, countess of, *see* Katherine of York
Devon, William Courtenay, 1st earl of, *see* Courtenay, William
divorce of Catherine of Aragon and Henry VIII; almsgiving by Catherine after, 129; Blackfriars divorce trial (1529), audience during, 9-10; childbearing struggles and, 18; christening cloth sought from Catherine, 55; continuity of household servants between Catherine and later wives, 40-1n. 79, 44; earlier married years and, 3; forced retirement of Catherine, 20; New Year gifts and, 105; performance of queenship by Catherine and, 156-7; piety of Catherine and, 124-5; previous marriage of Catherine to Arthur, 15; Princess Mary and, 3, 157; Royal Maundy of Catherine after, 136-7; sources affected by, 22; Spanish style of dress, Henry's declared dislike of, 69; Spanish wine, Catherine's difficulties obtaining, 38

INDEX

Dog[ge], James, 85 n. 77, 113
Dorset, Margaret Grey, marchioness of, *see* Wotton, Margaret
Dorset, Thomas Grey, 2nd marquess of, *see* Grey, Thomas
Douglas, Archibald, 6th earl of Angus, 19, 55, 154
dress, *see* clothing; livery; material culture
Dunbar, William, 23, 93, 112-13
Duwes, Giles, 12, 94, 113
Dymoke, Sir Robert, 109, 111

Edward III (king of England), 15, 63
Edward IV (king of England), 29, 31, 34, 156
Edward of Woodstock (Black Prince), 15, 53
Eleanor of Austria (queen of Francis I of France), 68
Elizabeth I (queen of England), 18, 35, 76, 114 n. 94, 135, 138
Elizabeth of York (queen of Henry VII of England), 24-5, 27-44; almsgiving, 129, 131; arrangement of marriages for siblings and other relations, 31-2; coronation, 32; death, 16, 28, 41, 44, 48 n. 11, 54; family and dynastic background, pp. xiii, xiv, 29-34; household, 32, 39-44, 117 n. 107, 132; influence on Catherine of Aragon and Margaret Tudor, 24-5, 27-9, 34, 36-7, 44, 71, 154; legacy regarding courtly hospitality and royal spectacle, 29, 34-9, 71; marriage of Margaret Tudor to James IV and, 16, 28, 36, 38-9; maternal interest in Catherine of Aragon, 27, 28; New Year gifts and, 105-6; organisation of wedding reception of Arthur and Catherine of Aragon, 35-6; political activities, 37-9; relationship with Margaret Beaufort, 30, 32, 38; Royal Maundy of, 137 n. 84, 138; Walsingham pilgrimage, 144
Elphinstone, Alexander, 1st Lord Elphinstone, 83, 116, 118-20
Elphinstone, Elizabeth, Lady, *see* Barlow, Elizabeth
Eltham Ordinances (1526), 86 n. 84, 127 n. 26

England: Anglo-French peace treaty (1518), 90; Scotland, relationship with, 14, 15-16, 19, 38 n. 69; stability of Tudor monarchy in, 14, 15, 29-30. *See also* Anglo-Spanish alliance; Field of Cloth of Gold.
Englefield, Thomas, 152
Erasmus, Desiderius, 11
Essex, Anne Woodville, countess of, *see* Woodville, Anne
Essex, Mary Bourchier, countess of, *see* Say, Mary
Essex, Thomas Cromwell, 1st earl of, *see* Cromwell, Thomas
Evil May Day apprentice boys, Catherine of Aragon and Margaret Tudor interceding for, 74

Faveraches, Richeldis de, 146
Felipez, Francisco, 95
Ferdinand of Aragon: Catherine as first female accredited ambassador, 17; death, 1 n. 2; and Elizabeth of York, 37-8; emblems of Catherine drawn from, 65 n. 94, 82; gifts sent to Henry VIII, 59-60; Henry VIII on Spanish-English marriages, 117; letters of Catherine, 42, 70; letters of Henry VIII, 49, 117; Mountjoy as English envoy, 117; negotiation of Catherine of Aragon's English marriages, 15; Scottish marital alliance considered, 14; successors, 1 n. 2, 14
Ferne, George, 132
Field of Cloth of Gold (1520): courtly hospitality and royal spectacle, 75, 79, 89; ladies of queen's household, 66-7; material magnificence, 25, 46, 60-9, 94
Fitzalan, Anne, *see* Percy, Anne
Fitzalan, Henry, 12th earl of Arundel, 118
Fitzlewis, Mary (Woodville), Countess Rivers, 32
Fitzwalter, Elizabeth Ratcliffe, Lady *see* Stafford, Elizabeth
Fitzwilliam, Mabel, 111
Flemish Book of Hours: re-gifted by Margaret Tudor, 95-6
Flodden Field, Battle of (1513), 19, 20, 55, 74-5, 91, 98, 110, 149-53

177

foot-washing on Maundy Thursday (*pedilavium*), see Maundy Thursday.
Forester, Sir Duncan, 104
Forman, Andrew (bishop of Moray), 91–2
Fortes, Katherine, 116 n.103
Foxe, John, 125
France: Anglo-French peace treaty of 1518, 90; Catherine of Aragon's efforts to ensure Anglo-Spanish alliance, 25, 60, 61–3, 67–8, 89–90; queen's almoner in, 131 n. 48; regency of Catherine of Aragon during Henry VIII's invasion, 20, 26, 149–53; traditional alliance with Scotland, 19. See also Field of Cloth of Gold; Charles VI; Francis I; Henry II; Louis XV.
Francis I (king of France), 63, 67, 75

games and gambling, see courtly hospitality and royal spectacle
Garneys, Christopher, 57–8
gender, see Royal Maundy; courtly hospitality and royal spectacle
gifts and gift-giving: between sovereigns, 59–60; deliverers of gifts, 109–11; Flemish Book of Hours re-gifted by Margaret Tudor, 95–6; gift-exchanges as patronage, 104–12; gifts from 'queen's own store', 111, 114; New Year gifts, 104, 105–12, 133; palfrey given to Margaret Tudor by Catherine of Aragon, 85, 96; plate and silver, 105, 106, 108, 109–10; re-gifting, 95–6, 107, 111–12; weddings as occasions for, 114–15. See also clothing; material culture.
Giustiniani, Sebastiano, 89
Glynn, John, 110, 114 n. 93, 149
Gonzaga, Francesco II, marquess of Mantua, 5
Grenville, Honor (Plantagenet), Viscountess Lisle, 101
Grenville, John, 10
Grey, Anne, 110
Grey, Eleanor, see St John, Eleanor
Grey, Sir John, 31
Grey, Katherine, 118
Grey, Lord Leonard, 10, 101
Grey, Margaret, see Wotton, Margaret

Grey, Thomas, Lord Harrington and 2nd marquess of Dorset, 32, 33–4, 36, 118 n. 113
Guevara, Dame Maria de, 116 n. 103
Guilliam (tabret player to Margaret queen of Scots), 94

Hall, Edward, 70, 86 n. 87, 125
Hamilton, Sir Patrick, 78
Harrington, Lord Thomas, see Grey, Thomas
Hastings, Anne, see Stafford, Anne
Henrietta Maria (queen of Charles I of England), 100
Henry (son of Catherine of Aragon and Henry VIII), 52, 79, 141, 145
Henry II (king of France), 150 n. 5
Henry VI (king of England), 8, 15 n. 57, 150
Henry VII (king of England): Burgundian influence on, 34–5; disguise and correct identification of king by queen, 81–2; Giles Duwes and, 113; family relations of Elizabeth of York, 32, 33–4; household of, 43, 81, 132; letter of Margaret Tudor, 97–8; on marriage of Catherine of Aragon and Henry VIII, 117; New Year gifts, 105–6; and political involvement of Elizabeth of York, 37; Royal Maundy, 135; stabilisation of monarchy and dynasty, 14, 16, 29–30; tournaments, 75; wedding ceremony of Arthur and Catherine of Aragon, 15, 36. See also Elizabeth of York.
Henry VIII (king of England): accession to throne, 16–17; Anne of Cleves, 82; Burgundian influence on, 35; education and upbringing, 12; Evil May Day apprentice boys, Catherine of Aragon and Margaret Tudor interceding for, 74; foreign styles of dress adopted by, 68; gifts given by Ferdinand of Aragon, 59–60; household, 43, 81; and James Carvenall, 132; Jane Seymour, 101; Katherine Parr, 44, 86 n. 82, 114, 150; Margaret Tudor's return to England, 55–60; marital adventures, Catherine's queenship as context for, 156–7; marriage to Catherine of

INDEX

Aragon, 1–3, 13, 19–20, 150; New Year gifts, 105–6; personal/social style of monarchy, 2, 86–7; piety and private devotions, 128; public and private marital relationship with Catherine of Aragon, 1–3, 150, 156–7; purported interest in Lady Hastings, 92, 99; regency of Catherine of Aragon during invasion of France, 20, 26, 149–53; Royal Maundy, 135, 136–7, 138; tournaments, 33, 75, 76, 79–80, 84; Walsingham, pilgrimage, 141, 145; wedding ceremonies of, 17n. 62. *See also* Anne Boleyn; Catherine of Aragon; divorce of Catherine of Aragon and Henry VIII.

Heron, John, 151

Hilton, Elis, 64, 152

Holland, William, 106

honour, 46, 56

hospitality, *see* courtly hospitality and royal spectacle

household: of Catherine of Aragon: continuity with later wives of Henry VIII, 40–1 n. 79, 44; and courtly hospitality and royal spectacle, 81, 86 n. 84, 93–5; as deliverers of gifts, 109–11; dismissal of members by king, 92, 99; at Field of Cloth of Gold, 64–7; ladies of, at Field of Cloth of Gold, 66–7; legacy of Elizabeth of York, 33, 39–44; livery, 60, 61, 64–5, 81, 94, 114; marriages arranged for, 115–18, 120; musicians, 93–5; patronage and gift-giving, 99, 101–2, 109–12, 113–15; procession to royal chapel, 127; regency of Catherine, 151–2; sources, 24. *See also* almoners; livery; patronage.

household: of Margaret Tudor: administration, 19; almoners, 131–4, 138; and courtly hospitality and royal spectacle, 81, 83, 85, 87 n. 90; legacy of Elizabeth of York, 9–44; livery, 65–6n. 96, 84, 104, 113, 133, 143–4; marriages arranged for, 115–17, 118–20; patronage and gift-giving, 102–3, 104, 107–8, 114–15; pilgrimage to St Ninian's shrine, Whithorn, 66 n. 96, 142–3; sources, 23, 24

Household Ordinances (1494), 106

households: continuity between Catherine and later wives of Henry VIII, 40–1 n. 79, 44; continuity of service between queens' households, 33, 39–44; dismissal of members of queen's household by king, 92, 99; of Elizabeth of York, 32, 39–44, 117 n. 107, 132; Eltham Ordinances (1526), 86 n. 84, 127 n. 26; of Henry VIII, 43, 81, 132; of James IV, 40, 87; of Katherine Parr, 44; ladies of, in courtly hospitality and royal spectacle, 72, 78, 80–1, 82–4, 90–1, 92–3; of Margaret Beaufort, 39, 41, 132; of Princess Mary, 44; of Mary Tudor, 42; musicians, 93–5; queen's symbolic position as mistress of, 87–8. *See also* almoners; Henry VII; Henry VIII; household of Catherine of Aragon; household of Margaret Tudor; James IV; livery; Margaret Beaufort; patronage; Princess Mary.

Howard, Agnes, duchess of Norfolk, 111, 114

Howard, Thomas, earl of Surrey, and 3rd duke of Norfolk, 31, 97–8, 110, 149

Huntingdon, Anne Hastings, countess of, *see* Stafford, Anne

Isabeau of Bavaria (queen of Charles VI of France), 56

Isabella (queen of Portugal), 5, 48 n.11

Isabella of Castile: and Christine de Pizan's *Treasure of the city of ladies*, 6; concerns about Catherine of Aragon at English court after death of Elizabeth of York, 28–9; correspondence with Elizabeth of York, 27, 28–9; education and upbringing of Catherine of Aragon, 11–12; Elizabeth of York and, 27, 28–9, 37–8; emblems of Catherine drawn from, 65; on giving away clothing, 114; and household of Catherine of Aragon, 42; martial skill, 151; negotiation of Catherine of Aragon's English marriages, 15; piety, 124; as queen regnant of Castile, 62; and Scottish marital alliance, 14

Isabella of France (queen of Edward III of England), 22 n. 87

179

Isabella of Portugal (Holy Roman Empress), 5
Isle of May, shrine of St Adrian at, 144 n. 122

Jack of Newbury (1597), 153 n. 26
Jakes (tabret player to Margaret queen of Scots), 94
James III (king of Scots), 77, 142, 150
James IV (king of Scots): Barlow-Elphinstone marriage, 119–20; bloody coat sent to Henry VIII by Catherine of Aragon, 110, 149; conducting business in royal chapel, 127; consummation of marriage to Margaret Tudor, 15 n. 58, 18, 52; death at Battle of Flodden Field, 19, 55, 91, 98 n. 4, 110, 149; and ecclesiastical benefices, 132 n. 52; Flemish Book of Hours given to Margaret Tudor, 95–6; household of, 40, 87; livery, 65–6 n. 96, 95, 108 n. 62; marriage to Margaret Tudor, 1–3, 13, 14, 15–6, 28, 36, 38–9; New Year gifts and, 105, 106–8; personal/social style of monarchy, 2, 86–7; pilgrimages, 53, 141–4, 144 n. 122; proposed as husband for Maria of Aragon (older sister of Catherine of Aragon), 14; proxy marriage ceremony of Margaret Tudor, 36; public and private marital relationship with Margaret Tudor, 1–3, 157; regency of Margaret Tudor, 19, 26, 55, 98, 149, 150, 153–4; Royal Maundy, 134 n. 67, 137 n. 83, 138–9; seeking Henry VIII's support for James Carvenall, 132; special relationship with earl of Surrey (English envoy to Scottish court), 97–8; tournaments, 75, 77–9, 82–4; wedding celebrations with Margaret Tudor, 77–9. *See also* Margaret Tudor.
James V (king of Scots), 7, 18, 19, 52, 55, 56, 60, 107, 116, 149, 153
James VI (king of Scots), 18
Jenny, Christopher, 118
Joan of Kent, 15
John III (king of Portugal), 14
John of Gaunt, 1st duke of Lancaster, 63 n. 85
Johns, Matthew, 102
Jones, Eleanor, 42, 108
Juan (son of Ferdinand of Aragon and Isabella of Castile), 14
Juana Enriquez of Aragon, 149
Juana of Castile (duchess of Burgundy and queen regnant of Castile), 14, 35, 37, 114 n. 92, 116
Justice, Richard, 43 n. 94, 67 n. 104, 94, 113, 152

Katherine of York (daughter of Edward IV; countess of Devon), 31, 32, 109
Kingston, Mary, 44
Kingston, Sir William, 103

Lancaster, John of Gaunt, 1st duke of, *see* John of Gaunt
Lennox, John Stewart, 3rd earl of, 114
Leszczynska, Marie (queen of Louis XV of France), 40
Levisay, Edmund, 43 n. 94, 114
Lindsay, Sir David, 93 n. 123
Lisle, Arthur Plantagenet, 1st Viscount (deputy of Calais), *see* Plantagenet, Arthur
Lisle, Honor, Viscountess, *see* Grenville, Honor
Litcham, rood screen of female saints at, 147
livery: courtly hospitality, royal spectacle, and, 81, 84, 94; of Margaret of Denmark, 40 n.5; of Margaret Tudor, 65–6 n. 96, 84, 104, 113, 133, 143–4; as material magnificence, 60, 61, 64–5, 65–6n. 96, 155; as patronage, 104, 113–14. *See also* Catherine of Aragon; Field of Cloth of Gold; material culture; James IV; Margaret Tudor.
Lollards, 123 n. 5
Louis XV (king of France), 40
Louise of Savoy, 62, 64, 66
Lovell, Sir Thomas, 152
Luke, Anne, 42
lying in, *see* pregnancy and childbirth

Maltravers, Lady Anne, *see* Percy, Anne
Mantua, Francesco Gonzaga II, marquess de, *see* Gonzaga, Francesco
Mantua, Isabella d'Este, marchesa de, *see* d'Este, Isabella

Manuel, Elvira, 15n58
Margaret of Anjou (queen of Henry VI of England), 8, 127, 144, 150
Margaret of Denmark (queen of James III of Scotland), 39, 40, 107, 137-8 n. 84, 142
Margaret Tudor: apartments, as queen of Scots, 86; audience and identity, 9-10; biographical information, 11-22; Catholicism, 124; childbearing struggles, 18, 48, 52-4, 55, 57, 82-3, 141-2; consummation of marriage to James IV, 15 n. 58, 18, 52; difficulties adjusting to Scottish court, 97-8; education and upbringing, 12-13; Elizabeth of York's influence on, 24-5, 27-9, 34, 36-7, 44, 71, 154; Evil May Day apprentice boys, interceding for, 74; Flemish Book of Hours re-gifted by, 95-6; gift-giving, 106-8, 112-13, 114-15; historical afterlife, 11, 19; historical reputation for vanity and frivolity, 56, 57; intervention to prevent James IV taking part in Battle of Flodden Field, 74-5; livery, 65-6 n. 96, 84, 104, 113, 133, 143-4; Margaret Beaufort and, 7, 38, 42; marital expectations, 13; marriage to Archibald Douglas, 6th earl of Angus, 19, 55, 154; marriage to James IV, 1-3, 13, 14, 15-6, 28, 36, 38-9; marriages arranged by, 115-17, 118-20; money problems of, 56, 97, 107; palfrey given by Catherine of Aragon, 85, 96; physical attractiveness, 66 n. 99; piety displayed on wedding journey to Scotland, 122, 130; pilgrimage to St Ninian's shrine, Whithorn, 54, 66 n. 96, 119-20, 141-4; as poetic focus, 93; political activities of, 1-2, 17-8, 19, 23; proxy marriage ceremony to James IV, 36; public and private marital relationship with James IV, 1-3, 157; as queen regent, 19, 26, 55, 98, 149, 150, 153-4; recovery of possessions from Scotland, 58-9; return to England, 1, 23, 25, 46, 55-60, 70, 80, 85-6, 95-6, 107; return to Scotland (1517), 95-6; and St Margaret of Scotland, 7-8; social skills and talents, 13; sources, 22-4; wedding celebrations with James IV, 77-9. See also courtly hospitality and royal spectacle; household of Margaret Tudor; James IV; material culture; patronage; piety.

Marguerite of Austria (regent of the Netherlands), 5, 62
Marguerite de Navarre, 116
Maria (queen of Portugal), 5, 14
Marie Antoinette (queen of Louis XVI of France), 40
marriages: of Arthur to Catherine of Aragon, 12, 14, 15; of Archibald Douglas, 6th earl of Angus, and Margaret Tudor, 19, 55, 154; consummation, of Arthur and Catherine of Aragon, 15 n. 58, of James IV and Margaret Tudor, 15 n. 58, 18, 52; Elizabeth of York's involvement in marriage arrangements, 16, 28, 31-2, 36, 38-9; French marriage proposal for Princess Mary, 62, 90; of Henry VIII and Catherine of Aragon, 1-3, 13, 19-20, 150; of James IV and Margaret Tudor, 14, 15-6, 28, 36, 38-9; of Mary Tudor and Charles Brandon, 21; proxy marriage ceremony of Margaret Tudor and James IV, 36; public and private marital relationship of Catherine and Henry VIII, 1-3, 13, 19-20, 150, 156-7, of Margaret Tudor and James IV, 1-3, 157. See also patronage; weddings.
Mary (daughter of Henry VIII and Catherine of Aragon, later queen of England): Christine de Pizan's *Book of the city of ladies*, 6 n.19; divorce of mother by Henry VIII, 3, 157; education and upbringing, 20-1; Field of Cloth of Gold, 62; French marriage proposal, 62, 90; household, 44; and Margaret Pole, 33; only surviving offspring of Catherine of Aragon, 18; phantom pregnancy, 51; Royal Maundy, 135; successful bid for throne (1553), 8
Mary (queen of Scots), 18, 150 n. 5
Mary of Guelders (queen of James II of Scotland), 7, 40
Mary of Guise (queen of James V of Scotland), 116, 144 n. 123, 150 n. 5

Mary of Hungary, 5
Mary Tudor (daughter of Henry VII):
    at court of Henry VIII, 21-2 n. 83;
    education and upbringing, 12; Flemish
    Book of Hours possibly given by
    Margaret Tudor, 95-6; gifts given from
    Catherine of Aragon's private store,
    111; household, 42; Margaret Tudor
    compared with, 21-2; at Margaret
    Tudor's public receptions after return
    to England, 70, 80; marriage to Charles
    Brandon, 21; as queen of France, 5,
    21, 70; and Walsingham pilgrimage of
    Catherine of Aragon, 146
Mary of York (daughter of Edward IV), 31
material culture, 25, 45-69, 155; elaborate
    headdresses, as Scottish fashion, 58;
    first pregnancies of Margaret Tudor
    and Catherine of Aragon, 48-55; gifts
    and gift-giving, 59-60; livery, 60, 61,
    64-5, 65-6 n. 96, 155; queen's body
    and, 45-8, 53; return of Margaret
    Tudor to England and, 46, 55-60; royal
    bodies compared to reliquaries, 47-8;
    significance of clothing, 45-8; Spanish
    fashion and Catherine of Aragon, 67-9;
    sumptuary laws, 47. *See also* Field of the
    Cloth of Gold.
Matilda (queen of Henry I of England), 7
Maundy Thursday and Royal Maundy, 25,
    123, 129, 134-9; gendered ceremonies,
    135-6, 137; *pedilavium* (foot-washing),
    134, 135, 136, 138, 139; Royal Maundy,
    25, 123, 129, 134-9, 147
Maximilian (Holy Roman Emperor), 79
Maxton, Charles, 102, 103
May, Isle of, shrine of St Adrian, 144 n.
    122
Medina del Campo, Treaty of (1489), 13
Memo, Dionysius, 89
miscarriage, 49, 50-1. *See also* pregnancy
    and childbirth.
'Moorish' women serving Margaret Tudor,
    83 n. 69
More, Ellen, 83 n. 69
More, Sir Thomas, 11, 113
Mountjoy, Lord William Blount, 4th
    Baron, *see* Blount, Lord William
Musgrove, Lady, 84, 93

music and dancing, 92-5

Neville, Anne (queen of Richard III of
    England), 15 n. 57
Neville, Sir Edward, 113
Neville, Katherine, *see* Stafford, Katherine,
    countess of Westmoreland
New Year gifts, *see* gifts and gift-giving
news and gossip, *see* courtly hospitality and
    royal spectacle
Norfolk, Agnes Howard, duchess, *see*
    Howard, Agnes
Norfolk, Thomas Howard, 3rd duke of, *see*
    Howard, Thomas
Noyon, Treaty of, 1

Observant Franciscans, 123, 131, 134 n. 67
Ogilvy, Sir Alexander, 108
Ogilvy, William, 83, 102-3
Order of the Bath (England), 79 n. 46
Order of the Garter (England), 63
Ormond, Thomas Butler, 7th earl of, *see*
    Butler, Thomas

palfrey: given to Margaret Tudor by
    Catherine of Aragon, *see* gifts and giving
Parr, Katherine (queen of Henry VIII of
    England), 44, 86 n. 82, 114, 150
Parr, Maud, 44, 86 n. 82, 114
Parr, Sir Thomas, 86 n. 82
patronage, 25, 97-121, 155; courtly
    hospitality, royal spectacle, and, 98;
    funding for, 103-4; of household
    members, 99, 100-1; ideals of, 99-100;
    informal nature, 101; livery as, 104,
    113-14; marriages arranged by queens
    as form of, 98, 115-20; relationship
    of queen with husband and, 97-103,
    120-1; rewards, 101-4; warrants, grants,
    and charters indicating, 101-2. *See also*
    gifts and giving.
pedilavium, *see* Maundy Thursday
Percy, Anne (Fitzalan), Lady Maltravers, 114
Perpetual Peace, Treaty of (1502), 16, 38
    n. 69
Philip of Burgundy (later king of Castile),
    14, 31, 35, 37, 94 n. 132
Philippa of Hainault (queen of Edward III
    of England), 53-4

INDEX

Phillips, Mistress [?], 114n. 93
piety, 25, 122–48, 155; almsgiving, 123, 128–34; Catholicism of Margaret Tudor, 124; divorce of Henry VIII and Catherine of Aragon and, 124–5; Margaret Tudor's wedding journey to Scotland, 122, 130; material culture and, 138; pre-Reformation context, 123–8; private devotions, 128; procession to royal chapel, 127; public expression of, 125–7, 134, 140; religious and political considerations affecting understanding, 124–5; Royal Maundy, 25, 123, 129, 134–9, 147; Virgin Mary, as model for queens, 5, 48, 126. *See also* coronation; Maundy Thursday; pilgrimages.
pilgrimages, 123, 139–47, 153
Plantagenet, Arthur, 1st Viscount Lisle, 10
plate and silver as gifts, 105, 106, 108, 109–10
Plomer, Christopher, 43 n. 94
Pole, Edith, *see* St John, Edith
Pole, Eleanor (Verney), 41, 43
Pole, Geoffrey, 43 n. 96
Pole, Margaret, countess of Salisbury, 32, 33, 43 n. 96, 111–12
Pole, Sir Richard, 32, 43 n. 96
Poyntz, Sir Richard, 111 n. 74, 113
pregnancy and childbirth: age of aristocratic/royal women at first birth, 18 n. 70; and Catherine of Aragon, 18, 48–52, 54–5, 82, 145; churching, 53–4; courtly spectacle and, 82–4; and Margaret Tudor, 18, 48, 52–4, 55, 57, 82–3, 141–2; New Year gift for Margaret Tudor before birth of first child, 107; phantom, 49, 50–1; pilgrimages related to, 141–7; sex of foetus, beliefs about when determined, 144 n. 124
Puebla, Roderigo de, 38
Pynson, Richard, 146 n. 138

queens and queenship in Renaissance Britain, 1–26, 154–7; audience and identity, 9–10; expectations and ideals, 3–11; households of queens, 33, 39–44; lives and historical afterlives of Catherine of Aragon and Margaret Tudor, 11–22; patronage and, 25, 97–121, 155; public and private marital relationships, 1–3; regencies, 26, 149–54 sources, 22–4; transactional nature of, 3–4. *See also* Catherine of Aragon; courtly hospitality and royal spectacle; Elizabeth of York; Isabella of Castile; Margaret Beaufort; Margaret Tudor; Mary Tudor; material culture; patronage; piety; regencies.

Radcliffe, Elizabeth, Lady Fitzwalter and countess of Sussex, *see* Stafford, Elizabeth
Ramsay, Sir John, 84
Rebelos, John de, 132
Redding, Mary, 42
regencies, 26, 149–54; of Catherine of Aragon, 20, 26, 149–53; of Margaret Tudor, 19, 26, 55, 98, 149, 150, 153–4; of Mary of Guise, 150 n. 5; of Katherine Parr, 150; Spanish, 149–50
reliquaries, *see* material culture
Réné of Anjou, 75
rewards, *see* patronage
Richard III (king of England), 29, 31
Richards, Griffith, 44, 64 n. 89
Richmond, Margaret Beaufort, countess of, *see* Beaufort, Margaret
Rivers, Anthony Woodville, 2nd Earl, *see* Woodville, Anthony
Rivers, Jacquetta de St Pol, Countess, *see* St Pol, Jacquetta de
Rivers, Mary Fitzlewis, Countess, *see* Fitzlewis, Mary
Robin Hood pageants and ballads, *see* courtly hospitality and royal spectacle
Rojas, Maria de, 116
Roper, Henry, 43 n. 94, 102
Ross, Alexander Stuart, *see* Alexander Stuart
Roule, Alison, 83, 103
royal entries, 18, 77–8
Royal Maundy, *see* Maundy Thursday

Sagudino, Nicolo, 45
St John, Edith (Pole), 32, 43 n. 96
St John, Eleanor (Grey), 32

St John's College, Cambridge, 30, 132
St. Margaret of Scotland, 7-8
St Pol, Jacquetta de, Countess Rivers, 35
saints: St Adrian's shrine, Isle of May, 144 n. 122; St Duthac's shrine, Tain, 144 n. 122; St Ninian's shrine, Whithorn, 53, 54, 66 n. 96, 119-20, 141-4
Salinas, Maria de, Lady Willoughby, 109, 110-11, 117-18, 146
Salisbury, Margaret Pole, countess of, *see* Pole, Margaret
Saxby, Elizabeth, 42
Say, Mary (Bouchier), countess of Essex, 33
Scotland: Battle of Flodden Field, (1513), 19, 20, 55, 74-5, 91, 98, 110, 149-53, losses in 23; Elizabeth of York's death anniversary marked, 28; potential dynastic alliance with Spain; relationship with England, 14, 15-16, 19, 38 n. 69; traditional alliance with France, 19. *See also* James III; James IV; James V; James VI; Margaret Tudor.
Scrope, Ralph, 31 n. 25
Scutt, John, 114
serpent's tongues, 107
servants, *see* households
Seymour, Jane (queen of Henry VIII of England), 101
Shorton, Robert, 132
Shrewsbury, George Talbot, 4th earl of, *see* Talbot, George
silver and plate as gifts, *see* gifts and gift-giving
Sinclair, Sir John, 93
Sinclair, Patrick, 78
Sinclair, William, 87
social activities, *see* courtly hospitality and royal spectacle
Spain: Burgundian dynastic connections, 35; female regency and lieutenancy in, 149-50; potential dynastic alliance with Scotland, 14. *See also* Anglo-Spanish alliance; Catherine of Aragon; Ferdinand of Aragon; Isabella of Castile.
Spanish fashion, *see* material culture
Spanish friars, and Catherine of Aragon, 128-9, 130-1

spectacle, *see* courtly hospitality and royal spectacle; material culture
Stafford, Anne (Hastings), countess of Huntingdon, 33, 92, 99, 111 n. 75
Stafford, Elizabeth (Radcliffe), Lady Fitzwalter and countess of Sussex), 32, 33, 99
Stafford, Edward, 3rd duke of Buckingham, 36, 92, 99, 109 n. 65, 112
Stafford, Katherine, duchess of Buckingham, *see* Woodville, Katherine
Stafford, Katherine (Neville), countess of Westmoreland), 92-3
Stewart, Alexander (archbishop of St Andrews and illegitimate son of James IV), 91
Stewart, Isabel, 114
Stewart, John, 1st earl of Atholl, 114
Stewart, John, 3rd earl of Lennox, 114
Stewart, William, 93 n. 123
Stuart, Alexander, *see* Alexander Stuart
Stuart, John, 1st duke of Albany, 23, 59, 154
Suffolk, Charles Brandon, 1st duke of, *see* Brandon, Charles
Suffolk, Edmund de la Pole, 3rd duke of, *see* de la Pole, Edmund
sumptuary laws, *see* material culture
Surrey, Thomas Howard, earl of and 3rd duke of Norfolk, *see* Howard, Thomas
Sussex, Elizabeth Radcliffe, countess of, *see* Stafford, Elizabeth

Taillefeir, Lucas (Luke Taylford), 40, 85 n. 77
Taillefeir, Thomas, 40
Tain, shrine of St Duthac at, 144 n. 122
Talbot, George, 4th earl of Shrewsbury, 110
Thomas (footman to Margaret Tudor), 97
tournaments, 75-80, 82-4
Tudors: creation of blended Tudor aristocracy, 30, 32, 33; family tree, p. xv; stability of Tudor monarchy in England, 14, 15, 29-30. *See also* Arthur Tudor; Elizabeth I; Henry VII; Henry VIII; Margaret Tudor; Mary (daughter of Henry VIII and Catherine of Aragon); Mary Tudor.

Vanegas, Inés (Agnes) de, 117

Verney, Eleanor, *see* Pole, Eleanor
Verney, Sir Ralph, 41, 43, 97
Victoria, Mistress (wife of Henry VIII's Spanish physician), 111 n. 75, 114
Virgin Mary: as model for queens, 5, 48, 126. *See also* Walsingham.
Vives, Juan Luis, 6 n. 17

Walsingham, shrine of the Virgin at, 141, 144-7, 153. *See also* pilgrimages.
Warbeck, Perkin, 118
Warham, William, (archbishop of Canterbury), 151
Wars of the Roses, 14
weddings: of Arthur and Catherine of Aragon, 1, 13, 15, 17 n. 52, 34, 35-6; Elizabeth of York's organisation of wedding reception for Arthur and Catherine of Aragon, 35-6; gift-giving, as occasions for, 114-15; Henry VIII's small and private wedding ceremonies, 17 n. 62; of Henry VIII and Catherine of Aragon, 15, 16-17; of James IV of Scotland and Margaret Tudor, 77-9, proxy marriage ceremony, 36. *See also* marriages.
Welles, John, 1st Viscount, 32
West, Nicholas, 127, 134 n. 67
Westmoreland, Katherine Neville, countess of, *see* Stafford, Katherine
Weston, Anne, 42
Whithorn, St Ninian's shrine at, 53, 54, 66 n. 96, 119-20, 141-4. *See also* pilgrimages.
Wild Knight and Black Lady, Scottish tournament of (1507/1508), *see* tournaments
Willoughby, Katherine, 118
Willoughby, Maria de Salinas, Lady, *see* Salinas, Maria de
Willoughby d'Eresby, William, 10th Baron, 1, 17-8
Wiltshire, Thomas Boleyn, 1st earl of, *see* Boleyn, Thomas
wine, English penchant for, 38
Wolsey, Thomas (cardinal; archbishop of York); Catherine of Aragon and, 20, 118, 132, 146, 152, 153; chapel, 132; and covered cup given by duke of Buckingham, 112; downfall and confiscation of papers, 23 n. 90; Field of Cloth of Gold and, 60, 62; Margaret Tudor and, 56, 95, 107; Maundy rituals, 136 n. 77
Woodville, Anne (Bourchier), countess of Essex, 33
Woodville, Anthony, 2nd Earl Rivers, 35, 129
Woodville, Elizabeth (queen of Edward IV of England), 29, 30-1, 35, 144, 156 n. 31
Woodville, Katherine (Stafford), duchess of Buckingham, 33
Woodville, Mary, *see* Fitzlewis, Mary
Woodville family, p. xiv, 30-1, 32, 34-5
Wotton, Margaret (Grey), marchioness of Dorset, 111 n. 75

York, House of, p. xiii, 30, 32
Young, John, 23-4, 78 n. 39, 122, 140

www.ingramcontent.com/pod-product-compliance
Lightning Source LLC
Chambersburg PA
CBHW070806230426
43665CB00017B/2505